THE RIGHT TO STAY HOME

THE RIGHT TO STAY HOME

How US Policy Drives Mexican Migration

DAVID BACON

BEACON PRESS, BOSTON

Beacon Press
25 Beacon Street
Boston, Massachusetts 02108-2892
www.beacon.org

Beacon Press books
are published under the auspices of
the Unitarian Universalist Association of Congregations.

16   15   14   13   8   7   6   5   4   3   2   1

This book is printed on acid-free paper that meets the uncoated paper
ANSI / NISO specifications for permanence as revised in 1992.

Text design by Wilsted & Taylor Publishing Services

Library of Congress Cataloging-in-Publication Data
Bacon, David.
The right to stay home : how US policy drives
Mexican migration / David Bacon.
    pages cm
Includes bibliographical references and index.
ISBN 978-0-8070-0161-5 (hardcover : alk. paper) —ISBN 978-0-8070-0162-2 (ebook)
1. Mexico—Emigration and immigration—Economic aspects. 2. Mexico—
Emigration and immigration—Social aspects. 3. Mexico—Commercial policy.
4. Forced migration—Mexico. 5. Poverty—Mexico. 6. Foreign workers—
United States. 7. Immigrants—United States. I. Title.
JV7401.B33 2013
325—dc23   2013001909

CONTENTS

INTRODUCTION

When I left the organizing staff of the United Farm Workers in the late 1970s, I took with me some functional working-class Spanish and a new worldview. I grew up in Oakland, California, and knew nothing about Mexican culture before I left the Bay Area to work in rural California and Arizona. In the union I began to learn—the UFW was a great teacher, and I'll always be grateful to the workers and organizers I met there for changing my life.

I was a pretty good organizer in a union that had some of the best. I helped workers pull together their committees and picket lines, and fight the foremen and the growers. I have good instincts and grew up in a left-wing family, so in many ways my own culture fit pretty well. And I really loved the union's culture. Holding hands and singing in union meetings! Eating lunch and talking in the grape rows or under the tangerine trees. No sleep.

Here's how the day went during just one campaign in Calexico and the Imperial Valley. We'd have meetings of worker/organizers til midnight, then meetings with the campaign leaders til one, then get up at three to get down to the Hoyo when workers were crossing the border, then drive in the dark up to Blythe, then talk for hours next to the field with workers waiting for the ice to melt on the lettuce, then house visits after work in Mexicali, and then the meetings in the evening all over again.

You get the idea. Exhausting. Inspiring. You learn a whole world in a short time.

The other thing I took with me leaving union staff, or rather didn't take with me, was money. I had to get a job quickly, to pay child support and just to live. So I went to Salinas to get a job picking strawberries. I couldn't last a week bending over that far, and my hands were far too slow. So I went over to Hollister to get a dispatch at the union hall to work the wine grape harvest at Almaden, then one of the world's largest wineries.

A thousand workers showed up the morning the picking started. I was the only white guy. Most knew each other from previous harvests, so they quickly formed crews and went to work. A few dozen were left, and from them each tractor driver picked the six who would pick behind his gondola. Finally there were just six left. It was like not getting picked for softball in junior high.

Our crew, the final six, made up the slowest pickers in Paicines, Almaden's long valley of grapevines south of Hollister. So with typical Mexican irony, we called ourselves Los Relampagos—the Lightning Bolts. We never made much more on the piece rate bonus than the hourly guarantee, and my crewmates were pretty impatient with me. Each crew of six splits credit for what they all pick, so the faster pickers basically carry the slower ones.

Almaden and the Hollister UFW office were self-administered by the workers' elected ranch committee. That was a tradition in the wine grapes and was also true of the union at companies like Christian Brothers and Paul Masson. In all these companies, workers themselves did most of the original organizing, helped by Jose Luna, a legendary worker/organizer who expected them to carry most of the load in running the union.

I earned my credit with my crewmates when the company decided to bust the number-one tractor driver on the Almaden seniority list, accusing him of sleeping on the job. By sending him back into the picking crews, he would have lost not only his place in the list but a good year-round job driving a tractor. His family would have been thrown out of their company-owned house.

I suggested that we hold a company-wide meeting in front of the office in Paicines at lunchtime and then refuse to go back to work until the company talked with us. Farmworkers organize work stoppages a lot, so the idea wasn't that strange. The company did agree to talk with us. We called in Bill Granfield from the Salinas UFW office, knowing that the managers needed to save face by seeming to agree with the union's official representative rather than with us, the workers. Bill, a good organizer, knew the game too and played his part well. Our driver got his job back, and after that my crew might not have been fast, but we were well loved, me included.

I lived in an SRO farm labor hotel in Hollister in a room found for me by Roberto San Roman, head of the ranch committee. When the picking was done, I drove over to Watsonville and got a dispatch out to a cauliflower crew. I worked in that crew for a good part of a year. It didn't pay too well—by the hour—but you can work standing up, cutting off the cauliflower heads with a machete and throwing them on the belt of the machine in front of you.

Here I learned something about Mexican culture that I still think and write about today, more than thirty years later. Our crew had a group of Oaxacans, the first I'd met (and probably among the first of the huge wave of folks who came to California from Oaxaca in the years that followed). They mostly ate lunch with each other and spoke a language I'd never heard but I knew wasn't Spanish.

We had a problem in this crew too. The foreman decided to stop giving us the whetstones we needed to sharpen our machetes. A dull machete makes the work many times as hard and messes the plants up too. So we decided to "forget" to bring our machetes with us one morning. When we went to talk with the Oaxacans, they all listened politely and then went off by themselves to talk about what we'd proposed. After a while, they came back and agreed.

The little *paro* did the trick. We got our stones back. And I could see that the way these (I learned later) Mixtec workers made their decisions was different. It wasn't each person on his or her own but the group acting like a community, making a collective decision that everyone implemented. Almost like a union within the union.

The experience resonated with me through the years after I left the fields to work in factories, then for other unions, and then as a journalist and photographer—the work I do today. In a life spent in the labor and immigrant rights movements, I seem to learn over and over again that the strength of indigenous culture is one of the most important resources these movements have.

This book looks at migration and work as they're experienced and discussed by migrant communities. Indigenous people play a very important part in that discussion. The way that experience is analyzed and the proposals people make are way ahead of the way migration and work are presented in the halls of government or in the mainstream media. If the dialogue on migration seems so poisonous in the United States, and so devoid of any ability to make political progress, it's in large part because this migrant and indigenous perspective is absent from it.

This is not a pitch for saying that migrants have the answer and all we need to do is to listen to their voices. There are millions of migrants and millions of voices. But the social movements of resistance to the brutal human cost of globalization in Mexico (and by extension, in other migrant-producing countries) and the movements for the human and labor rights for migrants in the United States and Canada, have made unique progress in the last two decades.

They've developed a framework for seeing the connection between the displacement of people in their countries of origin and the exploitation and repression of those communities in the countries where they go to work. Some of their proposals for human rights for migrants in the United States and Canada have won some attention. But the proposals in Mexico, especially for the right to not migrate, that is, for alternatives to forced migration, have not. And even more important, the link between the two has received no attention at all.

As Gaspar Rivera Salgado explains, migrant rights are connected to the right to not migrate. "Both rights are part of the same solution," he says. "We have to change the debate from one in which immigration is presented as a problem to a debate over rights." The suppression of rights in Mexico contributes to the pressure to migrate. The suppression of the rights of migrants in the United States and Canada makes their labor cheaper—a source of profit to employers.

This connection isn't just one of ideas. The movements of people on both sides of this global divide are connected as well. Whether it's the Frente Indigena de Organizaciones Binacionales fighting for indigenous rights or unions fighting mining companies and privatization, organizations and people themselves are crossing borders, seeking to implement both rights together.

This book tells some of that story. It looks at these problems and proposed solutions as presented by the participants in these efforts.

Each chapter except the last is also followed by longer narratives in which these participants speak for themselves—describing their experiences, analyzing the political and economic situation they face, and proposing the solutions as they see them.

Chapter 1 describes the impact of market reforms and free trade agreements in Veracruz, where the operation of Smithfield Foods makes the connections very clear. It shows the link between the displacement of people and their employment as migrant labor in North Carolina, and describes the way they tried to change their circumstances by organizing a union. That is also the effort of another group of Veracruzanos in North Carolina, tobacco workers, and the chapter concludes by looking at the use of guest worker programs and how they affect those efforts.

Chapter 2 looks at Oaxaca, where the debate over the right to not migrate is the most developed in Mexico. It describes the displacing activity of Canadian mining corporations and how that fits into the general economic reforms that have produced very high levels of rural poverty. The chapter then outlines the effort to win a government that seeks to help people find alternatives to forced migration, as well as the problems and criticism its officials encounter. Finally, it looks at a particular community, the Triquis, and the difficulties they face as migrants trying to return to their communities of origin.

Chapter 3 covers the repression of progressive unions in Mexico and the way this contributes to forced migration. It details the attacks on the long miners' strike in Cananea, the firing of forty-four thousand members of Mexico's oldest and most democratic union, and the proposals for a corporate-backed change to the country's labor law. Finally, it outlines a little of the history of cross-border solidarity between workers in Mexico and the United States.

Chapter 4 describes the criminalization of migrants once they've been displaced and forced to come to the United States. It examines the extreme anti-immigrant political hysteria in Arizona and the growth of the enforcement regime under the George W. Bush administration. It then recounts one of the most successful efforts to resist—the alliance between immigrants, African Americans, and unions in Mississippi, which has been able to stop many anti-immigrant proposals. Finally, it looks at the Utah compact, which seeks to implement on a state level the same corporate reforms proposed in the US Congress.

Chapter 5 looks at the development of immigration enforcement under the Barack Obama administration, especially as it has affected workers. It describes the growth of mass firings and the way immigrant workers and unions try to resist them. Finally, it assesses some of the alliances developed by immigrant workers in the last few years—with the Occupy movement to protest economic inequality, and with unions, as they struggle to overcome their own Cold War legacy.

Chapter 6 examines the long-term strategic effort by corporations to manage the flow of displaced people through guest worker and contract labor programs. It looks at the ways legal aid organizations have sought to help migrants, including guest workers. It describes the debate in Canada over its guest worker program, often held up as a model for future programs in the United States. It concludes with the debate over whether to reform these programs or to find alternatives to them.

Chapter 7 looks at the way that asserting the right to not migrate and the human and labor rights of migrants challenge the pro-corporate proposals made in all three countries—Mexico, the United States, and Canada. The book concludes by proposing that the right to not migrate is not so much an idea as a movement of people, and it suggests that their proposals can have a powerful impact on protecting and expanding peoples' rights.

The sources used in this book are generally given throughout the text. Much of the book is based on personal interviews with the author, but when quotes come from other sources, they are given. This book is not an academic presentation, although I'm very grateful for academic works I've used in the course of writing it and have credited them also. It tries to present the thinking of people and organizations in one wing of the labor and migrant rights movements and suggests that these views are worth exploring. It is meant to provoke discussion—there are even descriptions in a couple of chapters of the ways some of those discussions have already developed.

I don't claim to be an unbiased observer. I take the side of people in communities in Mexico trying to find alternatives to displacement and fighting for democratic political change. I'm on the side of immigrant workers and unions in the United States, whose struggle for rights and a decent life for families is one of the best hopes for change there as well. If this book helps to strengthen those movements, it will have served a good purpose.

For those interested in more information, the best sources include *La Jornada*, the Mexican left-wing newspaper, and also often the coverage in *El Milenio*. The Mexican press is much better at covering the United States, especially what goes on in immigrant communities, than the US press is at covering Mexico. Other good sources include two websites: the Americas Program and Mexican Labor News and Analysis. The academic studies mentioned in the text are all sources of important information. In the age of the Internet, it's easy to google the organizations mentioned in the book and make direct contact with them. I hope it inspires people to do that. A list of some of the sources used in this book follows the last chapter.

ONE

FROM PEROTE TO TAR HEEL

Pushing People out of Veracruz

On some warm nights, Fausto Limon's children wake up and vomit from the smell. He puts his wife, two sons, and daughter into his beat-up pickup, and they drive away from his farm until they can breathe the air without getting sick. Then he parks, and they sleep in the truck for the rest of the night.

Until the beginning of 2011, his mother went with them. Then her kidneys failed, and she went to the hospital, where she died. Limon and his family all had kidney ailments for three years before that. They kept taking medicine, he says, until finally a doctor told them to stop drinking water from the farm's well. After his mother died, they began hauling in bottled water. Once they stopped drinking from the well, the infections stopped too.

Less than half a mile from his house is one of the many pig farms built by Granjas Carroll de Mexico in the Perote Valley, a high, arid, volcano-rimmed basin straddling the Mexican states of Veracruz and Puebla. "Before the pig farms came, they promised they would bring jobs," Limon remembers. "But then we found out the reality. Yes, there were jobs, but they also brought a lot of contamination."

David Torres, a Perote native who spent eight years helping sows give birth in the farm's maternity section, estimates that by 2010 Granjas Carroll had eighty complexes, each with as many as twenty thousand hogs.

The sheds look clean and modern. "When I went to work there, I could see the company was completely mechanized," Torres says. But in back of each complex is a large oxidation pond for the hogs' urine and excrement. Driving through the valley, a plastic cover was visible on only one of several dozen lagoons. "Granjas Carroll doesn't use concrete or membranes under their ponds," Torres charges, "so the water table is getting contaminated. People here get their water from wells, which are surrounded by pig farms and oxidation ponds."

In a response to an article published in August 2010 in a Veracruz daily newspaper, *Imagen de Veracruz*, Granjas Carroll representative Tito Tablada declared flatly, "Granjas Carroll does not pollute." And Amy Richards, a representative for public relations firm Charleston Orwig, responding to an inquiry on behalf of Smithfield Foods—Granjas Carroll's parent company—added, "Our environmental treatment systems in Mexico strictly comply with local and federal regulations that are different than most other countries that encourage use of treated animal waste, at agronomic rates, as a key element of a nutrient management plan. Mexico encourages, and requires, anaerobic digesters and evaporation ponds."

Ruben Lopez, an *ejido* (communal land) commissioner in Chichicuautla, a valley town surrounded by hog farms, also charged that there are no membranes beneath the pools. The Commission for the Environment and Natural Resources of the Mexican Congress issued a report in February 2006 in which it accused Granjas Carroll of endangering the sixty thousand inhabitants of the Perote Valley. The dangers it listed included locating the ponds of excrement near sources of drinking water, pumping excessive quantities of water from the aquifer, failure to put membranes under the ponds, producing excessive amounts of methane, causing soil erosion, and undermining air quality with terrible odors. "The farms' consumption of water is greater than that of the entire population of the region," it said. According to Antonio Rodriguez, a former municipal councilor in Guadalupe Victoria in the heart of the valley, just one well on a Granjas Carroll property pumps out four hundred thousand liters of water a day to supply the pig farms.

Karina de la Paz Reyes, who wrote the article denounced by Granjas Carroll's Tablada, claims that the problems persist. In July 2011, she wrote that valley residents were up in arms at a Granjas Carroll proposal to expand the farms, alleging that the company had already acquired more than twelve hundred acres for another eighty shed complexes. "Although the company and local authorities deny responsibility, since this transnational enterprise located here," she wrote, "there have been persistent skin diseases, diarrhea, and a reduction in the water level in the wells, due to pig raising on an immense scale so close to population centers."

Granjas Carroll de Mexico is owned in large part by Carroll's Farms, a division of Virginia-based Smithfield Foods, one of the world's largest meatpackers. Company spokespeople point to the twelve hundred jobs it created in a valley where employment is scarce. But Limon counters that a third of its young people are leaving: "They don't see a future, and every year it's harder to live here." Carolina Ramirez, who headed the women's department of the Veracruz Human Rights Commission, says no official agency counts them, "but I'm sure many people have left."

Migrants departing the valley are joining a huge wave of migration from Veracruz that dates from the beginning of the 1990s—the start of the NAFTA era. The North American Free Trade Agreement took effect on January 1, 1994, the year the pig farms arrived and two years after Smithfield built the world's largest hog slaughterhouse in Tar Heel, North Carolina. Both operations have had an enormous impact on the lives of the people of Veracruz.

For over two decades, Smithfield has used NAFTA and the forces it unleashed to become one of the world's largest growers, packers, and exporters of hogs and pork. But the conditions created in Veracruz to help it make high profits, as one of Mexico's largest pig producers, also plunged thousands of Veracruz residents into poverty.

"In my town, Las Choapas, after I killed a pig, I would cut it up to sell the meat," recalls Roberto Ortega. "Whatever I could do to make money I did. But I could never make enough for us to survive." Eventually, he left Veracruz for the United States, where he again slaughtered pigs for a living. This time, though, he did it as a worker in Smithfield's Tar Heel plant.

North Carolina became the number one US destination for Veracruz's displaced farmers. Many got jobs in the Tar Heel slaughterhouse, helping Smithfield's bottom line by working for low wages on its US meatpacking lines. Some, like Ortega, helped lead a sixteen-year fight that finally brought in the union there. But they paid a high price. Asserting their rights also made them the targets of harsh immigration enforcement and a growing wave of hostility toward Mexicans in the US South.

The experiences of Veracruz migrants and farmers impacted by Perote pig farms show the close connection between US investment and trade deals in Mexico and the displacement and migration of its people. Protecting Mexico's environment, and the rights of migrants displaced by environmental and economic causes, requires making the connection between trade reform, environmental protection, and immigrant and labor rights.

Smithfield Goes to Mexico

In 1994, Carroll's Farms, a giant hog-raising corporation, created a partnership—Granjas Carroll de Mexico—with a Mexican agribusiness company, Agroindustrias Unidas de México. Together they set up the huge pig farm in Perote. Carroll's Farms had a joint partnership for many years with Smithfield Foods, the world's largest pork producer, including a seat on the Smithfield board of directors. In 1999 Smithfield, which now controls 27 percent of all US pork production, finally bought out Carroll's Farms entirely.

In 2004, the expansion of the swine sheds through the previous decade finally provoked a social movement that swept the Perote Valley. Pueblos Unidos—or United Towns, a coalition of local farmers—began in Xaltepec, where local residents started collecting signatures on a petition in protest. Veronica Hernandez was a teacher at the secondary school in La Gloria, the Perote Valley town where she was born. She was concerned about her students, who told her coming to school on the bus was like riding in a toilet. "Some of them fainted or got headaches," she charges. "In the morning, when it was time to eat, many couldn't because they still felt sick."

Hernandez not only signed the petition, she began to write leaflets urging Valley residents to get involved. "We said they weren't treating the pig excrement in a sanitary way," she recalls, "that they would leave dead pigs in the open air, which would attract flies. The flies were a potentially dangerous source of illnesses."

Jorge Morales Vasquez, a reporter for the Mexico City daily *Milenio*, later investigated the farms in 2009. He wrote that the anaerobic digesters referred to by Smithfield spokesperson Amy Richards were actually "just pits with a metal cover, where they throw the bodies of sick pigs or those that have been injured in fights or squashed in the sheds. In these holes dug in the earth, the bodies decompose, which becomes a source of contamination and the proliferation of flies. Carried on the wind, they travel into the community of La Gloria, where they then start living in people's homes." One resident, Maria Dolores Herrera, told Vasquez the flies were the size of killer bees.

The lack of any response from government officials increased the anger among Perote farmers. On April 26, 2005, hundreds of them blocked the main highway from Xalapa, Veracruz's capital, to Puebla. People from sixteen towns confronted the police and only lifted the blockade when officials said they'd talk with Granjas Carroll management.

That had no effect. The following November a construction crew in Chichicuautla, about to build another shed and oxidation pond, was met by a thousand angry ranchers. Police rescued the construction crew, but when they returned to the site, the people had disappeared with all the construction materials. In February of 2006, Atanasio Garcia Duran, Veracruz deputy for the left-wing Party of the Democratic Revolution, tried to inspect some of the Granjas Carroll facilities together with local farmers and a representative of the Federal Prosecutor for Environmental Protection, Francisco Briseno Cortes. Garcia Duran told reporters that he was threatened by guards, who followed the delegation and filmed the farmers who'd come to make complaints to the officials.

Finally, at a meeting in 2007 between the presidents of many valley towns and company officials, Granjas Carroll's Tito Tablada signed an agreement blocking any new expansion. The protests clearly worried the company, however. The following year Granjas Carroll filed criminal charges against Victoria Hernandez and thirteen other leaders in the state courts of both Veracruz and Puebla.

All were charged with "defaming" the company by accusing it of pollution.

One farmer, sixty-six-year-old Guadalupe Serrano, was denounced by the company as one of the troublemakers who'd blocked the highway. On April 8, 2008, federal agents came to his home, disguised as workers. The Perote mayor's personal secretary, Omar Hernandez, accompanied them. He got Serrano to leave his house by telling him the mayor wanted to appoint him director for public works. Once Serrano had walked out of his door, however, he was handcuffed and taken to jail in Xalapa, the Veracruz state capital. There was such a scandal over his arrest that the mayor fired Omar Hernandez.

In Veracruz, the charges were dismissed quickly, when a judge agreed the activists were exercising freedom of speech. "You can't negate the effects of the pig farms because the people are suffering from them," Veronica Hernandez explained. "That was the evidence, the reality test. Plus, we could show that the water table was dropping." Nevertheless, the fourteen had to spend the next two years registering with the court in Cholula, Puebla, every two weeks, to avoid being locked up. While those charges eventually were also dropped, they scared the farmers, and the protest movement diminished. Even several years later, Serrano, Veronica Hernandez, and their codefendants expressed great anxiety about the power of the company. "People saw us going through all of this, and it was very intimidating," she recalled. "They knew what it was about. They were afraid that if they continued protesting they'd be taken to jail too."

Then, in early 2009, the first confirmed case of swine flu, the AH1N1 virus, was found in a five-year-old boy from La Gloria, Edgar Hernandez. Two infants also died of what was diagnosed as pneumonia.

Pickup trucks from the local health department soon began spraying pesticide in the streets to kill the omnipresent flies. Health workers with backpack sprayers went house to house. Nevertheless, the virus spread to Mexico City, then to California. By May, 2,254 nonfatal US cases had been reported, while in Mexico forty-five people had died. Mexican schools closed, and public events were cancelled.

Smithfield denied the virus came from its Veracruz hogs. Mexican officials were quick to agree. A government statement claimed, "Neither in the farm, nor in the homes, did we see sick pigs or people. Neither did we see signs of respiratory disease." Tablada's statement to *Imagen de Veracruz* asserted, "Our company has been totally cleared of any links with the AH1N1 virus," and "the official position of the Secretary of Health and the World Health Organization leaves no room for doubt."

Meatpacking companies breathed a sigh of relief at Smithfield's exoneration. The US National Hog Farmer website reported that fear of the virus led to losses of $8.4 million per day for the first two weeks of the global scare.

In the valley, though, "no one believed it," Perote resident Limon recalls. "We all knew that such a brutal concentration of animals could result in illnesses. But we had to go on living here." Laura Carlson, journalist and director of the Mexico City–based Americas Program, warned, "The centrality of foreign investment in the Mexican economy creates a climate where transnational corporations with large investments can exercise coercive power over government agencies on all levels."

In August of 2011, however, Granjas Carroll representatives convinced Felipe Cortes Hernandez, the municipal president of Guadalupe Victoria, to grant a permit for building new hog farms. According to the lawyer for Pueblos Unidos, Abigail Marin, the director general for the state of Puebla, Laura Escobar, warned farmers not to get in the way. Nevertheless, representatives of eighteen town councils signed a declaration denouncing the new expansion plans. Referring to the 2007 agreement, they declared that "state and municipal authorities are trying to ignore and supplant the majority will of our communities . . . including even the threat to use public force [*granaderos*, heavily armed police] so that the company can continue to expand, against our will."

"It doesn't do any good to threaten to kill us," said one farmer. "We're already dying anyway. We're not going to let them build any more sheds. What we really want is for GCM [Granjas Carroll] to leave the valley."

By 2008, the Perote operation was sending close to a million pigs to slaughter every year—85 percent to Mexico City and the rest to surrounding Mexican states. By locating in the mountains above Veracruz, Mexico's largest port, trains could bring in imported corn for feed—two-thirds of the cost of raising hogs. US pork producers benefit from below-cost soybeans and corn, the key components of feed, which are subsidized in congressional farm bills. "After NAFTA," says Timothy Wise of the Global Development and Environment Institute at Tufts University, "corn was priced 19 percent below the cost of production." Lower feed costs, unavailable to Mexican producers, gave Granjas Carroll's hogs a competitive advantage.

But Smithfield didn't just import feed—it imported meat as well.

According to Alejandro Ramirez, general director of the Confederation of Mexican Pork Producers, Mexico imported 30,000 tons of pork in 1995, the year NAFTA took effect. By 2010 pork imports, almost all from the United States, had grown over twenty-five times, to 811,000 tons. As a result, pork prices received by Mexican producers dropped 56 percent. US pork exports are dominated by the largest companies; Wise estimates that Smithfield's export share is significantly greater than its 27 percent share of US production.

Imports had a dramatic effect on Mexican jobs. "We lost four thousand pig farms," Ramirez estimates. "On Mexican farms, each one hundred animals produce five jobs, so we lost twenty thousand farm jobs directly from imports. Counting the five indirect jobs dependent on each direct job, we lost over a hundred twenty thousand jobs in total. This produces migration to the United States or to Mexican cities—a big problem for our country."

John Womack, a professor of Latin American history and economics at Harvard, explains that NAFTA precipitated an economic crisis following its implementation in 1994. "Mexicans thought they could use the agreement to open up US markets, but once the dust settled, all of its banks belonged to US or Spanish investors," he says. "Mexico no longer had control over its economic policy. Foreign capital moved in, which changed the conditions of production and led to a vast wave of bankruptcies. Smithfield was one of many who saw opportunity in that."

Pork imports were still causing economic dislocation in 2012. In Queretaro, one of the main states for pig raising in Mexico, imports lowered pork prices so much that 70 percent of its production could no longer be sold locally—in fact, farmers have found the prices they receive per hog are now $19 to $25 less than the cost of raising them. "We're selling at competitive prices, but the US sells their [pork] products at very low prices in Mexico, and we really can't compete in Queretaro," said Alejandro Tinoco Ugalde, president of the state's Association of Pork Producers. "The imports are increasing every day more and more. We shouldn't prioritize imports without considering the state of small pork producers."

Corn imports also rose, from about 2 million tons to about 10.3 million tons from 1992 to 2008. Once Mexican meat and corn producers were driven from the market by imports, the Mexican economy was left vulnerable to price changes dictated by US agribusiness or US policy. "When the US modified its corn policy to encourage ethanol production," Alejandro Ramirez charges, "corn prices jumped 100 percent in one year."

"Small Mexican farmers got hit with a double whammy," Wise explains. "On the one hand, competitors were importing pork. On the other, they were producing cheaper hogs." Smithfield was both producer and importer. Wise estimates this one company supplies 25 percent of all the pork sold in Mexico.

Granjas Carroll enjoyed another advantage. The *Mexican News* online business journal explains that "production cost is very low because of the high ratio of pigs to workers. . . . The preparation of food and feeding of the pigs is completely automated, along with temperature control and the elimination of excrement."

Workers aren't employed directly by Granjas Carroll, however, according to David Torres. "Since we work for a contractor, we're not entitled to profit-sharing or company benefits," he says. "Granjas Carroll made millions of dollars in profits, but never distributed a part of them to the workers," which is required under Mexico's Federal Labor Law. Torres was paid 1,250 pesos ($110 US) every fifteen days and says the company picked him up at six every morning and returned him home at five thirty each night, often six days a week.

In Perote, the company was investing in an area where it wouldn't face the environmental cleanup costs it was forced to pay in the United States. In 1997, federal judge Rebecca Smith imposed the largest federal pollution fine to that date—$12.6 million—on Smithfield for dumping pig excrement into the Pagan River, which runs into Chesapeake Bay. Smithfield then had to upgrade the local water treatment facilities to handle the effluent from two plants.

That year the state of North Carolina went further, passing a moratorium on the creation of any new open-air hog waste lagoons, unless they were built with new, expensive waste-disposal technology. Smithfield had to agree to a production cap at its Tar Heel plant. Environmental groups advocated even stricter limits.

In 1998, the Environmental Protection Agency also proposed rules for animal-waste runoff. And in 2000, then state attorney general Mike Easley forced Smithfield to fund research by North Carolina State University to develop hog-waste treatment methods more effective than open lagoons. These requirements were criticized by Earl Bell, president of the North Carolina Pork Council, who claimed that "more regulations drive up the cost of production . . . [and] will hurt America's ability to export pork."

North Carolina is hardly a regulation-friendly state, but the outcry from communities enduring the stench and flies from the lagoons was so great that business lobbies retreated. In 2007, when Mike Easley (by then governor) signed SB 1465, a permanent ban on new lagoons, the Pork Council supported it.

In Perote, Smithfield didn't have to worry about US regulations. NAFTA had a side agreement, supposedly to raise Mexican environmental standards and increase their enforcement. No complaint was ever filed or action taken about hog farms, however. "The company can do here what it can't do at home," the Veracruz Human Rights Commission's Carolina Ramirez concluded bitterly.

And Veracruz Migrants Come to the United States

By the time of the swine flu epidemic, migration from Veracruz to the United States already had a two-decade history. The motivating force pushing people to leave was their need to survive. The World Bank, in a 2005 study made for the Mexican government, found that the extreme rural poverty rate of 35 percent from 1992 to 1994, prior to NAFTA, jumped to 55 percent between 1996 and 1998, after NAFTA took effect—the years when Roberto Ortega left Mexico. This could be explained, the report said, "mainly by the 1995 economic crisis, the sluggish performance of agriculture, stagnant rural wages, and falling real agricultural prices."

By 2010, fifty-three million Mexicans were living in poverty, according to the Monterrey Institute of Technology—half the country's population. About 20 percent lived in extreme poverty, almost all in rural areas.

Pork and corn imports were just part of a series of economic changes brought about by NAFTA and neoliberal reforms to the Mexican economy, such as ending land reform, that were made during the same period the treaty took effect. Companies like Smithfield benefited, but poverty increased also, especially in the countryside.

The growth of poverty, in turn, fueled migration. In 1990, 4.5 million Mexican-born people lived in the United States. A decade later, that population more than doubled, to 9.75 million, and in 2008 it peaked at 12.67 million. About 11 percent of all Mexicans now live in the United States. About 5.7 million were able to get some kind of visa, but another 7 million couldn't and came nevertheless.

As an agricultural state, Veracruz suffered particularly from Mexico's abandonment of two important policies. First, neoliberal reforms did away with Tabamex, a national marketing program for small tobacco farmers. A similar program for coffee growers ended just as world coffee prices plunged to record lows. Second, Carlos Salinas de Gortari, the country's most corrupt president, pushed through changes in Article 27 of the Constitution in the late 1980s, dismantling land reform and allowing the sale of *ejidos*, or common lands, as private property.

Waves of tobacco and coffee farmers sold their land because they could no longer make a living on it. Many became migrants. Granjas Carroll, however, could not only buy land for its swine sheds but also found a ready supply of displaced rural labor to staff them.

Simultaneous changes in the United States accelerated migration. In 1986 Congress passed the Immigration Reform and Control Act, expanding the existing H2 visa program and creating the current H-2A program, which allows US agricultural employers to bring in workers from Mexico and other countries, giving them temporary visas tied to employment contracts. Growers in North Carolina became large users of the program, especially through the North Carolina Growers Association. Displaced tobacco farmers from Veracruz became tobacco workers in the Carolinas.

"Many Veracruzanos came because we were offered work in the tobacco fields, where we had experience," remembers Miguel Huerta. "In Veracruz, we spent our lives working in hot, tropical weather in the tobacco fields. The tobacco harvest here in North Carolina takes place in extreme heat too, and we're used to that." Huerta also points out that growing families were trying to make a living from a limited amount of land. Since families were already living close to survival, with only very limited help from the government, the pressure of a growing population also fueled migration.

"The majority of the people from Veracruz live off of the land," he explains. "Many families have simply outgrown their plot of land. The family size continues to grow, but the land doesn't, and it isn't enough to feed the new members of the extended family. This forces the family to move and look for other options. The land is fertile and perfect for agriculture in Veracruz, and there is a lot of work, but it isn't enough for everyone." His own migration to North Carolina had its roots in that pressure. "I come from a family of *ejidatarios* [farmers who share communal land rights]. When you have a ten-acre parcel of land, that's only enough for one family. But my parents had seven children, and we had children. Our family could survive off of the land, but not get an education. This is why we came to this country. Our son was able to go to school and now has a good job."

Once people began working in North Carolina's tobacco fields, they began to put down roots. "Then people who'd been contracted just stayed, because they didn't have anything in Mexico to go back to. After the tobacco harvest, workers spread out to other industries," Huerta recalls.

As the pool of Veracruzanos grew in North Carolina, it attracted migrants like David Ceja. He was eighteen and living on a ranch outside Martinez de la Torre, two hours from the Perote Valley. Ceja remembers that when he was a small child, his family had ten cows, as well as pigs and chickens. Even then, he still had to work, and they sometimes went hungry. "But we could give milk to people who came asking for it. There were people even worse off than us," he recalls. "Sometimes the price of a pig was enough to buy what we needed, but then it wasn't. Farm prices were always going down." His family had no money to plant trees or crops. "I didn't really want to leave, but I felt I had to," he recalls. "I was afraid, but our need was so great."

In 1999 his parents sold four cows and two hectares of land, and came up with enough to get him to the border. There he found a *coyote*—someone who smuggles people across the border—who took him across for $1,200. He arrived still owing for the passage. "I couldn't find work for three months. I was desperate," Ceja says. He feared the consequences if he couldn't pay, and took whatever jobs he could find on the street until he finally reached North Carolina. There he found friends, got the identification he needed for a real job, and went to work at Smithfield's Tar Heel packinghouse. "The boys I played with as a kid are all in the US," he says. "I'd see many of them working in the plant."

Roberto Ortega remembers that there were hundreds of people from Veracruz in the Tar Heel plant when he worked there in the late 1990s and early 2000s. They'd have community get-togethers, eat seafood, and play their state's famous *jarocho* music on wooden harps and guitars. "Almost the whole town [of Las Choapas] is here," he says. "Some are supervisors and *mayordomos*, and they bring people from the town."

As an academic in the 1990s, Carolina Ramirez studied migration to North Carolina before taking her position at the Veracruz Human Rights Commission. Labor recruitment was a big factor, she found. "There were recruiters in many Veracruz towns," she remembers. "There were even vans stationed in different places, and a whole system in which people were promised jobs in the packing plants. It was an open secret."

Smithfield spokesperson Amy Richards responds, "With one exception [a management trainee program], Smithfield Foods does not travel to, nor advertise in, other countries or outside of our local communities to actively recruit employees for our various facilities around the country."

"These companies are very powerful and can do anything," Veracruzano Miguel Huerta responds. "They hire legally and illegally. They can go to Mexico and bring as many employees as they want and replace them when they want." Poverty, though, was the real recruiter. It created, as Ceja says, the need. "We all had to leave Veracruz because of it," Ceja emphasizes. "Otherwise, we wouldn't do something so hard."

The Union Campaign in Tar Heel

The Tar Heel slaughterhouse kills and dismembers thirty-two thousand hogs every day. Meatpacking is demanding and dangerous work. People stand very close together as animal carcasses speed by, cutting the hogs into pieces. In their white aprons, hairnets, and masks, workers wield extremely sharp knives, slicing through meat, sinews, and bone with the same motion, hundreds of times each hour.

The plant's first workers were mostly African Americans. From the moment it opened in 1992, many objected to the high line speed, and the injuries that proliferated as a result. Even in North Carolina, where union membership and wages are low, Smithfield's wage level gave the company problems. It was hard to attract local workers, especially with a growing reputation for job-related injuries. Once people were hired, many quickly wanted more money for such exhausting and dangerous labor. The United Food and Commercial Workers (UFCW) began helping workers organize a union almost as soon as the lines started running. What followed was one of the longest and most bitter fights in modern US labor history.

In 1994 and 1997, the UFCW lost two union representation elections, the latter thrown out because of company intimidation tactics. In 1997, the head of plant security, Danny Priest (later a Smithfield general manager), told local sheriffs he expected violence on election day. Police in riot gear then lined the walkway into the slaughter-house, and workers had to file past them to cast their ballots. At the end of the vote count, according to charges filed with the National Labor Relations Board, union organizer Ray Shawn was beaten up inside the plant.

Priest and the other security guards were later deputized and maintained a holding area in a trailer on the property, which work-ers called the company jail. During the campaign, one couple was "arrested" when security discovered a pair of smoldering gloves in a trashcan. "They took us to a jail the company had," one recalled, and then to the county lockup. "It was to intimidate us since we were both actively organizing in the plant. They wanted to get rid of us."

In the mid-1990s, the percentage of immigrants in the slaughter-house began to rise. As new migrants, people from Veracruz were desperate and hungry. Most were undocumented. Keith Ludlum, one of the plant's few white workers, was fired for union activ-ity in 1994. He says, "After Smithfield ran through the workforce around here, you started seeing a lot more immigrants working in the plant. The company had to make that happen. They thought, the undocumented will work cheap, they'll work hard, and they won't complain."

Carolina Ramirez describes the Veracruz immigrants as "docile at first, because they didn't have the experience." For employers, she explains, "these people were a safe workforce. They didn't under-stand their rights or the system here. But they got the message—don't organize. Don't think for yourself. If you comply, your job is assured. They would work fast for fear of losing their jobs, because there was no alternative."

Nilsa Morales, a Veracruz native, slipped and fell on the greasy floor in 2004, twisting her arm and shoulder, which were already injured from using an electric knife all day. The company doc-tor forced her to return to work, a common complaint. "I kept on working in spite of the pain," she remembers, "because I needed the money. People depend on me. But there came a moment when I just couldn't stand the pain anymore." She left her job, and the company cut off her insurance. "Many workers put up with the pain and keep on working. They don't say anything because they're afraid of being fired."

"They pressured you so you'd work faster and produce more," Ortega recalled. "You felt like knifing the foreman. Many wanted to throw their knives at his feet and just leave. But if you are the support of your family you put up with it. 'I am not going to leave my work,' you say to yourself. 'Who will pay me then?'" Eventually, people didn't put up with it. In the early 2000s, the UFCW sent in a group of organizers, who began helping workers find tactics to slow down the lines. They set up a workers' center in Red Springs and offered English classes after work. When Ortega was fired on trumped-up charges, he began making visits to the homes of other workers. In 2003, the night cleaning crew refused to work, keeping the lines from starting the following morning. David Ceja helped organize another work stoppage a year later.

By 2006, Mexican workers made up about 60 percent of the plant's five thousand workers. As immigrant protests and demonstrations spread across the country that April, hundreds left the plant and marched through the streets of Wilmington. On May Day, only a skeleton crew showed up for work.

That spring, Smithfield enrolled in the Department of Homeland Security's IMAGE program, in which the government identifies undocumented workers, and employers agree to fire them. The program enforces a provision of the 1986 Immigration Reform and Control Act, employer sanctions, which prohibit employers from hiring undocumented workers. All workers in the United States since then have had to fill out I-9 forms declaring their citizenship or immigration status when they're hired. Employers can now check the information provided by consulting an electronic database called E-Verify. Smithfield spokesperson Amy Richards says, "We do all that the law requires, and more, in assuring that our workforce is authorized to work in the US. In addition to complying with the Form I-9 process, all of our plants are members of E-Verify."

In October 2006, Smithfield announced it intended to fire over three hundred workers, alleging they had bad Social Security numbers, presumably because they were undocumented. When terminations started, hundreds of other workers walked out, forcing the company to rescind the firings temporarily.

Just months before, after a twelve-year legal battle, the company had been forced to rehire Keith Ludlum. "It was really empowering to see all those workers stand up together," he recalls, "probably one of the best experiences of my life." It had an effect on African American workers too. They collected four thousand signatures, asking the company for the day off on Martin Luther King Jr.'s birthday. When managers refused, four hundred black workers on the kill line didn't come in. With no hogs on the hooks at the beginning of the lines, no one else could work either. The plant shut down again.

Nine days later, agents of Immigration and Customs Enforcement (ICE) detained twenty-one Smithfield workers for deportation, questioning hundreds more in the lunchroom. Fear was so intense that most immigrants didn't show up for work the following day. A few months later, another raid took place. Some of the detained workers were later charged with federal felonies for using bad Social Security numbers.

Meanwhile, ICE agents swept through Mexican communities, detaining people at home and in the street. Ludlum and union organizer Eduardo Peña followed the ICE agents with video cameras, but they couldn't stop the terror the raids engendered. Ludlum, Peña, and other union activists believe the company cooperated in the IMAGE program and immigration enforcement because the Veracruzanos were no longer useful. "The workforce that was in the shadows was expecting rights, expecting to be part of the community," Ludlum says. "That's not what they wanted. They wanted a workforce that would be quiet and do what they were told."

Terry Slaughter, an African American union supporter, calls it "a tactic by Smithfield, a dirty low blow. The company knew who they were hiring."

Eventually, the immigrant workforce shrank by half as people left. Union organizing stalled. But then, led by Slaughter, African American workers stopped the plant again by sitting all day in the middle of the kill floor. They put union stickers on their hard hats and began collecting signatures demanding union recognition. Helped by widespread community support and impending lawsuits, the company agreed to a union election that would bar its old bare-knuckle tactics. When the ballots were finally counted on December 11, 2008, the union won. Today Ludlum is president of UFCW Local 2208, and Slaughter is secretary-treasurer.

A Veracruzana, Carmen Izquierdo is on the union executive board. "In the union it doesn't matter if you're undocumented, if you have papers or not," she says. "We should all be respected because we are human beings, and because of our work. All the workers here, whether or not we have papers, have rights." Ludlum and Slaughter say line speed is slower now, and workers can rotate from one job to another, reducing injuries. They no longer fear company doctors will send them back to work if they're hurt. David Ceja felt the union gave workers a tool to change conditions. "I'm glad it came in," he said. "We worked hard to get it."

But he's not there to enjoy it. Now he works as a mechanic in a local garage, and his band plays weddings and quinceñeras. His brother Marcos wants him to come back to Veracruz, where the family used the money David sent from his job at Smithfield to plant fruit trees on their ranch. Roberto Ortega and his wife, Maria, left North Carolina when the hostility toward immigrants got worse, and they couldn't find work. Juvencio Rocha, head of the Network of Veracruzanos in North Carolina, says bitterly, "After we contributed to the economy, they didn't want us here anymore. They even took our driver's licenses away."

Demands for Change, on Both Sides of the Border

Smithfield didn't invent the system of displacement and migration. It took advantage of US trade and immigration policies, as well as Mexican economic reforms. And at crucial moments in each country, it found cooperative governments willing to bend those laws and policies for its benefit.

For a while, farmers in Perote Valley were able to stop expanding swine sheds. Migrant Veracruzanos did help to organize a union in Tar Heel. But there was no balance of power in this system. Today, those farmers and migrants continue to face that same imbalance as they try to defend their land, their jobs and their rights.

"From the beginning NAFTA was an instrument of displacement," says Juan Manuel Sandoval, a professor at the National Institute of Anthropology and History in Mexico City and cofounder of the Mexican Action Network Opposing Free Trade. "The penetration of capital led to the destruction of the traditional economy, especially in agriculture, and produced a huge labor reserve in Mexico. People had no alternative but to migrate. The system helps corporations make profit, which is relocated to the United States. And it produces displaced people, who are needed by the US economy."

Sandoval sees that many US industries are now dependent on this army of available labor. "Meatpacking especially depends on a constant flow of workers," he says, "because of the very intense system of production, and the high rate of injuries. Mexico has become its labor reserve." The Mexican government, meanwhile, has a growing stake in sending workers abroad, Harvard historian Womack believes. "Mexico has no economic policy anymore," he says, "no plan or goal of directing investment toward industries which would hire Mexican labor." According to Tim Wise and Betsy Rakocy of the Global Development and Environment Institute at Tufts University, "The confluence of agriculture, trade, immigration, and labor policies have pushed cheap commodities south and driven people north."

The remittances (money sent home) by the 11 percent of Mexico's population living in the United States, which were less than $4 billion in 1994 when NAFTA took effect, rose to $10 billion in 2002, and then $20 billion three years later, according to the Bank of Mexico. Even in the current recession, Mexicans sent home $21.13 billion in 2011. Remittances total 3 percent of Mexico's gross domestic product, according to Frank Holmes, investment analyst and CEO of US Global Investors. They are now Mexico's second largest source of national income, behind oil.

Those remittances support families and provide services that were formerly the obligation of the Mexican government. This alone gives the government a vested interest in the continuing labor flow. Raul Delgado Wise, a professor at the University of Zacatecas, charges that "rather than a free-trade agreement, NAFTA can be described as . . . a mechanism for the provision of cheap labor. Since NAFTA came into force, the migrant factory has exported [millions of] Mexicans to the United States."

But today, on both sides of the border, people are demanding change in the laws and policies that contribute to that displacement. Fausto Limon's right and ability to stay in Mexico, on his ranch in the Perote Valley, depends on ending the problems caused by the operation of Granjas Carroll. He has become a leader of Pueblos Unidos and hopes to find a counterweight to the company's influence by joining forces with other Mexicans who've also suffered environmental destruction from corporate mines and dams. In July of 2011, he went to Acapulco for the seventh national assembly of Afectados Ambientales (Environmentally Affected). The Afectados declare their mission is to build a national movement "to fight for life in our homes, our lands, our waters, and our territories." It's part of a broader movement connecting similar groups throughout Latin America.

But Limon has no money for planting, and his family was driven out of the government's PROCAMPO program of payments to farmers when the protests started. He shares the poverty created by meat and corn dumping, followed by price spikes to consumers, with farmers throughout Mexico. The trade system that allows this state of affairs to continue will inevitably produce more migrants—if not Limon himself, then perhaps his children. The fabric of sustainable rural life at his Rancho del Riego is being pulled apart.

In the United States, many migrant rights networks believe rational immigration reform must change US trade policies that contribute to displacing people. The TRADE (Trade Reform, Accountability, Development, and Employment) Act, proposed in Congress by Representative Mike Michaud (D-ME), received support from many of those groups because it would hold hearings to reexamine the impact of NAFTA. Such hearings might cover provisions like the treaty's environmental side agreement, which did nothing to restrict the impact of Granjas Carroll on Perote Valley. The bill would also ban negotiations of new trade agreements that lead to the violation of environmental and labor rights.

Another proposal, called the Dignity Campaign, goes one step further and would ban agreements that lead to displacement, like that caused by pork imports or the cross-border investments that created the Perote pig farms. Instead it proposes an alternative immigration bill based on human and labor rights. It would also repeal employer sanctions, the immigration law that led to firing and driving so many Veracruz migrants from the Tar Heel plant.

"Employer sanctions have little effect on migration," says Bill Ong Hing, a law professor at the University of San Francisco, "but they have made workers more vulnerable to employer pressure." Hing investigated the impact of employer sanctions and raids in the Swift meatpacking plants, located across the country, for the UFCW. "The rationale has always been that this kind of enforcement will dry up jobs for the undocumented and discourage them from coming," he explains. "However, they actually become more desperate and take jobs at lower wages. This can lead to an overall reduction in the average wage level for millions of workers, which is, in effect, a subsidy to employers."

"When you make someone's status even more illegal," Carolina Ramirez adds, "you just make their living and working conditions worse. Jobs become like slavery. And if there are no remittances, kids in Veracruz can't go to school or to the doctor. All the social problems we already have get worse. And all this just provokes more migration."

"We would be much better off if we ended employer sanctions and changed our trade and economic policies so they don't produce poverty in countries like Mexico," Hing concludes.

The walkouts in Tar Heel and the marches in the streets of Wilmington in 2006 show a deep reservoir of support for basic changes in the conditions facing immigrants. In Perote Valley, farmers are equally determined to prevent the expansion of pig farms and the destruction of their environment. In many ways, their efforts are linked together, not just by the fact that they're carried on by people from the same state, facing the same transnational corporation. They're fighting the same system.

"We are fighting because we are being destroyed," said Roberto Ortega. "That is the reason for the daily fight, to try to change this."

A Union for Tobacco Workers

As a hot August sun beats down on a field in Nash County, North Carolina, Manuel Cardenal moves down his row almost at a run. He pauses for a second in front of each tobacco plant, breaking off the new shoots at the top. He calls them *"rotoños."* They have to be removed so that the growing strength of the plant will flow into the leaves below, making them broad and heavy. Cardenal understands the way tobacco plants grow, and knows what must be done to make them productive. He used to have a farm of his own in Esteli, the best-known tobacco region of Nicaragua, a country famous for cigars.

Five other workers like him race down their own rows, deftly choosing and plucking out the right parts of the right plants. To do this well, rancher Corey (they don't know their employer's full name) says they have to use their bare hands. Gloves would be too encumbering, he says, and might damage the plants. In addition, they're being paid a piece rate. The workers have to work fast just to make the minimum wage. Corey says the whole field has to be finished by the end of the day.

By one in the afternoon, the temperature has reached 102 degrees. Cardenal's arms shine with sweat. Since six that morning, when they went into the field, the hands of all six workers have been covered with a sticky green tar—the residue of tobacco juice and gum from the leaves. The same thing that gives cigarettes and cigars their kick, the nicotine, is not just present in the tar but also permeates even the dust in the air. Anyone walking into the field starts to feel that heady sensation you get from smoking the first cigarette of the day. "I feel it as soon as I start work," Cardenal says. "Then, after my body gets used to it, I can hardly feel it at all. But I know I'm absorbing it all day." The other workers say they still feel light-headed, even though hours have passed since they started work. When the heat reaches its peak, they sometimes feel nauseous as well.

Another component of the sticky tar is the residue of pesticides sprayed on the plants. Growers aren't supposed to send workers into the field for seventy-two hours after they spray. Some do anyway, but even past that limit chemicals remain on the plants' sticky leaves. "I know I'm getting exposed, but I don't know what I'm exposed to," Cardenal says. "On my own farm I'd at least know what I was using to kill insects. But here I have no idea, and the growers never tell us."

The reason all six workers know so well the operations needed to grow tobacco is that they all come from the tobacco regions of Mexico and Central America. They've all worked in those fields at home. Ruben Barrales and Manuel Buendia come from Veracruz, where tobacco leaves even form part of the coat of arms of Alamo, Buendia's hometown. Maynor Gonzalez, his brother Ismail, and Francisco Escobar all come from Santa Rita in Honduras. That town is an hour from San Pedro Sula and the port of Puerto Cortez, where Honduras manufactures and exports its cigars.

Migration to North Carolina from Honduras and Nicaragua is relatively recent, but the flow of people from Veracruz dates back to the mid-1980s. The Veracruz flow is connected to the passage of the Immigration Reform and Control Act, and later the implementation of NAFTA. Central American migration, with its origin in the exodus of refugees from its civil wars, got a big boost following the passage of the Central America Free Trade Agreement (CAFTA).

Once the Immigration Reform and Control Act took effect in 1986, US growers could recruit workers in other countries and bring them to the United States on H-2A work visas. Those workers can only work for the length of their employment contract—less than a year—and then must leave. They can only work for the grower or contractor who hires them.

Importing contract labor to the United States on temporary work permits was halted when the notorious bracero contract labor scheme was ended in 1964. The H-2A visa program, however, reopened the door. Soon after it took effect in 1986, hiring agents for North Carolina growers appeared in Veracruz, offering people the chance to work in the United States on the guest worker visas. In the tobacco regions, they found plenty of takers.

Once their original work contracts ended, many H-2A workers simply stayed in the United States without visas and became undocumented. Over time, others came north on their own to join friends and relatives already living in North Carolina. A pool of Mexican workers began to grow, most from Veracruz. Eventually they were joined by people arriving from Central America as well, displaced by CAFTA. That agreement took effect in 2005, unleashing the same economic forces NAFTA set loose earlier on rural communities in Mexico.

While recruitment of H-2A workers continues, most farmworkers in North Carolina's tobacco fields today are undocumented. A 2011 report by Oxfam America, *A State of Fear: Human Rights Abuses in North Carolina's Tobacco Industry*, estimates that of the hundred thousand farmworkers in the state, only 9 percent have H-2A visas. Almost all the rest have no legal immigration status, Cardenal and his five coworkers among them. According to the US Department of Labor, 7 percent of the nation's 1.4 million farmworkers have H-2A visas, while 53 percent have no visa at all.

Of the 103 workers interviewed for the Oxfam report, almost all were undocumented. A quarter said they were paid wages less than the legal minimum. A majority reported the same physical symptoms Cardenal and his coworkers describe—a syndrome called green tobacco sickness—and most had no gloves or other protective equipment. Only a third said there were toilets in the fields where they worked. Every year, North Carolina's Department of Labor reports the death of several field laborers from heat exposure. Most farmworkers in North Carolina live in labor camps, which are like small company towns where workers depend on the employer for housing, transportation, and food. Almost all those surveyed complained of problems like dilapidated barracks, inadequate showers and toilets, lack of heat or ventilation, and insect infestations.

Conditions for H-2A workers are better than those described by the undocumented, primarily because most belong to a union, the Farm Labor Organizing Committee (FLOC). In 2004, FLOC signed an agreement with the North Carolina Growers Association (NCGA) and the Mt. Olive Pickle Company. The union had mounted a long corporate campaign against Mt. Olive, since it was a non-union competitor to union pickle producers in Ohio and the Midwest, where FLOC had contracts.

Until the FLOC contract, North Carolina's H-2A workers were held in a form of low-wage bondage. Federal law requires growers to pay an "adverse effect" wage to H-2A workers, supposedly set high enough so that it doesn't depress local wage standards. North Carolina growers, however, were well known for paying less than the legal minimum, and North Carolina Legal Aid filed many complaints against them. Even today, most growers using the program pay the minimum wage or slightly above.

To enforce the low-wage regime, NCGA maintained a blacklist, called in its employee manual a "record of eligibility [that] contains a list of workers, who because of violations of their contract, have been suspended from the program." The 1997 NCGA Ineligible for Rehire report listed 1,709 names. The reasons for ineligibility given most often were abandoning a job or voluntary resignation. Legal Aid, however, charged that when workers were fired for complaining, they were given a paper to sign saying they'd quit voluntarily. Among the names were also many whose reason for ineligibility was given as "lazy," "slow," "work hours too long," "work too hot and hard," or "slowing up other workers." Workers were warned not to talk with legal aid attorneys, according to numerous legal cases, and were even told to burn the pink legal aid know-your-rights books in a trash barrel at the association office.

The NCGA was organized in 1989 by Craig Eury and Kenneth White, who were fired that year as rural representatives of the North Carolina Employment and Security Commission, the state's unemployment office. The two then set up businesses in North and South Carolina, Kentucky, Tennessee, and other states for importing guest workers. In 2003 they brought in over ten thousand workers, recruited in Mexico by Manpower of America, which used local *enganchadores*, or recruiters.

When Mt. Olive signed with FLOC in 2004, NCGA signed as well, since it was the recruiter of the workers employed by the growers who grew the cucumbers for Mt. Olive pickles. As a result of the agreement, FLOC was then able to police the recruitment system. North Carolina is a right-to-work state, which limited the union's power over hiring, however. Today a grower has the right to make a decision about whom he or she hires, but the union maintains a se-niority list. If a worker isn't rehired by a particular grower at the start of the season, the union can get the NCGA to find him or her another job. The union has a grievance system, and workers can make com-plaints about the kind of health and safety problems they previously had to suffer through in silence and fear. The Oxfam report notes that in 2010 FLOC processed more than seven hundred complaints.

The contract, especially the monitoring of hiring, came at a high price. In 2004, FLOC opened an office for that purpose in Monterrey, Mexico. On April 9, 2007, Santiago Rafael Cruz, sent by the union to staff that office, was tied up, tortured and murdered. To this day, the Mexican government has been unable to bring his killers to justice. There is little doubt, however, that he was murdered because the union was trying to stop the bribes extorted by the *enganchadores* from workers, who had to pay the bribes to get hired.

Six thousand H-2A workers brought to North Carolina every year are the heart of FLOC's membership in the state. When workers fall under the union contract, FLOC represents them, regardless of their immigration status. Some contract growers employ both H-2A and undocumented labor. FLOC members do more than pick cucumbers for pickles, however. NCGA growers also grow tobacco, the state's most important crop. Of FLOC's seven thousand North Carolina members, 80 percent work in tobacco as well as cucumbers. That gives the union a base for organizing the tobacco industry, using the same corporate and boycott strategy it used to gain agreements with Mt. Olive and other multinational food corporations.

This time, FLOC's adversaries are the world's largest cigarette manufacturers—Philip Morris, Lorillard Tobacco Company, and Reynolds American. None of them actually own land or grow to-bacco themselves. They contract with growers and buy what they produce, at a price these manufacturers totally control. Some grow-ers contract for workers through NCGA, while others hire workers themselves, usually through labor contractors. The NCGA work-ers all have H-2A visas, while those working for labor contractors are mostly undocumented.

"Conditions for tobacco workers are worse than those for farm-workers anywhere else in the country," says Baldemar Velasquez, FLOC's president. The fact that union members hired through the NCGA are H-2A workers makes NCGA growers economically uncompetitive, he maintains: "They have to provide better conditions, from the adverse effect wage rate to paying Social Security and workers' compensation." With Mt. Olive, all growers supplying pickles to the company have to abide by union conditions and pay the same wages. Tobacco, however, is a much larger business, in which NCGA growers with the union contract are competing with non-union growers. A union contract for the whole tobacco industry would force growers to pay the same wages, essentially taking labor costs out of competition.

Since the vast majority of the farm labor workforce in tobacco is undocumented, an agreement with the big cigarette manufacturers would have important differences from the first contract with Mt. Olive and the NCGA. One question is whether undocumented workers would be represented by the union if the industry is forced to sign a master agreement. Velasquez says he's out to organize all workers, regardless of status. "Just because someone's undocumented doesn't mean they don't have rights," he declares. Another complexity is the ability of manufacturers to dictate prices to growers. After the US government abandoned its marketing regulations for tobacco, growers lost much of their leverage for negotiating those prices. "Typically, the farmer must sign the contract as written [by the manufacturer] or else lose the chance to grow tobacco during the upcoming season," the Oxfam report notes. One grower told investigators that "[in] 2010 our crop is going to bring us half a million dollars less than it did in 2009." Growers today have only one way to respond to price pressure: get workers to produce more for lower wages, while spending even less on their food, housing and health. That exerts a continuing downward pressure on wages and conditions in the fields.

H-2A workers have become more expensive than undocumented workers in North Carolina, not because of changes in the H-2A program, but because of the union contract. In every other state, where

H-2A workers have no union protection, their wages and conditions are often no different from those of undocumented workers. On many ranches they're employed and housed together.

Some North Carolina growers see advantages in using H-2A workers, especially if competing growers must do the same. One told the Oxfam investigators, "You want to know if you are going to pour all this money into these crops, that if you do everything you are supposed to, you are going to have the labor there till the end of the year to get that crop out of the field. . . . When you hire, you know, a crew leader, an undocumented worker, you are running the risk they are going to leave you before you finish, you run the risk they're going to leave when you need them the most."

What makes the program desirable to employers, however, also makes workers vulnerable to employer pressure. The means used to make workers dependable—the employment contract, grower control of recruiting and hiring, and the ability of employers to deport workers by firing them—deprive workers of power. In 2007 the Southern Poverty Law Center's report *Close to Slavery* said the program was structurally flawed because workers "are bound to the employers who 'import' them. If guest workers complain about abuses, they face deportation, blacklisting, or other retaliation." Regulations to protect workers "exist mainly on paper. Government enforcement . . . is almost non-existent."

The Oxfam report recommends expansion of the H-2A program, claiming this would improve wages and conditions. However, allowing growers to import more workers simply means that more workers will endure the abysmal conditions described in the "Close to Slavery" report. Even in North Carolina, where H-2A conditions are relatively better, the reason for that improvement is not the work visa, but the fact that workers have a union contract. Without a strong union, conditions would quickly return to what they were before 2004. Yet the Oxfam report makes no recommendation that tobacco manufacturers sign a union contract.

In the end, the choice faced by Cardenal and the five other migrants in the Nash County field is simple. Stay home and go hungry, or come to the United States and survive. Bad conditions and lack of legal status are no deterrent. These workers are not unsophisticated about the situation they face in the United States. Nor do they lack knowledge about the perils of farm labor. They simply have very little power to change their situation other than by leaving home and migrating to North Carolina.

Cardenal asks about dibromochloropropane, or DBCP, an agricultural pesticide that was used by Dole Corporation on banana plantations in Nicaragua for many years. The chemical was found to have caused sterility among farm laborers. He cites it as an example of the possible dangers of working in the United States, where he comes in contact with plants and chemicals without knowing their effects. "Some people got money to settle their legal cases," he explains, "but the price they paid was very high. They never had children. How do I know that years from now some chemical on the leaves here won't cause me a problem like that?"

A strong union would make sure he knows the potential dangers from pesticides. A higher wage, not tied to a piece rate, could allow him to work more slowly using gloves, instead of absorbing nicotine through his bare hands. And a union contract could protect him if he went to rancher Corey and demanded these things, keeping Corey from firing him, evicting him from company housing, and even deporting him. At present, whether Cardenal comes into the tobacco field as an H-2A worker or without any visa at all, he runs the risk of retaliation if he demands better conditions. Undocumented workers can always be threatened with the *migra*—US immigration enforcement—while H-2A workers lose their visa along with their job if their boss fires them.

The choices in this field are very circumscribed. But envisioning a more liberating solution for the workers here is not hard. If NAFTA and CAFTA were renegotiated or repealed, people would have a better chance to earn a decent living at home, making migration only an option, not a necessity. A green card for tobacco workers—a residence visa instead of an H-2A employment contract or no visa at all—would give them greater labor and social rights. Workers with enforceable organizing rights would face less difficulty requiring huge corporations to sign union agreements.

The toxic and deadlocked politics of Washington, DC, call these solutions impossible. At the same time, US immigration policy is largely shaped by the desire of US employers for labor, limiting what's possible for Cardenal and his workmates. But shouldn't migration produce strong communities of people fully able to assert their rights in the United States or Canada? And can't people have a choice between migration and staying home in healthy communities in their countries of origin? Or must displacement and migration be geared to supplying labor to cigarette manufacturers at a price they want to pay?

You Don't Need to Be a Doctor or Scientist to Smell the Stench

The Story of Fausto Limon

Fausto Limon lives in the Perote Valley, where Smithfield Foods has built a huge hog-raising complex. He is a leader of the resistance to the hog farms.

My family has been living in the *municipio* of Perote for generations. My ancestors were landowners, and they had a big hacienda in Alchichica, where they built a church that's unique, different from all the rest in Mexico.

My great-grandfathers went off to fight with Pancho Villa during the Revolution. Then, even before the land reform came, they divided up the hacienda into small parcels. My grandfather then bought his own ranch, where we live today, called Rancho Riego. My father built a stone house here during the 1950s. He was very taken with modern ideas about design and construction, and there's nothing like it.

Today we grow corn, beans, wheat, carrots, tomatoes, and tomatillos—at least we would if we had the money. That's what we used to grow. Today I hardly have enough money to plant a crop of beans, which is what we have in front of the house. We farm thirty-eight hectares, which is enough to support a family. There were six of us, but there's only five now since my mom died of a kidney infection.

Before the *granjas* [pig farms] came, they said that they would bring jobs. But then we found out the reality, the way things really are. Yes, there were jobs, but they also brought a lot of contamination.

The *granjas* came in '94 and '95. What we experienced at first was the stench. The air smells like rotten meat. The wind has a chemical smell. I can't really describe how bad it smells. At night we'd begin to vomit, and we'd get into my pickup truck and drive until we couldn't smell it any longer, and we'd all sleep in the truck.

Then the taste of the water from my well changed. We had very good water before, but everyone in my family began to suffer from kidney infections. Two and a half months ago, we went to a doctor who told us we should stop drinking the well water. We began to drink bottled water. Since then we haven't had to take any more medicine for our kidneys. Before that we were taking it every fifteen or twenty days.

There are a lot of flies now. Some time ago we also had a lot of savage dogs, who were attracted by the dead bodies of pigs from the farms. They'd just bury them right below the surface of the earth, and the dogs would dig them up. There were many of them. We were raising ostriches, and they killed five of the six we had on the ranch.

Once people began to understand the reality, we began to hold meetings and form a group, Pueblos Unidos, to defend what is ours. I was one of the first people, because I was living in the middle of it all. The reason for the protests was the stench, and the pollution in the air, the ground, and in the aquifers. In the area where I live, the water table is about 8 meters below the surface now. When they dig the holes for their oxidation ponds, they don't use a membrane or filter, so what's in the pond travels into the aquifer. The ponds are as deep as the level of our aquifers.

In 2003–2004, they bought land near my own farm. The company bought land from *ejidos* [collectives formed during the land reform] mostly, and some from small farmers. When they announced they were expanding the unit there, the people got together, and we wouldn't let them build it. Earlier there'd been an expansion in Totalco, and people stopped it from expanding there also.

We sat in and blocked the highway, because they were beginning their expansion plans again for the farm next to my ranch. We actually let cars through, but we slowed them down. There were more than a thousand of us. We had an effect, because it stopped the construction of more farms.

We also collected signatures, and sent appeals to government authorities, but to this day we've never received any real answers. There was a meeting with the authorities from Puebla and Veracruz in Chichicuautla. At that meeting we signed an agreement, but the company went on functioning and treating us as they always had.

Now they're saying again they're going to expand. We'll see what the people decide to do. The municipal president in Guadalupe Victoria in Puebla wants to give the company permission to do it. At a meeting with the subsecretary of administration for the state of Puebla, people told me that she said the company was going to expand no matter what.

The people are saying now that they're not going to let the company put in more farms. I don't know exactly what they will do, but if they say they won't let the company build more *granjas*, then for sure they won't let it happen.

Our back is to the wall. I'm glad to see the people waking up to the pollution here. You don't need to be a scientist or doctor to smell the stench or see how it's filtering into our water and earth. The authorities and the company say they're not polluting. But everyone here can see it. When they say the pollution is not getting into the water, no one believes it.

There was a lot of pig-growing here before the *granjas*. We used our pigs as kind of a savings account, and because we could feed them the corn we were already growing. They were something we could sell if we needed money. But now there's very little.

You have to vaccinate pigs so they don't get sick, three times for different illnesses. When the pig farms came, they stopped selling the medicine, and lots of our pigs died. The medicine's not available here anymore. They don't sell it.

Once one of the people working at the *granja* told me I should get rid of my pigs, and they'd give me sheep to raise instead. But to this day I've never seen a sheep from them. I'm probably a sheep for believing him.

Many people have left for other countries. It's also because of the lack of jobs here. People leave in groups, and invite others to go with them—groups of three, four, even ten people. They risk crossing the border without documents, and many lose their lives. It's a big problem, and getting even bigger.

We all want the company to leave. We don't want it here and we don't see any other solution.

We're Here Because of the Economic Crisis

The Story of David Ceja and Guadalupe Marroquin

David Ceja and Guadalupe Marroquin were both born in Veracruz and migrated to the United States, where they went to work at Smithfield Food's Tarheel plant.

DAVID CEJA

My father and brother are *ejidatarios* [farmers on communal land] near Martinez de la Torre, in Veracruz. They have some land, but never enough money to cultivate it. That's why I left, in order to get some money so that we could farm. As a child I was already working in the fields, just to buy shoes, or a book or pencil for school. It was hard to find enough for everyone, so I suffered all through my childhood.

It was hard just to get bread, much less a piece of meat, because it was all so expensive. As they say, we ate tortillas with salt. But we could give milk to people who came asking for it. There were people even worse off than us. Now the boys I played with are all here. I'd see them working in the plant.

At first we had some fruit trees—oranges and bananas—and about ten cows. We had some pigs and chickens we'd sell to get sugar or salt. Sometimes the price of a pig was enough to buy what we needed, but then it wasn't. Farm prices were always going down. Everyone was hurting almost all the time.

The fruit we were growing was for the US, but then when they'd stop eating it, or they'd have some requirement we couldn't meet, we couldn't sell what we were growing. The free trade agreement was the cause of our problems. They were just paying as little to farmers as they could. When the prices went up, no one had any money to pay. After the crisis, we couldn't pay for electricity—we'd just use candles at home. But when you see that your parents don't have any money, that's when you decide to come, to help them.

In the ranches where we lived, *coyotes* would come by offering to take us north. I was eighteen years old when I left, in 1999. When we started thinking about coming to the US, we couldn't see how to come up with the money we needed. We'd look at what we had and it didn't add up to much. My parents sold four cows and two hectares for the money to get to the border. Then I walked across the river from Tamaulipas to Texas and walked through the mountains for two days and three nights.

The *coyote* cost $1,200. I couldn't find work for three months. I was desperate and afraid of what would happen if I couldn't pay. I had to stay and work in Texas until I paid him off, and then some friends told me to go to North Carolina to harvest tobacco. In Veracruz we'd heard there was a slaughterhouse there. While I was working in the tobacco fields friends gave me a hand, and I was hired. They all come from the area near where I lived in Martinez de la Torre. Lots of people from Veracruz worked at Smithfield.

GUADALUPE MARROQUIN

I grew up on a ranch in Las Choapas, in Veracruz. Our family grew rice and corn and sold pigs when the price was high. But prices were usually low, and my father complained that when the crops were harvested the prices always fell. Whenever we thought we could get ahead, the prices would fall.

Later, I worked on a rubber plantation. I was never able to go to school, because we didn't have any money. I got married in 1981, and my husband and I worked in the fields. We had a small piece of land, and we'd raise corn, cows, and pigs. Sometimes we could get a good price, but mostly we couldn't. My four kids were born in the 1980s. I didn't want them to be illiterate. I could read and write a little, but I wanted something better for them, so I began to put them through school.

In 2000, my oldest girl started college. She took the exam to get a subsidy for low-income families, but that wasn't enough. Plus, I had the other kids getting older too. My goal was to get them all through school.

So I came to the US with a *coyote*. I took a bus, first to Mexico City and then to Naco, Sonora. We spent three days in an empty house, sleeping on the floor, men and women together. I didn't know any of them, and I was worried by all the stories I'd heard about women getting raped and robbed. We were all waiting for the *coyote* to get enough people together for the trip.

Then one afternoon he took us down into a ravine. We climbed into a pipe, crawling on hands and knees, one person behind the next. The pipe was only about four feet around, with sewage running at the bottom. We inched forward in total darkness, in terrible, dirty-smelling water.

We crossed in the sewers that run between Naco, Sonora, and Naco, Arizona. I was very scared, but I needed to make it across. It was very dark, and the *coyote* warned us not to go off to the side or we'd get lost. I prayed to the saints that I would come out alive. But I had such a need to come that I wouldn't stop. I dreamed before we left that I was stopped by the *migra*, but when I showed him my saint, he let me pass. It cost me $2,000 to cross the line.

I arrived in Lumberton, North Carolina, on a Saturday, went to Mass, and gave thanks to God on Sunday and went to work in the fields on Monday. With the first money I made in the states I bought a saint and gave him to the church there. A lot of people from my town live in Lumberton. They helped me get here, gave me a place to stay, and told me about the job at Smithfield. I bought identification from friends and went down and applied for a job there.

On the line, I worked on cutting out the liver and heart. It was very hard, and I had to learn how to use the knife. The line went very fast, and when the knife was dull, the work was very difficult.

DAVID CEJA
I worked at Smithfield for seven years. I went to work on the stomach line, and after eight months they put me on the loin line, making $8.25 an hour. They just put us on the line and we had to learn fast. The loin line had a lot of problems, and they pressured us to work fast.

Our supervisor began shouting at us and using gross insults. Then he put another person into our work area, and there wasn't enough room for us all. It was dangerous because the line moves so fast, and we were going to cut him, or cut ourselves. When we protested to the supervisor, he began yelling at us for not doing a good job. When he called out to me, he used a bad word, instead of my name. We protested to the Human Resources department, but they never did anything.

The supervisor said, "If you don't want to do your job, the door is really big," meaning, go look for another job. We said they were treating us like burros, like slaves. But this isn't a job for a burro.

So we agreed that we'd stop the line. We'd done it before, but it hadn't changed anything. The line slowed for a week, but then they started speeding it up again. We didn't know anything about the law, but I told my friends that I knew people who could help us, from the union. People were scared to talk with them. But I said they knew what we could do. There were people working with the union who'd been workers inside the plant too.

We had meetings in a field near San Pablo. They suggested writing a letter first, so we put all our complaints into it. We asked for better safety because the way we were working was very danger-ous, due to the speed of the line. The majority of people on our line signed, about eighty people.

We took the letter to HR at break time. Some were afraid, but I told them, if you're afraid all the time, nothing will happen. They'll just keep treating us like slaves. We were shaking when we got to the office, but we explained the purpose of the letter. The managers said they'd give us an answer in a week or two.

Two weeks later they chose ten people and took us to HR. They asked who had helped us with the letter. I said we'd written it. Fi-nally they said they'd slow the line down. The next week we were really happy, but after two or three weeks, they speeded it up again. That's when I told my friends, we need a union. We needed an orga-nization to support us.

I'm glad it came in. We worked hard to get it.

GUADALUPE MARROQUIN

I worked on the line for nine years. Then I got a letter from Motor Vehicles that said that my license was no good. I got very scared because there had been raids, and people were being fired because they didn't have good IDs. So I quit my job before something worse happened to me.

Lots of people from Mexico have lost their jobs here, and many have been deported. Others get arrested for drunk driving or domestic problems, and then are picked up and deported too. Sometimes the *migra* goes to the apartment houses where we live and rounds people up. There are not nearly as many Mexicans living here as there used to be. People have moved to other states, with their whole families. Some restaurants have even closed.

But I have faith in God, and I still need the money to send home for my children. I've been here for eleven years, and when it's their birthdays or Christmas, we just talk on the telephone. I feel very sad and alone on the holidays. But I've fulfilled my commitment. I came to help my children, and with faith I can do it.

Now I work in a restaurant, making tacos for workers. They call me Doña Lupe de los Tacos. Since I came here I've never been without money. When someone gets deported, their family often will ask me to help pay their bills. Unemployment went up because of the raids, so we have a lot of collections to help those families.

So far the authorities haven't bothered me. But many of my friends believe they act in a very unjust way towards us. Everyone has come here like me, sacrificing a lot.

DAVID CEJA

I became a supervisor also, but they wanted me to put pressure on the workers. I asked to go back to being a regular worker, but they said there was no other job for me. They said, "There's the door, you can leave." I came from the line. I know what it's like. I know what your body feels like when it's tired. If workers say they can't do it, then they can't, so I couldn't just force them to work faster.

Then the company began to hire more white and black people. I don't have anything against them. We all need to work. But the company wanted them producing right away, and expected me to put pressure on them. The managers just wanted me to make them work.

During this time the *migra* arrived. I don't know if the company had an agreement with ICE [Immigration and Customs Enforcement], but they came before the union election, and they scared the people. When someone was called into the office, they were afraid and sometimes just went home instead.

The big raids happened while I was on vacation. When I came back people just weren't there. Workers said supervisors had sent them up to the office where the *migra* was waiting, and they never came back. Then managers began to tell me to send such and such a person to the office. I'd tell the worker, go if you want, but if you don't want to, go home, because the *migra* might be there waiting for you.

They wanted me to send workers to the office where I was afraid the immigration agents would be waiting for them. I thought it was better for me to leave, so I wouldn't have to turn in my *compañeros*. These big companies always want people to be scared, so that they can keep control. That's why there's so much intimidation. Once people unite, the company starts to tremble, so they say, the *migra's* coming, or they're going to check your papers. The company attitude is, you're here to work, so just go to work.

The company knew we didn't have papers. They need the workers, and we need the work. If the government would give us permission to work things would be much better. We'd have labor rights. But we had to buy papers in order to work. I bought my papers for $700, ten years ago.

It's really because of the economic crisis that we're here—all the Veracruzanos. It's the poverty that recruits us. We all had to leave Veracruz because of it. Otherwise, we wouldn't do something so hard. But I never let them humiliate me. I always fought for my rights.

TWO

CURSED BY GOLD OR BLESSED BY CORN

Communities Resist Canadian Mining Companies

When Fausto Limon, Veronica Hernandez, and the other Perote Valley residents began battling Smithfield Foods over environmental contamination and the political repression that followed, their problems weren't unique. In many parts of Mexico, large corporations take advantage of NAFTA and economic reforms to develop a megaproject in a rural area. These projects often threaten or cause environmental disaster. Communities affected by the environmental and economic impacts are uprooted, and their residents begin to migrate. The projects themselves are defended against protests from poor farmers and townspeople by the federal government, whose economic development policy for decades has prioritized corporate investment.

This is particularly true for communities facing the vast expansion of huge industrial mining projects. One such project is the proposed Caballo Blanco gold mine near the Veracruz coast, which has faced stormy opposition. Even sharper conflicts have broken out over mines in Oaxaca. In one community, San Jose del Progreso, indigenous leaders have been assassinated and the town deeply divided since the mine began operation.

These conflicts shape the political terrain in which indigenous people are seeking alternatives to displacement and forced migration. The companies and their defenders promise jobs and economic development. But affected communities charge that far more people lose jobs and their livelihoods as a result of negative environmental and economic consequences. Meanwhile, the exodus of displaced migrants grows ever greater.

Oaxaca is also the state where the debate over how to end displacement and forced migration has become more intense than almost anywhere in Mexico. In part this is because poverty there, by many measures, is greater than in almost any other state except Chiapas. At the same time, the political movements that advocate for the right to not migrate, and for the human rights of migrants, are growing in political strength. They were part of the upsurge that defeated the Institutional Revolutionary Party, or PRI, and elected Gabino Cue governor in 2010. Now that administration is under pressure to make concrete progress in finding alternatives to displacement. One indigenous community, the Triquis, have precipitated a political crisis, as many demand a political solution that can make it possible for displaced people to return home.

In Veracruz, the Caballo Blanco mine was proposed during the six-year term of Governor Fidel Herrera, who left office in December 2010. A Canadian corporation, Goldcorp Resources, initiated exploration for two huge open pit excavations halfway between the state capital, Xalapa, and the Gulf Coast. The company, with headquarters in Vancouver, and its Mexican subsidiary, Minera Cardel, were virtually given a concession of more than seventy-seven square miles by the federal government.

The Herrera administration was notorious for allowing the Zeta drug cartel to operate freely. Even Mexico's right-wing president Felipe Calderon at one point told reporters, "I believe Veracruz was left in the hands of the Zetas. I don't know if it was involuntary, probably, I hope so." Both Calderon, leader of the conservative National Action Party (PAN), and Miguel Angel Yunes, the party's candidate for governor, were bitter over Angel Yunes's defeat by Herrera in 2004. Yunes later told reporters that Herrera "handed over the police and police command to these criminal groups, and everyone in Veracruz knows it." Even the Zeta's rival Sinaloa cartel made a video in which they called Herrera "Zeta Numero Uno."

Herrera's laissez-faire attitude also applied to corporations like

Goldcorp and Smithfield. Mexican environmentalist Tulio Moreno Alvarado compared the Caballo Blanco proposal to the Granjas Carroll pig farms. "The way the mine worked to overcome its opponents was very similar to that of the marginalized communities of Perote, although it's important to understand that the damage the mine will leave behind is incomparably greater than what the pig farms will cause." He estimated that Caballo Blanco's impact would extend over seventy-five square miles.

Edgar Gonzalez Gaudiano published an analysis of the mine in the local newspaper, *La Jornada Veracruz*, in which he estimated that the mine would produce a hundred thousand ounces of gold a year, with a value of about $1,660 an ounce at May 2012 prices, or $166 million. Goldcorp would operate two huge open pits. The ore would be treated with cyanide, a strong poison, to leach out the metal. Cyanide bonds with the gold, essentially dissolving it. Later the gold is separated out, leaving a large amount of cyanide-laced wastewater. That runoff is held in huge open-air ponds.

Gold mining with cyanide is a very dangerous process, yet more than 90 percent of all gold extracted worldwide relies on its use. In Romania in January 2000, a dam on one such pond broke and about thirty-five million cubic feet of toxic wastewater and mud poured into the Danube River. The plume of cyanide traveled downstream, through Hungary and the former Yugoslavia, to the Black Sea, killing everything it touched. It was called the worst environmental catastrophe since the nuclear meltdown in Chernobyl.

At Caballo Blanco, each ton of ore would produce only half an ounce of gold, so mountains of cyanide-treated tailings would quickly rise around the pit and the wastewater ponds. According to the *Diario de Xalapa*, another local newspaper, leaching out the gold would require almost four hundred million cubic feet of water per year, depleting the aquifer on which rural farming communities depend. The wastewater itself would not only be unusable to residents but would poison plants and animals if it ever escaped the ponds.

An even greater danger might come from Mexico's only nuclear power plant, Laguna Verde, less than ten miles away. The ore would be broken loose from the earth by virtually continuous explosions, using up to five tons of explosives a day. This section of Veracruz is geologically part of a volcanic region that includes some of Mexico's most famous dormant volcanoes, including Orizaba, less than a hundred miles away, and the Cofre de Perote, which is even closer.

Even before people from the towns closest to the mine, Actopan and Alto Lucero, began to protest, they said they'd been threatened in order to get them to sell their land to Goldcorp. Beatriz Torrez Beristan, an activist with the Veracruz Assembly and Initiative in Defense of the Environment (LA VIDA, in its Spanish acronym), reported to *La Jornada Veracruz* that in a public hearing on the project, "they never said anything, but they came up to us at the end and told us they were afraid, that they'd been intimidated and felt forced to sell their land. There is definitely intimidation here, and they're criminalizing social and environmental protest."

As Granjas Carroll did in Perote, Goldcorp promised jobs and said the environment would be restored after the gold and metals had been extracted. "But we know that this can't be," Torres told reporter Fernando Carmona. "It's impossible to restore an ecosystem that has been so damaged. You can cut down a tree and plant another, but you'll never restore the complex ecological chain, with its many trees, birds and water."

In February 2012, a Pact for a Veracruz Free of Toxic Mining was signed at a statewide assembly of environmental activists. "The 300–600 fulltime jobs they promise for six years can't compensate for the thousands of jobs that will be lost in pig raising and sustainable tourism in this region of Veracruz," it declared. People signing the pact committed themselves to distributing accurate information about the exploitation of natural resources, alerting communities about potential threats, initiating legal actions, and organizing peaceful demonstrations. Signers pledged support to communities that resist, and called for dialogue with authorities and companies based on respect for people and the environment. Other groups, including Red Mexicana de Afectados por la Mineria, or Mexican Network of Communities Affected by Mining, and Red Mexicana de Accion Frente al Libre Comercio, or Mexican Action Network on Free Trade, also organized opposition to Caballo Blanco.

Environmental damage from the mine is potentially so great that on February 28, 2012, during Veracruz's environmental day, Herrera's replacement, Governor Javier Duarte de Ocho, announced he was opposed to its operation. But one of the biggest problems faced by local municipalities, where people still have some power, and even states with leaders who respond to popular pressure, is that municipalities and states don't make the basic economic decisions in Mexico. That power is in the hands of the federal government. On March 13, 2012, Goldcorp announced it had received its first environmental impact report from SEMARNAT, Mexico's federal Secretariat of the Environment and Natural Resources, a major step toward operating the mine. Then, in May, SEMARNAT denied the company permission to start work. Nevertheless, LA VIDA warned that Goldcorp would undoubtedly appeal any denial, and that in any case other Canadian-owned mines in Mexico simply operated without all the required permits.

Federal acquiescence to Goldcorp would not only be unsurprising—it is the corollary to its policy of virtually giving away Mexico's mineral wealth. In 1992, Mexican president Carlos Salinas de Gortari modified the country's mining law. This was the same year he also changed Mexico's land reform law to allow the sale of former communal (ejido) lands. Both changes were intended to allow foreign corporations to invest in huge projects in Mexico, and to protect those investments. A year later, just before NAFTA took effect, the ceiling on the amount of foreign investment that could be allowed in "strategic" industries (like mining) was eliminated.

Changes continued under Salinas de Gortari's successors, with both the PRI's Ernesto Zedillo and the PAN's Vicente Fox increasing the number of mining concessions given to foreign corporations like Goldcorp and to huge Mexican mining cartels like Grupo Mexico. Taxes on mining operations were eliminated. Companies only had to make a symbolic payment for each hectare of land granted.

According to Carlos Fernandez-Vega, whose business column, Mexico SA (Mexico, Inc.), runs in the left-wing Mexico City daily La Jornada, the amount of land given in concessions reached 61 million acres at the end of Fox's presidency in 2006, and then more than

doubled, to 126 million acres, in just the first four years of his successor Felipe Calderon's term. "In the two PAN administrations, about
26 percent of the national territory was given to mining consortiums
for their sole benefit," Fernandez-Vega charges. He based his column
on a study by Mexican academics Francisco Lopez Barcenas and
Mayra Montserrat Eslava Galicia of the Autonomous Metropolitan
University in Xochimilco.

In 2010, Fernandez-Vega explains, Calderon granted almost 10
million acres in concessions, in exchange for which the Mexican
government received US$20 million. The foreign and domestic cor-
porations given the concessions made US$15 billion that year (a 50
percent increase from the previous year). Those earnings were 750
times what they paid for the concessions.

The Mexican Constitution, with its roots in the revolution of
1910–1920 and the nationalist government of Lazaro Cardenas of the
late 1930s, puts forward goals for mining and other economic activity. They include, states Lopez Barcenas, "using natural resources for
social benefit, creating an equitable distribution of public wealth, encouraging conservation, and achieving a balanced development for
the country leading to improved conditions of life for the Mexican
people." The new mining law, however, says any potential resource
must be utilized, which gives the exploitation of resources preference over all other considerations.

"Concession holders can demand that land occupied by a town
be vacated, so that they can carry out their activities," Lopez Barcenas writes. "If land is used for growing food, that has to end so
that a mine can be developed there. Forests or wilderness are at the
same risk. This legal requirement also applies to indigenous people. Their land used for rituals or sacred purposes, which contribute to maintaining their identity, can be leveled or destroyed. This
provision violates ILO Convention 169, which protects indigenous
rights."

Language in the mining law now "prohibits states and municipalities from imposing fees on mining activity, and therefore deprives
them of any income from those activities that might benefit them,"
he says. It even prohibits them from charging fees for permits for the
use of land or roads.

Killings in San Jose del Progreso

In Oaxaca, that policy opened the door to another Canadian company, Vancouver-based Fortuna Silver, which began drilling exploration holes in a previously mined area of San Jose del Progreso. San Jose is a small town in the municipality of Ocotlan, an hour south of the state's capital. Its twelve hundred residents speak Zapotec, an indigenous language that was already centuries old when the Europeans colonized Mexico.

Fortuna Silver began exploration in 2006, and five years later its mine went into full production. According to Flavio Sosa Villavicencio, a state deputy from the Party of Labor, the company told him that in 2011 it produced 490,555 ounces of silver and 4,622 ounces of gold. That production has a 2012 market value of $15.7 million for the silver ($32 per ounce, US) and $7.6 million for the gold ($1,660 per ounce, US). In 2012, Fortuna expected to produce 1.7 million ounces of silver and 15,000 ounces of gold. It estimated peak production at 3.2 million ounces of silver and 25,000 ounces of gold annually, worth $143.9 million at 2012 prices. Sosa Villavicencio said annual profits from the mine would reach 468 million pesos, or US$39 million.

That's not as big as Caballo Blanco would be. But San Jose del Progreso lies in a valley filled with small indigenous towns, many of which have already lost more than half their inhabitants to migration. In an environment of economic desperation, money from the mine has a big impact.

Bernardo Vasquez, an opponent of the mine and director of Coalition of People United in the Ocotlan Valley (COPOVU), explained to Canadian journalist Dawn Paley the way the company distributed its largesse: "They gave out fifty energy saving stoves that are unused because they only gave them out to buy people off, but also they never worked, so the people are still cooking in the traditional way, and as nice as the new stove is, people are used to their way of doing things. It's an investment that's basically thrown away, they made ecological toilets, some use them others don't. It's a very reduced vision that the company has; it's like a package that they apply in every country, and they think that people in every country are going to respond the same way."

Some residents enjoyed the benefits, while the mine opponents organized demonstrations to protest. The town became divided— there are even two taxi stands on its main square, one for mine supporters and the other for opponents. Vasquez said the division extended into the schools, the health center, and to the municipal offices. In the meantime, the traditional organs of government in San Jose del Progreso buckled under the stress.

In 2009, the mine was blockaded by three hundred people for over a month. Twice that number of police eventually descended on the demonstrators with dogs, guns, tear gas, and a helicopter. People were beaten and two dozen arrested. In another confrontation that year, the mayor and the town's health director were killed. Father Martin Garcia Ortiz, a priest opposed to the mine, was kidnapped by supporters, beaten, and later arrested. He left town as a result. "Things are so broken that there's no other way out. The only way, I think, is that the company leaves," he told Paley.

Then, in January 2012, a group of opponents confronted a work crew laying water pipes, accusing them of building a water system for the mine. Police were called again, and this time they shot and killed Bernardo Mendez, one of the leaders of COPOVU. Abigail Vasquez, Bernardo Vasquez's sister, was wounded. After that, the town's mayor fled, and the municipal offices were closed. Bernardo Vasquez demanded that the municipal government be dissolved and the mayor removed.

Bernardo Vasquez, an agronomist, said he'd been threatened at least a dozen times by members of an armed group in the town, and the state Human Rights Commission issued an order of protection for him. However, while he was returning home on the evening of March 15, 2012, gunmen forced his pickup truck off the road and murdered him. His brother Andres and Rosalinda Canseco were both wounded and hospitalized.

The following day, two COPOVU representatives, Jorge Sanchez and Eustasio Vasquez, in a press conference reported by the Oaxaca daily *Noticias,* said the killing was the work of *"guardias blancas,"* or paramilitaries, supported by the company. "We've seen them give money to people in the community who are against us and create a group called 'Protecting Our Rights.' These are people who now have new cars, when before they had nothing. They are the *guardias blancas* who kill and threaten." The two criticized Oaxaca's governor, Gabino Cue, for saying that the violence was an internal problem within the community.

Fortuna denied responsibility. The company's CEO, Jorge Ganoza, told Canadian media, "We, as a company, and our team in Oaxaca, are saddened by these senseless and continued acts of violence in the town of San Jose, related to a long-standing political struggle for local power. It is in no way related to our activities or involves company personnel."

Despite the state's fractious politics, community and social organizations throughout Oaxaca came together to condemn the assassination. Servicios para una Educacion Alternativa A.C. (Services for an Alternative Education, or EDUCA) said the violence was a consequence of the government's development policy. "Oaxaca has been converted into an arena for experimentation with the imposition of megaprojects at any cost," it stated. "The multimillion profits of the big mining companies, and the human and social costs, will be paid as always by those 'conflict-loving Indians,' as they insultingly call those who defend their communities."

The National Assembly of the Environmentally Harmed (Afectados Ambientales) also noted that the government had received photographs and other evidence documenting the activity in San Jose of Protecting Our Rights, but had not acted to prevent the violence. The state teachers' union, a militant chapter within the more conservative national union, also condemned Vasquez's assassination: "We support the three demands of the people of San Jose del Progreso: the disappearance of the armed groups, punishment of the intellectual and material authors of the killing of Bernardo Vasquez, and the immediate closing of the Cuzcatlan mine," it declared.

In his interview with Paley before his assassination, Vasquez connected the mine's operation with the displacement of San Jose's residents. "There's no reason to negotiate with the company," he told her. "There's no parameters to say, 'Okay, we'll propose some productive projects or development projects,' and then the next day I'll have to leave my village."

Instead of bringing prosperity, the mine sharpened the crisis that is already the reason many Zapotecos leave the towns of Oaxaca's central valleys to find jobs cleaning office buildings in downtown Los Angeles. "What the mine has left to Oaxaca is bitterness, death, the disarticulation of our community and a devastated environment," mourned Sosa Villavicencio, the Party of Labor state deputy. "That's the only thing the indigenous people of San Jose del Progreso will have once the useful life of the mine has ended."

The murder of Bernardo Vasquez was also condemned by the leaders of another Oaxacan town resisting mining projects, Capulalpam de Mendez in the Zapotec Sierra Juarez region. "The death of a *compañero* affects us a lot because we are organized together in one brotherhood, and it's as though they killed a member of our family," said Rodolfo Hernandez Cosmes, former secretary of Capulalpam's Commission for Communal Welfare.

In March 2012, its municipal leaders demanded an end to the mining activity in the area of the Natividad mine and the cancellation of all the concessions given to its owners, another Canadian company called Continuum Resources, in Oaxaca and the Sierra Juarez region. Between 2004 and 2006 Continuum Resources was given mining concessions for 123,000 acres in Sierra Juarez, most covering communal lands.

The residents of Natividad, the tiny town at the mine site, were promised that the mine would bring jobs and economic development. Over half the six hundred inhabitants have never completed elementary school, and a quarter of their 160 homes still have dirt floors. But the mine had a huge environmental impact. While mining in the area has a two-hundred-year history, for almost all of that time it took place on a much smaller scale with primitive methods. Hernandez Cosmes says that ecological problems became much worse in the last decade, after the Natividad mine opened in 2002. Just four years later, in 2006, water problems grew so bad around the mine that the federal Prosecutor for Environmental Protection ordered all work at the mine to stop.

Community leaders accused the mine of having damaged the aquifers on which they depend, and said thirteen springs had disappeared. "A community without water has no life on which future generations can depend," a communal statement declared. Residents feared that continued operations would lead to drying up the last spring in the community of three thousand indigenous Zapotec people.

Water in the local river runs yellow and has a terrible smell, according to Capulalpam residents. The current Communal Welfare secretary, Javier Garcia Juarez, says that in 2011 some of the dams holding back ponds of toxic residue from earlier mine operations collapsed. Tons of waste contaminated communal land belonging to the town, and trees in the local forest were stained grey with the chemicals that had been used to separate gold and silver from the ore extracted from the mine. That impact was particularly devastating for Capulalpam, which was declared "a magical town" by the federal government's secretary of tourism. In the Sierra Juarez there are over two hundred species of orchid, including some that are in danger of extinction. People still sight jaguars, while monkeys, parrots, and toucans are common, along with pumas, white-tailed deer, and the dwarf magpie.

Despite this biodiversity, in 2011 another mining company, Minera Teocuitla, arrived in the community accompanied by agents of the Agrarian Reform department. Minera Teocuitla is a subsidiary of Sundance Minerals, whose business model involves developing mines next to other mining projects, even closed ones. The company proposed an exploration project called Geranio directly north of the Natividad mine. Mine and government representatives demanded a meeting with community residents to authorize a new exploration contract. On April 10, 2011, however, the Zapotec community's general assembly announced it would not support the project. Their statement: "The community of Capulalpam, exercising our rights as an indigenous and farming municipality, refuses permission to the companies Natividad, Minera Teocuitla, Continuum Resources, Arco Exploration or companies using any other name to carry out exploration or exploitation of minerals in our land."

In the midst of turmoil over the mine, in 2008 Sierra de Juarez communities were further convulsed by an uproar over a study conducted by a team of anthropologists, headed by Peter Herlihy of the University of Kansas' geography department. According to the Union of Organizations of the Sierra Juarez of Oaxaca (UNOSJO), two years earlier Herlihy had gained communities' cooperation in a mapping project called Mexico Indigena. The project not only set out to map the region's physical geography but also land ownership and the social and political organizations of its inhabitants. Herlihy told the towns that Mexico Indigena was sponsored by the American Geographical Society, Kansas University, Kansas State University, Carleton University, and the Universidad Autonoma de San Luis Potosi. Another study sponsor was the Secretariat of Environment and Natural Resources (SEMARNAT), responsible for regulating mining and preventing ecological harm.

Lack of transparency about the project's intentions soon began to alienate some of the Sierra communities, including Santa Cruz Yagavila and Santa María Zoogochi, as well as UNOSJO itself. The researchers then concentrated on San Miguel Tiltepec. All are about fifteen miles from Capulalpam and the Natividad mine.

After Aldo Gonzalez, a leader of UNOSJO, began investigating the project, he discovered that its sponsors included not only the academic institutions and SEMARNAT, but the Foreign Military Studies Office (FMSO) of the United States Army. Participating in the study was Radiance Technology, a military intelligence contractor. The project itself turned out to be part of a larger effort, Bowman Expeditions, a geographical research project also financed by the FMSO. The army integrates these projects into its Human Terrain System, which forms part of a global counterinsurgency strategy.

The Mexico Indigena project then published its maps on the Internet, in English, not a language accessible to most residents, who speak Spanish, and many of whom are monolingual in Zapotec. The database included the names of individual residents and details about the boundaries and uses of the individual plots of land in each community surveyed.

Gonzalez was disturbed by the possibility that the project was intended to help authorities head off, or deal with, community mobilizations opposing development projects. "[These projects] have been the source of protest by people and communities who are being robbed of their land, water, and decision-making power. Then conflicts are engineered by those who want to stop any opposition to their activities," he said. A statement by UNOSJO declared that it "is against this kind of [research] project being carried out in the Sierra Juárez and distances itself completely from the work compiled by the México Indígena research team. We call upon indigenous peoples in this country and around the world not to be fooled by these types of research projects, which usurp traditional knowledge without prior consent. Although researchers may initially claim to be conducting the projects in 'good faith,' said knowledge could be used against the indigenous peoples in the future."

Oaxacans Debate Poverty and Migration

Another political activist in Oaxaca who condemned Bernardo Vasquez's assassination is Bernardo Ramirez, elected the binational coordinator of the Binational Front of Indigenous Organizations (FIOB) at its assembly in 2011. For Ramirez and FIOB, the kind of development represented by mining projects is no answer to the displacement of farmers. In Oaxaca, 41 percent of the people make their living from agriculture. Mining jobs account for only 0.28 percent of state employment.

The mines promise jobs, but they produce very few, while their social and environmental cost is high. The projects benefit not the residents of local communities, but the shareholders of large corporations, which exercise enormous influence on the federal government. State governments also cooperate closely, especially in states controlled by Mexico's current ruling party, the Institutional Revolutionary Party (PRI), or its former ruling party, the conservative National Action Party. With federal and state support, corporate projects move forward in spite of local opposition. Both Veracruz and Oaxaca were governed by the PRI for decades, and as of 2012, Veracruz still is.

FIOB leaders contend that this kind of economic development not only doesn't stop the displacement of communities, but in fact causes it. Displaced people, in turn, migrate through Mexico, and eventually to the United States and Canada, seeking survival. For almost half a century, migration has been a main fact of social life in hundreds of indigenous towns spread through the hills of one of Mexico's poorest states. That's made migrants' rights and their living and working conditions central concerns for communities like Santiago de Juxtlahuaca, in the Mixteca region. For these communities, the right to travel to seek work is a matter of economic survival.

In June 2009, dozens of farmers left their fields, and women weavers their looms, to debate another right, the right to stay home. In Juxtlahuaca's community center, two hundred Mixtec, Zapotec, and Triqui farmers, and a handful of their relatives working in the United States, made impassioned speeches asserting this right at an FIOB assembly. Hot arguments echoing from the cinderblock walls of the cavernous hall ended in numerous votes. People repeated one phrase over and over: *derecho de no migrar*—the right to not migrate. Asserting this right challenges not just the inequality and exploitation facing migrants, but the reasons why people have to migrate to begin with. Indigenous communities were pointing to the need for social change to deal with displacement and the root causes of migration.

Although FIOB is a binational organization, since the late 1990s its assemblies have been held every three years in Mexico. In part, this is a practical matter. Indigenous farmers can't easily come up with the money to travel as delegates to meetings in the United States. Even if they could, getting visas would be virtually impossible. US consulates suspect that poor Oaxacans trying to visit California are just looking for a way to cross the border to stay and work. Consequently, FIOB's Mexican assemblies always draw far more delegates from Mexico than from the United States, and have been shifting the organization's center of gravity, and its political activity, to the south.

FIOB, however, actually had its origin on the US side of the border, when the wave of Oaxacan migration north reached California's central valley, Los Angeles, and San Diego in the mid-1980s. At its founding on October 5, 1991, it was called the Frente Mixteco Zapoteco Binacional, because the migrant stream came at first mostly from Oaxaca's Mixtec and Zapotec towns. Soon it had to change its name, though, when Triquis, Chatinos, and other indigenous groups joined the wave of migration. It became the Frente Indigena Oaxaqueña Binacional, the Binational Indigenous Oaxacan Front. Then, in the mid-2000s, the name changed again, to the Frente Indigena de Organizaciones Binacionales, or the Binational Front of Indigenous Organizations, after including indigenous migrants from states like Puebla, Guerrero, and Michoacan.

The Frente's growth rode a wave of increased assertiveness among indigenous people in Mexico itself as a result of the Zapatista uprising in Chiapas. That began on January 1, 1994, the day NAFTA went into effect. FIOB immediately mounted actions to pressure the Mexican government to refrain from using massive military force to crush the uprising. From Fresno to Baja California to Oaxaca, Frente activists went on hunger strikes and demonstrated in front of consulates and government offices. Their experience solidified the organization's binational character, sparked the development of cross-border tactics and contributed to its activist identity.

Organizing Oaxacan migrants around their rights as workers became a bedrock activity for the FIOB in California. It developed a strategic alliance with California Rural Legal Assistance (CRLA), which started an Indigenous Farmworkers Project. FIOB leaders like Rufino Dominguez and Irma Luna, Jesus Estrada and Lorenzo Oropeza became community outreach workers for CRLA, helping farmworkers enforce minimum-wage laws and basic protections for their working conditions.

In 1993, the Frente began serious organizing in Oaxaca itself. "We began with various productive projects such as the planting of the Chinese pomegranate, the forajero cactus, and strawberries," Dominguez explained, "so that families of migrants in the US would have an income to survive." Those efforts grew into five separate offices in the state, and a membership base larger than that in the United States, expanding to more than seventy towns. In 1999, the Frente entered into an alliance with the PRD and elected Romualdo Juan Gutierrez-Cortez to the state Chamber of Deputies in a district in the Mixteca region. "For the first time we beat the *caciques* [rural political bosses]," Dominguez declared proudly.

About five hundred thousand indigenous people from Oaxaca live in the United States, three hundred thousand in California alone, according to Dominguez. Many of these men and women come from communities whose economies are totally dependent on migration. The ability to send a son or daughter across the border to the North, to work and send back money, makes the difference between eating chicken or eating salt and tortillas. Migration means not having to manhandle a wooden plough behind an ox, cutting furrows in dry soil for a corn crop that can't be sold for what it costs to grow it. It means that dollars arrive in the mail when kids need shoes to go to school or when a grandparent needs a doctor.

Oaxaca is one of the poorest states in Mexico, where the government category of extreme poverty encompasses 75 percent of its 3.4 million residents, according to EDUCA. *Migration and Poverty in Oaxaca*, a study by Ana Marguerita Alvarado Juarez and published by the Institute for Sociological Investigation at the Autonomous University Benito Juarez in Oaxaca, says Oaxaca consistently falls far below the national average for every measure of poverty and lack of development. Alvarado Juarez based her study on Mexico's 2000 census, as reported by the National Council of Population (CONAPO). While nationally 9.4 percent of Mexico's people are illiterate, in Oaxaca 21.5 percent are, she found. Nationally 28.4 percent of students don't finish elementary school, but in Oaxaca 45.5 percent, or almost half, never complete it. Nationally 4.8 percent of Mexicans live with no electricity, 11.2 percent live in homes with no running water and 14.8 percent walk on dirt floors. In Oaxaca, those numbers more than double—to 12.5 percent, 26.9 percent and 41.6 percent, respectively. Only in Chiapas, Mexico's poorest state, do children get less schooling then Oaxaca's average of 6.9 years per person.

The Mexican minimum wage varies between 62.3 pesos in Mexico City or Baja California, and 59.08 pesos a day in states like Oaxaca (in 2011). Half of Mexicans make less than twice that, meaning that they make less than US$10 a day. In Oaxaca, over two-thirds of wage earners (71.9 percent) make less than twice the minimum.

Displacement of people from Oaxacan communities tracks the growth in poverty in recent decades. In 1990, the net migration from

Oaxaca was more than 527,000 (people leaving minus people arriving or returning). In 2000, that number grew to more than 662,000. In the five years between 2000 and 2005, despite a high birth rate, Oaxaca's population only grew 0.39 percent. Eighteen percent of its people have left for other parts of Mexico and the United States.

But displacement and migration don't affect all communities equally and instead are concentrated in certain parts of the state. Alvarado Juarez found that from 1990 to 2000, 45 percent of the state's municipalities, accounting for 17.4 percent of its population, had negative growth. The towns that lost population were rural ones with fewer than fifteen thousand inhabitants, and were mostly indigenous. Some 52.9 percent of the population lives in rural areas, and 41 percent make their living from agriculture. Oaxaca has 20 percent of all indigenous people in Mexico, who make up 32.5 percent of the state's population. Displacement is concentrated in the Sierra Norte and Valles Centrales regions, site of the Capulalpam and San Jose del Progreso mining projects, as well as the Mixteca. All are overwhelmingly corn-farming regions. According to CONAPO, of Oaxaca's 570 municipalities, 182 are considered to have a "very high" degree of economic marginalization, and 270 have a "high" degree—together making up 80 percent of the state's municipalities.

Alvarado Juarez concluded that "marginalization and economic conditions have an influence on the decision to migrate, although there are other characteristics that make migration possible." Among the conditions that encourage migration, she pointed to four factors: high levels of poverty and marginalization, decline in the rural economy affecting more than half the economically active population, the lack of well-paying jobs made worse by lack of skills and illiteracy, and family and social networks that link community residents with migrants who have already left.

As a result, according to the Indigenous Farm Worker Study conducted by Rick Mines (who for many years headed the US government's National Agricultural Workers Survey), there are 120,000 indigenous Mexican farmworkers in California. Counting the 45,000 children living with these workers, the Mexican indigenous farmworker population in California makes up a total of 165,000 people.

The vast majority come from Oaxaca—in fact, one-third of the seven hundred thousand farmworkers in California come from Oaxaca and southern Mexico. In 1990 it was only 7 percent. Mines's survey just covers farmworkers; a huge number of Oaxacan indigenous migrants also migrate to California cities.

Mines documents this population's growth, from about 35,000 indigenous farmworkers in the early 1990s to 120,000 in 2008. As a result, linguistic diversity in California has exploded, and the state's farmworkers today speak twenty-three indigenous languages. Nine of every ten indigenous farmworkers are Mixtecs, Zapotecs, or Triquis, but their numbers also include Amusgos, Chatinos, and others. There are so many indigenous people that California has at least seven Guelaguetza festivals every year—the annual celebration that showcases the colorful dances and varied music of the indigenous people of Oaxaca, Puebla, Yucatan, Guerrero, Michoacan, and other states. In some farmworker towns, like Greenfield and Hollister, public libraries hold special events to recognize the indigenous culture of the local agricultural workforce.

The growth in numbers has not meant an increase in the economic well-being of indigenous Mexican migrants, however. Mines's survey found that indigenous families were earning an average of $13,750 per year. Meztizo families (nonindigenous Mexican migrants) had an income that was almost double, $22,500. Of all farmworkers in California, indigenous workers receive the lowest pay. According to Mines, one-third of those he surveyed earned above the minimum wage ($8 per hour), one-third reported earning the minimum and one-third less than the minimum—a wage that violates California state law.

Most indigenous families live in crowded conditions in apartments or trailers. The survey found they paid $400 to $700 a month in rent in coastal agricultural valleys like Salinas or Santa Maria, and $280 to $350 in the central San Joaquin Valley. But in some areas, particularly in Sonoma and northern San Diego Counties, some indigenous migrants, especially the most recent arrivals, live outside in tents—even under trees. During the harvest in many California valleys, workers sleep in their cars in parking lots or even in the fields themselves.

The indigenous immigrant community is very young. The average age of a person crossing the US-Mexico border today is twenty. In 2010, the study found the typical indigenous migrant had only been in the United States for three years. Reflecting the statistics for Oaxaca itself, the majority of Mexican farmworkers in California have only six years of education. Young people who are older than eleven when they come to the United States often don't go to school, and many work in the fields. But younger Mexicans in California have more education than older people, reflecting an increase in education access once they arrive. Children born in the United States from indigenous families have an average 11.5 years of school.

All of these statistics highlight the desperate living situation for many farming families in Oaxaca—despite bad housing, low wages, and discrimination in the United States, migration is not just preferable but sometimes the only recourse promising survival. "There are no jobs here, and NAFTA made the price of corn so low that it's not economically possible to plant a crop anymore," Rufino Dominguez asserted in an interview at the 2008 FIOB assembly. "We come to the US to work because we can't get a price for our product at home. There's no alternative."

NAFTA did indeed change Mexican national economic policy. Together with the economic reforms that accompanied it, the treaty didn't just eliminate earlier programs for finding markets for the products grown by farming families, like those for the tobacco and coffee farmers of Veracruz. It eliminated food sovereignty and self-sufficiency as a goal of economic development. In its place it substituted development based on exports, a policy that, in the countryside, favored large landholders producing for export over small ones producing for a national market. That affected especially indigenous communities, which often hold land in common, as well as agricultural communities based on the *ejidos* established by earlier agrarian reform policies.

The impact of NAFTA on farming was widely predicted in Mexico, and the government was forced to come up with agricultural subsidy programs that would, at least on paper, compensate for entirely predictable losses. Jonathan Fox of the University of California at Santa Cruz analyzed those transfer payment programs, starting with their basic assumptions. "Many believed," he said in a presentation made at an international forum on migration held in Oaxaca in April 2011, "that with the commercial opening produced by NAFTA and its low-priced corn imports, corn would lose its central place in the country's agriculture, while many of the hundreds of thousands of small producers who grow it would be displaced. This prediction characterized the subsidy programs in Mexico of the last fifteen years, and justified giving $20 billion in payments directly to farmers to compensate them and help them adjust to NAFTA between 1994 and 2009. As was predicted, imports increased greatly. But corn continued to be the most important crop in Mexico, in terms of the volume of production, the number of producers, and the area under cultivation. At the same time, many producers abandoned farming."

Underlining this basic contradiction, Fox found that while Mexico's spending on farming doubled between 2001 and 2008 alone, employment in agriculture plummeted by 20 percent, from 10.7 million to 8.6 million. The problem, according to Fox, was that the money wasn't invested in helping small producers, much less directed to those communities where the crisis of falling rural income was leading to the greatest displacement, and consequently, emigration. Some subsidy programs, like Ingreso Objectivo, actually favored the states of northern Mexico rather than the poorest ones of the south. "Ingreso Objectivo directly subsidizes the production of a small number of the biggest ranchers in the country," he asserted. "This highlights the huge support for the operations of large processors and distributors, including transnational producers like Cargill and Maseca. With the exception of PROCAMPO, the sharp concentration of agricultural subsidies in the hands of a few privileged recipients is increasing economic inequality."

PROCAMPO—Programa de Apoyos Directos al Campo, or the Farmers Direct Support Program—is the program set up in theory to benefit small producers and distributes payments to 2.5 million farmers, mostly those who grow corn. "Nevertheless, the way resources are distributed is not progressive, and is designed to pay more to farmers who have more land," Fox charged. "In practice, the majority of the poorest producers (who have less than five hectares [twelve acres]) are completely excluded." Over time, PROCAMPO itself has accounted for a smaller and smaller part of the agricultural budget, and the amount it pays to farmers per hectare has also declined. "On the other hand, the losses suffered by small Mexican farmers receiving PROCAMPO have grown," he said. "This is a result of falling corn prices produced by increased US corn imports (actually dumping, at prices below the cost of production)." Fox concluded that "the agricultural program intended most to benefit corn producers, and the most inclusive one, has not only excluded the majority of its intended population, but is slanted to favor the richest producers."

A Government Committed to the Right to Not Migrate?

It is no wonder that at the FIOB assembly of 2008 indigenous farmers concluded that, without large-scale political change, their communities would not have the resources for productive projects or economic development that might provide a decent living. Towns like Juxtlahuaca don't even have wastewater treatment. Rural communities rely on the same rivers for drinking water that are also used to carry away sewage. "A typical teacher earns about 2,200 pesos every two weeks [about US$220]," says Jaime Medina, a reporter for Oaxaca's daily *Noticias*. "From that they have to purchase chalk, pencils, and other school supplies for the children."

"We need development that makes migration a choice rather than a necessity—the right to not migrate," said Gaspar Rivera Salgado, who was elected to a three-year term at the 2008 assembly as FIOB's binational coordinator when Rufino Dominguez stepped down. Rivera's father and mother still live on a ranch half an hour up a dirt road from the main highway going toward the coast, in the tiny town of Santa Cruz Rancho Viejo. There his father, Sidronio, planted three hundred avocado trees a few years ago in the hope that someday their fruit would take the place of the corn and beans that were once his staple crop. He's been fortunate—his relatives have water, and a pipe from their spring has kept most of his trees, and those hopes, alive. Fernando, Gaspar's brother, started growing mushrooms in a FIOB-sponsored project and even put up a greenhouse for tomatoes. Those projects, they hope, might produce enough money that Fernando won't have to go back to Seattle, where he worked for seven years.

This family has come closer than many to achieving the right to not migrate. For the millions of farmers throughout the indigenous countryside, not migrating means doing something like it. But finding the necessary resources, even for a small number of families and communities, presents FIOB with its biggest challenge. This was the source of the debate at its Juxtlahuaca assembly, where Gaspar Rivera Salgado declared, "We will find the answer to migration in our communities of origin. To make the right to not migrate concrete, we need to organize the forces in our communities, and combine them with the resources and experiences we've accumulated in sixteen years of cross-border organizing." Fernando, the greenhouse builder and mushroom farmer, agreed that FIOB has the ability to organize people. "But now we have to take the next step," he urged, "and make concrete changes in peoples' lives."

Organizing FIOB's support base in Oaxaca meant more than just making speeches. As Fernando Rivera Salgado pointed out, communities want projects that raise their income. Over the years, FIOB has organized women weavers in Juxtlahuaca, helping them sell their textiles and garments through its chapters in California. It set up a union for rural taxis, both to help farming families get from Juxtlahuaca to the tiny towns in the surrounding hills and to provide jobs for drivers. Artisan co-ops make traditional products, helped by a cooperative loan fund.

In the Mixteca, where Juxtlahuaca is located, the PROCAMPO payments are distributed by officials who favor supporters of the Institutional Revolutionary Party, or PRI, which ruled Oaxaca from the time the party was formed in the 1940s until the 2010 state election. One objective debated at the FIOB assembly was organizing community pressure to win more of these resources. But the subsidies were viewed with suspicion by activists familiar with the strings tied to them, and the effect of the funding on communities themselves. "Part of our political culture is the use of *regalos* [gifts], or government favors, to buy votes," Gaspar Rivera Salgado explained.

"People want *regalos*, and think an organization is strong because of what it can give. When people demand these results from FIOB, do we help them or not? And if we do, how can we change the way people think? It's critical that our members see organization as the answer to problems, not a gift from the government or a political party. FIOB members need political education."

FIOB leaders don't think the organization can turn its back on peoples' expectations, however, warned Romualdo Juan Gutierrez Cortez. "We aren't the only organization in Oaxaca—there are 600 others. If we don't do it, they will." But for its entire existence, FIOB has been a crucial part of the political opposition to Oaxaca's PRI governments. Gutierrez Cortez, a schoolteacher in Tecomaxtlahuaca, was FIOB's Oaxaca coordinator until he stepped down at the Juxtlahuaca assembly. He has also been a leader of Oaxaca's teachers union, Section 22 of the National Education Workers Union, and of the Popular Association of the People of Oaxaca (APPO).

In June 2006, a strike by Section 22 led to a months-long uprising, led by APPO, which sought to remove the state's governor, Ulises Ruiz, and make basic changes in development and economic policy. The uprising was crushed by federal armed intervention and dozens of activists were arrested. According to Leoncio Vasquez, an FIOB activist in Fresno, "The lack of human rights itself is a factor contributing to migration from Oaxaca and Mexico, since it closes off our ability to call for any change." In 2008, as FIOB was holding its assembly, teachers again occupied the central plaza, or *zocalo*, of the state capital, protesting the same conditions that had sparked the uprising two years earlier.

Gutierrez himself was not jailed during the 2006 turmoil, although the state issued an order for his detention. But he'd been arrested before. Following his term in the state Chamber of Deputies, Gutierrez was imprisoned by then-governor Jose Murat until a binational campaign won his release. While the spurious changes against him were quickly dropped, his real crime was insisting on a new path of economic development that would raise rural living standards, and on the political right to organize independently for that goal.

While APPO wasn't successful in getting rid of Ruiz and the PRI in 2006, Gaspar Rivera Salgado believed that "in Mexico we're very close to getting power in our communities on a local and state level." He pointed to Gutierrez's election as state deputy and, later, as mayor of his hometown San Miguel Tlacotepec. Other municipal presidents, allied with FIOB, had also won office, and a political coalition was forming with the common goal of getting rid of the PRI.

FIOB delegates agreed in 2008 that the organization would continue its alliance with the PRD. Nevertheless, that alliance was controversial, partly because of the party's internal disarray. "We know the PRD is caught up in an internal crisis, and there's no real alternative vision on the left," Rivera Salgado said at the time. "But there are no other choices if we want to participate in electoral politics, so we're trying to put forward positive proposals. We're asking people in the PRD to stop fighting over positions, and instead use the resources of the party to organize the community. We can't change things by ourselves. First, we have to reorganize our own base. But then we have to find strategic allies.

"Migration is part of globalization," he emphasized, "an aspect of state policies that expel people. Creating an alternative to that requires political power. There's no way to avoid that."

The discussion moved from agitation and critique of failed government economic policies to expectations of concrete change in 2010, when Gabino Cue, former mayor of Oaxaca city, was elected governor. Cue had run against Ulisses Ruiz in 2004 and, by most accounts, would have won a clean vote. Election fraud in indigenous communities, however, put Ruiz into the governorship, and set up the insurrection in Oaxaca's streets two years later. In 2010 Cue was nominated again, this time by an unwieldy coalition of the PRD and the PAN, whose virtually sole point of unity was the desire to knock out the PRI. When the polls closed this time, Cue emerged the winner.

Despite criticism on the Left of the PAN-PRD alliance, the hopes and aspirations of Oaxacan political activists ran very high after the election. The magazine *El Topil* (named after a term referring to positions of responsibility in indigenous communities) published by

EDUCA, put out a special issue, prefacing it by saying, "This political moment opens an extraordinary opportunity to 'rethink Oaxaca.' No other moment of our recent history has freed such high expectations about what our government could do."

Aldo Gonzalez used his contribution to the special issue to focus attention on the crisis of rural communities, especially displacement. "Farmers in Oaxaca today are older than at any other time in our history," he wrote. "The lack of support for farming in Mexico forces their children to migrate in search of survival, abandoning their land and crops. Oaxaca isn't self-sufficient in food any longer." Gonzalez also pointed out that the mega-development projects promoted by the federal government, instead of creating employment and rising living standards, undermined them because they were "designed from outside, and imposed on indigenous territories," intended to benefit investors instead of communities.

"They have been met with protests by people and communities whose land and water have been taken," Gonzalez declared. "The new government cannot let them pass by unnoticed, despite the fact it has no decision-making power over them. Oaxaca is only governable if the government listens, pays attention to and supports that protest, and doesn't criminalize it."

Finally, Gonzalez urged the government to support a more self-sustaining form of agriculture that might provide a basis for people to remain on the land. "Many communities are making agreements to return to the production of their own food," he noted, "in spite of the fact that it might cost more than buying it from the outside. The next government should support food sovereignty and self-sufficient farming, not the agroindustrial model that's heating the planet. We don't need charity and handouts, but a policy of real support for indigenous Oaxacan farmers."

Following the election, Governor Cue held a meeting with FIOB leaders from both Oaxaca and California, in which they proposed measures to implement the right to not migrate. "We are going to create an Oaxaca in which migration isn't the fated destiny of our rural and urban population," he promised. FIOB's binational coordinator, Gaspar Rivera Salgado, responded, "FIOB has struggled for twenty years for the rights of migrants, and now we want to fight for the right to not migrate, to change people's actual living conditions so that migration isn't their only alternative."

Cue appointed Rufino Dominguez, FIOB's former binational coordinator, to head an office charged with defending the interests of migrants, the Instituto Oaxaqueño de Atencion al Migrante (the Oaxacan Institute for Attention to Migrants, or IOAM). And when FIOB held its next binational assembly in 2011 in Oaxaca city, the gathering was opened by speeches from Dominguez and other officials in the new state administration.

The FIOB delegates from California came to this assembly feeling that the organization had to prioritize resistance to the escalating attacks on migrant rights in the United States. California FIOB chapters had earlier debated and adopted one of the most advanced and progressive proposals for immigration reform made by any migrant organization in the United States. It is much like the Dignity Campaign program, but after an extensive series of internal discussions, FIOB included additional provisions based on its historical opposition to guest worker programs, and its defense of the cultural rights of migrant indigenous communities.

As early as its 2005 assembly, FIOB passed a resolution condemning guest worker programs. That set it apart from many migrant rights organizations in the United States at the time, many of whom were willing to accept new programs (supposedly with greater rights for migrants), in exchange for legalization for the undocumented. In Mexico at that time, the government was calling for the negotiation of a new bracero program. Jorge Castaneda, a former leftist who became foreign minister in the PAN administration of Vicente Fox, said what Mexicans cared about was getting a chance to work in the United States, and that this could be achieved by trading bracero programs for legalization, which he called the "whole enchilada." Dominguez charged at the time, "Migrants need the right to work, but these workers don't have labor rights or benefits. It's like slavery."

Rivera Salgado, who guided the development of FIOB's immigration program during the California discussions, connected migrant rights with the right to not migrate. "Both rights are part of the same solution," he explained. "We have to change the debate from one in which immigration is presented as a problem to a debate over rights. The real problem is exploitation." The new position emphasized language rights for migrant communities—unsurprisingly, since FIOB fought for translation rights in California courts in the 1990s, at a time when Oaxacan court proceedings didn't guarantee them (and still often don't).

Mexican members, mostly from Oaxaca, but some also migrants living in Baja California, came to talk about the right to not migrate. Cue's election and Dominguez's appointment had changed the relationship between FIOB and the government dramatically. Instead of governors who arrested and attacked FIOB leaders, Cue's secretary for social development was on the stage as the assembly opened, reminding delegates of his long relationship with them.

But the real change wasn't ceremonial. Delegates from Oaxaca had high expectations that the new state government, and especially its migrant affairs office, would be able to move the right to not migrate from slogan to reality. That was a tall order. The federal government, with its neoliberal, free-market, anti-labor policies, sets the parameters for economic development in Mexico, regardless of what states do. Nevertheless, farmers demanded some way to stay on their land, and to sell their crops for a price that could keep them going from one year to the next. Many delegates also wanted to raise organic crops, protect Oaxaca's corn from genetic contamination, and undo the damage of deforestation. Oaxacan women weavers and indigenous artisans saw their production as another potential road freeing them from forced migration, and needed more support for it.

The hundred-plus delegates tried to combine these related elements into a political program, and then into action capable of realizing it. It was debate and discussion, not among academics discussing migration, but among people living it as a daily reality.

That year Rivera Salgado, one of the few delegates around when FIOB was organized twenty years earlier, stepped down as binational coordinator. Some positions were filled by Oaxacan migrants living in California, but the new coordinator, Bernardo Ramirez, lives in the heart of the Mixteca region of Oaxaca. In addition, the Oaxaca regional coordinator is a leader of the state teachers' union. Ramirez worked five seasons in the fields of the United States, an experience shared with most FIOB delegates. His election, however, signaled that the organization's center of gravity was moving even more firmly into Mexico.

A few months later, at the state's celebration of the International Day of the Migrant on December 16, Dominguez, now director of the IOAM, paid tribute to the contributions of the braceros. The ceremony honored the first of Oaxaca's migrant workers to travel to the United States, from 1942 to 1964, and the women who cared for the families they left behind. Around the balconies of the interior courtyard of the Palacio del Gobierno, the ornate colonial state capitol building, hung photographs showing the lives of current migrants from Oaxaca working as farm laborers in California. Migrant rights activists, artisans, and public officials spoke about the important role migration continues to play in Oaxaca's economic, social, political, and family life.

"Our starting point is to understand the need for economic development," Dominguez told them, "because the reason for migration is the lack of work and opportunity in people's communities of origin. If we don't attack the roots of migration, it will continue to grow. There's a fear of investing in our own people, but there's no other way. We have to have economic development and respect for the human rights of migrants as they come and go."

The celebration illustrated one element of IOAM's accomplishments in its first year under a post-PRI administration. Earlier, the institute had registered and identified the approximately 4,470 Oaxacans who had worked in the United States during the bracero period. Those still living (2,508) were very old; the Cue administration gave 10,000 pesos (about US$800) to each worker, or to their surviving family members. In a small way, the gesture sought to compensate for the fact that braceros had money deducted from their wages while working in the United States, which then disappeared once they returned to Mexico. In the 1990s and 2000s, former braceros filed suit in both Mexico and the United States to recover the lost wages, and the federal government was eventually forced to set aside 3,816 million pesos in a fund to pay compensation—money the braceros are still fighting to receive.

IOAM sought to become more active in migrant communities in the United States as well. Dominguez made several trips in which the institute offered help in obtaining birth certificates and other documents needed by migrants abroad. Although there were glitches in the implementation of those services, IOAM nevertheless sought to become a source of much more concrete help than it had been in the past. Its desire to be more closely involved in helping migrant families was put to the test when two Oaxacan brothers died as they were cleaning an underground tunnel in a recycling station near Bakersfield, in California's San Joaquin Valley. Oaxacans in the Valley expected the institute to help send the men's bodies home, which it did, and Dominguez met with California state health and safety authorities, who filed legal charges against the company.

IOAM expressed the basic political program of the administration in its report describing its first year of work: "This administration has the objective of creating conditions for socioeconomic development that permit Oaxacans to not abandon their communities of origin in search of better opportunities. The right to not migrate constitutes the fundamental basis of this administration's program in relation to migration issues. We have therefore coordinated our efforts and actions in order to promote local development, productivity, and the creation of jobs."

The report then described the investment of 1.6 million pesos in a program that helped 320 women to get more training in developing new styles for artisan products. IOAM worked on a program for housing improvement in communities with high rates of emigration, despite suffering budget cuts from an unsympathetic federal government. Together with activist teachers from California's Sacramento State University and the Davis campus of the University of California, the institute facilitated a training program for teachers of migrant education that trained seventeen instructors. These teachers work in US districts in New York, California, and Michigan, where thirty-seven hundred Oaxacan students are enrolled.

IOAM personnel, including Dominguez and Romualdo Juan Gutierrez Cortez, also worked on the problems faced by migrants crossing into the United States, as well as Central American migrants passing through Oaxaca itself. IOAM helped produce radio spots giving information to would-be border crossers, including a Saturday broadcast called *The Migrant Road*. In Ciudad Ixtepec, it helped create a Grupo Beta police team responsible for investigating and halting the widespread robberies and rapes suffered by Central American migrants. That team reported giving food, medical attention, and refuge to 361 people. And facing the high rate of deportations from the United States (about one million during the first two and a half years of the Obama administration), IOAM helped to repatriate 22,454 Oaxacan deportees during its first six months of operation.

IOAM also signed an agreement in January 2012 with the United Food and Commercial Workers Union (UFCW), which has been organizing guest workers in Canada on farms and in food processing facilities. Dominguez and UFCW president Wayne Hanley agreed to cooperate to protect the labor rights of Oaxacans working in Canada. "Mexican migrants, above all Oaxacans, who are the majority," said Hanley, "make huge contributions to Canadian society and its economy. So it's only fair that our union should recognize this and work with Mexican institutions to help them gain better wages and working conditions."

The union announced it would set up ten support centers in Canada together with the Alianza de Trabajadores Agricolas (Alliance of Farm Workers). The centers, staffed by Spanish-speaking personnel, would offer training in legal, labor, housing, health and human rights, and maintain a free phone line migrants could call from anywhere in Mexico or Canada. The training would also allow workers to understand those rights before they left Oaxaca, Dominguez said. "In IOAM we have to investigate the human rights situation of Oaxacans in Canada," he explained, "and also make sure they understand those rights and how to enforce them. That's a role we're going to develop."

Here also, however, the state of Oaxaca is pursuing a course that collides with federal policy, which sometimes discourages workers in Canada and the United States from demanding wages and unions that would make them less attractive to employers. If fewer Canadian and US employers seek to import Mexican workers, the remittances flowing back to Mexico from those workers' wages might decline. Federal economic policy depends on those remittances to pay for health care, education, housing, and other social costs, and they now vary between $25 billion to $30 billion annually, about 1.5 percent of the country's entire GNP.

Can the Triquis Go Home?

Those in poor communities don't always see migration as an answer to their problems. Alvarado Juarez says her study shows that the poorest people don't necessarily migrate. "An important number of Oaxacans . . . see migration as the hope to overcome the poverty in which they find themselves. But we're not saying that only the poorest people are those who leave their communities," she says. "In the Mixteca, one of the state's poorest regions, 130 municipalities, with 84 percent of the population, have a very high or high degree of marginalization [poverty]. But only 21 percent have a high degree of migration; 56 municipalities, with 36 percent of the population, have a low degree of migration."

Oaxacan activists emphasize that migration is not just a function of poverty. Lack of political and human rights also contributes to the pressure to leave. One of the sharpest challenges faced by the state's new government is ensuring that the right to propose different courses of development isn't suppressed. This is not just a question of what the government might do in response to future protests, but whether those responsible for the suppression of previous protests, including incarcerations and deaths during the teachers' strike in 2006, will go unpunished.

On the sixth anniversary of the strike, Azael Santiago Chepi, then general secretary of the Oaxacan teachers union Section 22, declared angrily, "The assassins are still free, and [former governor] Ulises

Ruiz enjoys his freedom too, but despite that, the people of Oaxaca, not just the teachers, reject impunity for the looting of the state and for the killings." The union called for the creation of a truth commission to hold the perpetrators responsible. In a speech before the teachers' commemorative march, Governor Cue acknowledged that the government had been guilty of "serious violations" of human rights. This public recognition, he said, meant that it was committed to guaranteeing those acts would not be repeated and those committing them would not enjoy impunity.

Shortly afterward, the state government arrested a suspect in the killing of US journalist Brad Will, who was shot while filming a demonstration during the 2006 strike. State attorney general Manuel de Jesus Lopez announced that the accused assassin, Lenin Osorio Ortega, had worked for the state government while Ulises Ruiz was governor. Will's murder occurred at the height of the protests, and the day after he was shot the federal government sent troops to occupy Oaxaca City, escalating the violence. Twenty-six Mexicans were killed during the strike and protest. Numerous arrest warrants were issued, and some political activists went to the United States to avoid imprisonment. Ruiz's government originally arrested one of Will's fellow protesters for the murder and held him in prison for a year, releasing him only when it became obvious that the arrest was a cover-up. No further investigation was made into the case until after the Cue administration took office.

Political violence not only takes place during demonstrations and strikes, but has been used in the political system itself. It can force people into migration when even poverty itself doesn't. This has been the experience of the Triquis, an indigenous people living in the Mixteca region, amid their efforts to overcome the violence that has plagued their communities for almost half a century. The solution to the problem of the violence in these communities is as much a part of ensuring the right to not migrate as the problem of finding alternative means for economic development.

Just before Christmas 2011, the women and children who'd spent seventeen months living on the sidewalk outside the Palacio del Gobierno (the state capitol building) in Oaxaca announced they were going home. In the spring of 2010, these refugees had abandoned their homes in San Juan Copala, the ceremonial center of the Triqui people. Many houses were burned after they left. Stringing tarps and ropes across the palacio's outdoor colonnade, they set up their *planton*, an impromptu community of sleeping and cooking areas across the sidewalk from the zocalo, the central plaza of Oaxaca city. On the surface, it looked like the settlements of the Occupy protesters that spread across the United States in the fall of 2011. But rather than fighting to remain in their tents, as the Occupy squatters had up north, the Triqui families in the planton were fighting for the right not to live in their tents, for the right to go home.

In December they announced an agreement with representatives of Governor Cue, who'd promised to protect the families if they returned to San Juan Copala. Still, many questioned whether they could really go back safely. Even more importantly, they asked what might bring an end to the violence that has claimed the lives of at least five hundred people over the last four decades. This question is not just debated on the sidewalk by the zocalo, or only in Oaxaca. It is also asked, albeit in whispers, by Triqui migrant farmworkers in Baja California and Sinaloa in northern Mexico and in Hollister and Greenfield in California's Salinas Valley.

Mixtecos have been leaving Oaxaca for decades, driven mostly by the endemic poverty of the Mexican countryside. The Triquis, however, who are equally poor and live in the same region, had other motives for fleeing Oaxaca. Their migration began when the violence in their communities made life unbearable. Once displaced, they began to migrate within the Mixteca region, then within Oaxaca, and then within Mexico. They traveled north, following other Oaxacans to San Quintin in the 1980s and then, in the 1990s, to California.

There Triqui migrants might have escaped the violence, but they could not escape the political presence of the groups they were fleeing. Wherever they went, representatives of the Movement for the Unification of the Triqui Struggle (MULT) and the Social Welfare Group of the Triqui Region (UBISORT) still required people to pay monetary quotas and participate in mobilizations.

The violence in the Triqui region is in large part a result of politi-

cal conflicts manipulated by the state government, the PRI and even
the military. Although communal violence had been a factor before
then, the social structure and the political organizations in Triqui
communities began to change in the 1970s. Local political bosses, or
caciques, formed alliances with the PRI and functioned as the party's
local agents. The *caciques* provided votes and were given money in
their role as local government officials. Jorge Hernandez Diaz and
Leon Javier Parra Mora, in *Violence and Social Change in the Triqui Region*, a book published in 1994 by the Benito Juarez Autonomous University of Oaxaca, explain that since that time, "those who controlled
the largest part of the budget had the greatest prestige and power."

In the late 1970s, Triqui activists sought to break the *caciques'* hold.
In the conflicts that followed, one political faction even appealed to
the army to occupy San Juan Copala, after which the military used
its presence to support groups siding with the PRI. Those opposing
the PRI organized the Movement for the Unification of the Triqui
Struggle, or MULT, in 1981. The year before, Mexico's first local government independent of the PRI had been voted into power in Juchi-
tan, a city in the isthmus of Oaxaca. The political organization there,
the Confederation of Workers, Farmers and Students of the Isthmus
(COCEI), was an ally of MULT as it attempted to break the PRI's
power among Triquis.

This struggle took place, not just in voting booths, but through
assassinations and murders. "MULT was a grassroots organization
to fight the *caciques* over control of land, forests, and other natural
resources," says Rivera Salgado. "The *caciques* were so violent that
MULT members had to arm themselves. Eventually, those armed
men became a paramilitary group." Hernandez Diaz says MULT at
first "was practically an underground organization" and was accused
by the PRI of being agents of Cuba or Nicaragua, which MULT activists hotly denied. "We were born and raised in Yosoyuxi and Ras-
trojo, and no one can deny it," one responded at the time.

"But what began as a grassroots organization became something different," Rivera Salgado continues. "There was no transition to a civil society form of organization." In 1994 Triquis angry
with MULT over the continuing violence or still loyal to the PRI

formed the Social Welfare Group of the Triqui Region, or UBISORT, which also then began fighting MULT for political control of Triqui communities.

The state used money to manipulate and control both MULT and UBISORT. By 2002, MULT already administered a budget of several million pesos, through the Oportunidades program of subsidies for poor people, in the towns under its control. UBISORT did the same in areas where it was in power. And while MULT was aligned with other left-wing parties in Mexico through the 1990s, when Governor Jose Murat took power, he engineered a political realignment, bringing MULT closer to the PRI.

In 2003 MULT formed a political party, the Party of the United People (PUP), and in 2004 it ran its own candidate in the election which pitted Gabino Cue, then mayor of Oaxaca, against Ulises Ruiz, the candidate of the PRI, who was elected. Many observers accused PUP of acting as a spoiler to keep the PRI in power. When the teachers' strike took place two years later, MULT leaders were accused of threatening strikers and telling them to go back home.

Meanwhile, UBISORT acted as a political support base for the PRI. "A civil war went on between them," Rivera Salgado says. In 2006, Raul Marcial Perez, a leader of UBISORT, was assassinated. Then in October, 2010, Heriberto Pazos, the head of MULT/PUP, was gunned down in the streets of Oaxaca City. Many others were killed during these years of violence and retribution.

Adelfo Regino Montes, a Mixe indigenous leader, traces the violence in the Triqui region to "political submission, territorial disintegration, economic exploitation, racial discrimination, and exclusion in every aspect of daily life." After Mexico won its independence, Triquis controlled three *municipios*, or counties, where they were the majority. That gave them some degree of political power. After the Mexican Revolution, however, two of the *municipios* were dissolved, and much of the community's autonomy was lost.

"San Juan Copala itself was no longer a *municipio*," explains a Triqui activist in California, Elvira Santos (whose name has been changed). "Many *mestizos* [people of mixed indigenous and Spanish ancestry] didn't want Triquis to have power. They introduced alco-

hol and arms in order to gain control of the land and resources."
Today they still own much of the best agricultural land in the region, Santos says, and the *caciques* protect them with repression and
violence. Triqui *municipios* "were dispersed into districts where non-
indigenous people are the majority," Regino Montes said in a 2010
Jornada column. "The big majority of Triqui communities have been
excluded from any decisions that affect their lives and destinies, undermining their autonomy and freedom to make their own choices.
Those decisions remained in the hands of the *caciques*, the state and
federal governments, and the party leaders of the PRI."

In the only *municipio* that remained in Triqui hands, San Martin Itunyoso, Antonio Jacinto Lopez Martinez, a MULT leader, was
elected president in 2004, but then couldn't take office because of
threats and fled to the nearby city of Tlaxiaco. In October 2011, as
he was crossing the street there with two members of his family, a
gunman shot him in the head. "The violence is created by a lack of
the assertion of the rule of law. But the government has excused its
failure to stop it with such racist ideas as 'Triquis are savages and
uncivilized,'" Rivera Salgado charges.

In 2007, Triqui activists created the autonomous *municipio* of San
Juan Copala, inspired by the experiences of the Zapatistas in nearby
Chiapas. In doing so, Regino Montes wrote in *La Jornada*, "They re-
created the system of indigenous self-government, the only real possibility for peace in the region."

"They were looking for a political alternative," adds Rivera Salgado, "and they used the political process. They weren't armed. And
they won in a clean election." Santos, though, is less convinced that
supporters of the autonomous *municipio* were unarmed. "There is
a general culture of violence," she says. "People establish leadership that way. It will take a great deal to change that culture, and all
groups are implicated."

The autonomous *municipio* had roots in a split from MULT, called
MULT Independiente, or MULTI. Both UBISORT and MULT saw
this group as a threat, and eventually laid siege to the town, which
went on for months. A number of residents were killed. On April 27,
2010, a caravan of Mexican and European human rights activists set

out for San Juan Copala. They were stopped at a roadblock, where gunmen began shooting. Beatriz Alberta Carino Trujillo, a Mexican human rights activist, and a Finnish supporter, Tyri Antero Jaakkola, were murdered. The others fled into the hills. Human rights lawyer Gabriela Jimenez Rodriguez said she was captured by hooded men who told her they were from UBISORT and MULT. "They told us that no one could pass here, that it was their territory." Finally, she and others were released. Police recovered the two bodies, but never tried to enter the town.

On August 22, three more people were killed and two wounded while driving to nearby Santa Cruz Tilapia, where residents were also trying to establish an autonomous *municipio*. One was the town leader, Antonio Ramirez Lopez, who was seventy-eight years old. Then, in September, five hundred paramilitaries surrounded San Juan Copala and told supporters of the autonomous *municipio* they had twenty-four hours to leave. "That wasn't just a threat," Reyna Martinez, one of the town's leaders, told *La Jornada*. "They did the same thing in San Miguel Copala, where they killed twelve of our colleagues in the city hall. Neither state nor federal authorities dare even to come into San Juan Copala."

Oaxaca's governor at the time, Ulisses Ruiz, said there were no gunmen, deaths or disappearances in the Triqui region, and no need for protective measures for residents. By that time, families who'd fled were already living in the planton outside his office, and some had gone to Mexico City to set up a similar planton there. "They got us to leave," said another leader, Marcos Albino Ortiz, "but that doesn't mean we've given up."

When Gabino Cue finally beat the PRI in 2010, UBISORT campaigned for the PRI. MULT's PUP ran its own candidate again, viewed by many as another attempt to draw votes from Cue. After the election, Cue put Regino Montes in charge of the state Secretariat of Indigenous Affairs. The women in the planton didn't stop demonstrating against the government, however, and the violence continued. In August 2011, three MULTI members were killed in Agua Fria. Their bodies were brought to the planton for a public funeral. In October, Reyna Martinez was arrested with two dozen others for occupying a piece of land near the airport, in an act of civil disobedience. They demanded that the new state government provide protection to allow their return to San Juan Copala, pay for the destruction of peoples' homes there, and arrest those responsible for the killings. And in December, women and children in bright red huipils marched through Oaxaca City, demanding the government accept the conditions.

In response to the pressure, Rufino Juarez, an UBISORT leader, was arrested in May for killing MULTI activist Celestino Hernandez Cruz a year earlier. Cue's administration then issued arrest orders for a number of others, but none were detained, with one exception. Authorities did arrest a MULTI founder and retired teacher, Miguel Angel Velasco, accusing him of arranging the disappearance of two young women belonging to MULT in 2007.

Nevertheless, Marcos Albino Ortiz said the state government had fulfilled half of what it agreed to. "We're going back to San Juan Copala, and we're talking with the communities there to ensure they support our decision. Our objective is to pacify the region." He said representatives of the Interamerican Commission for Human Rights, which issued orders of protection for many of the activists, would accompany them. About 135 families had received some restitution for their burned homes by December, he added.

The families waited a month, and then at last set out to San Juan Copala, about eight hours away. When their caravan reached the Triqui region, however, just outside the tiny hamlet of Yosoyuxi, a police cordon blocked the road, preventing their further advance. While the women and children stood on the blockaded highway, chanting and singing, their leaders met with state government representatives in the nearby city of Tlaxiaco. Government secretary Jesus Martinez Alvarez prevailed on leaders of the caravan to halt their progress, and send ten delegates to a community meeting held the next Sunday in San Juan Copala. The displaced families vowed they intended to return nevertheless. Martinez Alvarez countered that the return should be delayed while the needs of Copala residents were met, such as health, education, and social development. These issues, he said, were the underlying cause of violence in the area. But the families were left in the middle of the highway, in the same place where the attack occurred on the caravan two years earlier. They still had not returned to San Juan Copala by November of 2012, at the time this book was written.

To ensure peace in San Juan Copala, some police presence there is unavoidable, at least in the short run, Rivera Salgado believes. "The litmus test is whether the government will create the conditions in which people can go home," he says. "You can't change overnight a situation that's existed for thirty years. In the short term, they have to disarm the armed people. This can create political space. But military occupation is not a long-term solution. People need to become a force for change themselves." Following the ambush of the first caravan, Regino Montes asserted: "The solution must be the recognition and respect, in law and in action, for the process of Triqui autonomy." Since Cue's election, one of Oaxaca's biggest political questions is the ability and will of the government to implement that recommendation.

Meanwhile, migration has had a high cost for Triquis. "They faced tremendous racism and prejudice," Rivera Salgado charges. "They're always the outsiders, treated like savages." Over the course of some twenty-five years, so many have fled the political murders plaguing their homeland that they've formed towns like Nueva Colonia Triqui, or New Triqui Town, in Baja's San Quintin Valley. In that *colonia*, or in California's Triqui neighborhoods, people ask whether peace is possible, and if it were, would they go home too?

"People left looking for a better future, but they worry about the safety of their families at home," says Triqui activist Santos, pointing to the fear that many Triquis share of reprisals for speaking publicly, not only against themselves but also against their families in Oaxaca. "They'll think twice before going back, because the conflicts and the same armed groups are still there."

In northern Mexico, migrants found farm labor camps with dirt floors and no electricity. When they wanted homes for children and families, Triquis and other indigenous migrants had to mount land invasions, build houses on federal land, and then await the police sent to evict them. In one of the most celebrated cases, Julio Sando-val, a Triqui leader from Yosoyuxi, was imprisoned for two years in the penitentiary in Ensenada for helping families settle in Cañon Buenavista, about two hours south of the US-Mexico border.

When Triqui migrant farmworkers arrived in Greenfield, in Cali-fornia's Salinas Valley, the local police and legal system condemned them for cultural practices like home births or early marriages, or for drinking in public, normal activities in their communities of ori-gin. Eventually they reached agreement with the local police chief, who even set up a desk in the police station for Triqui leader Andres Cruz to provide translation. Then some town residents, who saw the migrants as unwelcome invaders, tried to fire the chief. The Triqui community in Greenfield by then numbered three thousand peo-ple, according to community activists. Helped by the United Farm Workers, migrants marched through town to assert their right to live there.

Peace in Oaxaca may encourage Triqui migrants to return, but going home is not easy. To begin with, no one can afford to go back just to take a look to see if the violence has really ended. Nor has the fear of violence there diminished. In the last few years, five Triqui families even won political asylum, helped by San Francisco's Law-yers Committee for Civil Rights.

In addition, the Triqui community is more affected by the lack of legal immigration status than most. Triqui migration hit the United States after the amnesty of the 1986 Immigration Reform and Con-trol Act, so most arrived after it was too late to apply. Going back home is a permanent decision, not a temporary visit. People can cross the border back into Mexico, but returning to the United States is a much bigger problem. It's increasingly expensive—at $5,000 for a *coyote*, the border crossing is now three or four months' wages for a farmworker. Plus, it's more dangerous every year, as people get pushed by increased enforcement to cross in the most remote sec-tions of the border.

"Most migrants get much harsher treatment now," says Rivera Salgado. "The current enforcement policy is based on excluding them, through violence and jail at the border, and isolation and fear in their community. The idea is to make life so hard for them in the US they'll have to leave. But where are they supposed to go?"

Nevertheless, Santos believes, "I think a lot of people would go home if they could. Our land is very productive, and as farmworkers here we've seen new crops that we could grow in Oaxaca. But we need jobs and schools there, and especially security. Right now, we don't know if we can even hope for that. Some of us have lost hope. Our governments have made these promises before. It would be good if it were true this time, but we have to see if their actions match their words."

"And where is home?" asks Rivera Salgado. "Lots of Triquis have grown up in San Quintin or Greenfield by now. Yet the first generation still yearns for connection to San Juan Copala. It is part of their identity and sense of belonging. Everybody needs that."

If We Don't Attack the Roots of Migration, It Will Continue to Grow

The Story of Rufino Dominguez

Rufino Dominguez migrated from San Miguel Cuevas, in Oaxaca, in the 1980s, first to Sinaloa and Baja California, then to Fresno, California. He became binational coordinator of the FIOB in 2002 and is now director of the Oaxacan Institute for Attention to Migrants.

The Oaxacan Institute for Attention to Migrants [IOAM] was created eleven years ago by then-governor Jose Murat Casab, responding to the demand that the state pay attention to the problems of migrants. I was appointed director by Governor Gabino Cue Monteagudo on November 26, 2010. I couldn't sleep the night he called because it was a difficult decision for me, and my family was opposed to it because they live in California. They reminded me that I already had a job there. Nevertheless, I decided to do it, because it was a chance to understand the way the government works here on a deeper level, and to be closer to my people and land and know them better. I know California and the US well now, having lived there many years, but less so Oaxaca and Mexico.

The institute has many limitations, in its budget and in the way previous administrations looked at migration. They created the institute just for migrants in the US. Have we just paid attention to migrants in the US because they send dollars home? We do have to work effectively with migrants in the US, but I see four kinds of migrants.

There are thousands who pass through Oaxaca from Central America, mostly on their way to different places. They've suffered systematic violations of their rights. We can't tell the US govern-ment, or the governments of California and other US states, to respect the rights of our people who are living there, if we ourselves are not respecting the rights of migrants here in Oaxaca. So in the first place, I said, we were going to have to pay attention to the human rights of migrants in transit.

Then there are many people who migrate within our state, who work in regions of Oaxaca, like Papaloapan for instance, where there's a lot of pineapple and sugar cane. Many migrants work on the coast, too, in coconut plantations. There are about thirty thousand migrants who circulate within the state, and we've never paid attention to them. But we will now, because they are migrants too.

Another three hundred thousand live in Mexico City and states in the North, like Sinaloa, Sonora, and Baja California. The institute hasn't paid attention to them in the past. What good was it to them? Sometimes the problems of migrants within Mexico are even greater than those we have in the US.

And then the public policies about migrants in the United States were always made here. That is, the government in Oaxaca said it would do such-and-such. For example, they'd say they organized many Guelaguetza dance festivals or sporting events there. But the state government only gave its support to certain groups, while there are many others that also organize these events. We never consulted the people who actually live in the US about our activity there, or asked for their opinions. We want a different vision, a more level or equal relationship, where we're not dictating policies because we're the government, but asking people for their input and opinions. When I got to the institute they only had big plans. I want smaller ones that are concrete and specific, and that reflect our values.

We're not going to continue doing the same things that were being done before. We're going to do more, we have a vision for our work, we're committed to it, and we have a budget for implementing different programs. Our starting point is to understand the need for economic development, because the reason for migration is the lack of work and opportunity in people's communities of origin. If we don't attack the roots of migration, it will continue to grow. There's a fear of investing in our own people, but there's no other way. We have to have economic development, and respect for the human rights of migrants as they come and go.

It is a big challenge to implement economic development in Oaxaca when the federal government determines most things about development policy and is committed to free trade policies. The federal government should support our efforts, but it is more worried about declining remittances than it is about creating jobs in our own country.

It's become part of our culture to depend on remittances from migrants in the US, and we're talking not just about communities, but about the federal government itself, which is afraid that they're declining. The states in Mexico fear the same thing. But there's not a culture of investing those remittances, so that they can generate jobs and production. How can we change this, to invest in something productive that can create jobs? That's what I'm trying to get us to discuss here in Oaxaca, so that people will invest what they're receiving.

It's not possible to continue exporting migrants to the United States, especially when the remittances are falling. We understand that lots of states are sending migrants. I can't imagine that the twenty thousand people who tried to cross the border from January to now [October 2011] were just from Oaxaca. So if there isn't a similar effort in the rest of them, what good does it do just to try here? But we have to start somewhere, and we're here in Oaxaca. I don't know if we'll have an impact on other states or the federal government. But I do know that many of the initiatives I see that try to work on this problem are starting here.

The federal government has the responsibility to create safe conditions and jobs. Yet it doesn't accept responsibility for the economic development that could change this. At the same time, we've become so dependent on the remittances migrants send back to their families. The silence about this is a disgrace.

In March 2011 alone, four thousand migrants were sent back after trying to cross into the US. That tells us that there's still a huge number of people trying to cross, and that the number isn't getting any smaller. The economic pressure on people to migrate, and the violation of human rights on the border, are still part of our reality. Migrants are raped and beaten, and recruited into criminal gangs. Over three hundred Oaxacans have disappeared, and we don't know if they're alive or dead. Their families haven't heard from them. Our state is responsible for them, along with the federal government.

So we also have to tell people about the risks of migrating. In Durango and Tamaulipas they've found hidden graves of many migrants, and the surprising thing is that the big majority killed with such cruelty are Mexicans. It's not just a risk to cross the border into the US. You're risking your life migrating here in your own country. We have to create a willingness at all levels of government to say honestly to migrants that they are risking their lives. People also need to understand that the economic crisis in the US hasn't gotten any better. When you get there, your chance of finding work is worse than ever, and there's a lot of competition for jobs. This has to be part of explaining the risks of migration too. It should be part of implementing the right to not migrate, while protecting the ability to migrate safely, making sure that people's dignity and human rights are respected.

We are trying to expand the three-for-one program, in which migrants contribute 25 percent of the costs of public works projects in their home communities, and the government contributes the rest. Last year, for example, the previous administration only invested 12 million pesos in this program. This year we'll invest twenty-two million. Who's governor makes all the difference. We're doubling the investment, and migrants can see we're working with them. Next year it will be more than thirty million, so it's going up. In the past the money was always used for public works, like building schools, churches, community centers, and roads, and that's good. Maybe we can't give the same resources to economic development, but we want to raise the question. Last year they didn't invest in any productive projects [economic development projects in which people produce farm products or other goods]. This year we're investing three million. That's not a lot, but it's a big difference, because it's the first time the state has invested any resources in productive projects.

We are not going to try to dictate what kind of development projects should be carried out in our communities. Communities themselves know what they want to work on, and what's viable. We have to send them engineers who can study what can be improved. Many migrants who are returning home learned a lot when they were in the US or northern Mexico—how to plant strawberries, raise turkeys and chickens, or to work in bakeries. Why can't they use their knowledge here? The system for irrigation in the US is very advanced. That can be applied here.

When we talk about productive projects, that can be bakeries, fruit and vegetable fields, even the revival of artisan work and Oaxacan cuisine. How can we export these things to the US, complying with their food standards, so that migrants there can consume them and generate jobs and production for the people here? We have *totopos, tasajo,* and foods that haven't been exported, and there's also *mezcal,* of course. There are many things we could export. We're not even talking about the Anglo Saxon market in the US. Twenty million Mexicans live there and consume. A million Oaxacans. With that market, we could really begin something here.

So I think the communities have to propose what they want to work on, what they have experience doing. What works depends on the climate, on what there's demand for, but these decisions belong to the communities. In the past when there was money, the decision was imposed by the government, and we don't want to do that. We want the communities to say what they want to do, how they want to do it, and then our job is to find the financing and technical assistance. We want the 3 million we invested this year in productive projects to become 12 million next year. We're targeting four main regions from which people are migrating—the Mixteca, Valles Centrales, the Sierra Sur, and Sierra Norte. There are other regions, too, but I think we have to begin here. It's not a lot of money, so we have to focus. The purpose is to lower the migration of young people and of families to the US.

Today I'm traveling everywhere, trying to find out what people want. One idea, for instance, is an insurance program that can pay the cost of bringing home the remains of someone who dies in the

US. Many migrants in the United States, Sinaloa, and Baja California don't have birth certificates. In California alone we've sent three thousand, but we have to do much more. In Baja California, it was two thousand, sent free of charge to migrants. It's a huge job that's hard to organize, but we feel we're accomplishing a lot for people when we do it.

There's still resistance in parts of the state with the same power structure that lost the last election. There's a lack of understanding that migration is a complex, difficult problem. Some of the people in the present government don't understand either how important it is. At the institute, we'll work with everyone, all the other parts of the government. The governor has said it: we have to work together in a coordinated way. But that's hard for some to accept. It's difficult, it's complex, but the good part is that I'm working with everyone, and that's the way it should be.

We're also working with all different kinds of organizations, including FIOB, but way beyond it. In California we've added our grain of sand to the Guelaguetzas organized by Lazos Oaxaquenos de San Jose, the Organizacion Regional de Oaxaca Los Angeles, the Unidad Popular Benito Juarez de Bakersfield, and the Centro Binacional para el Desarrollo Indígena Oaxaqueno. That should be our policy, working with everyone, because we are the government of everyone. If we just gave FIOB money for organizing their event, we'd be repeating the mistakes of the past governments. Our policy is always to work with everyone who asks for our support, and we'll continue to give it without basing it on ideology, political party, or religion. As they say, Oaxaca for everyone, a government for everyone. Now we have to put it in practice.

As a migrant myself, I don't agree with how migrants have been used there. The labor of migrants in the US has been used throughout its history. They tell us to come work, and then when there's an economic crisis, we're blamed for it. This policy of attacking migrants has never stopped in the United States. They accuse us of robbing other people's jobs, and our rights are not respected. These new state laws in Alabama, Florida, South Carolina, Arizona, and elsewhere are not just anti-immigrant but inhuman.

Relations with the US are the responsibility of the federal government, but I think it should be more aggressive in defending the human rights of migrants. It has the responsibility for this. At the same time, states in the US do not have the right to pass the kind of laws we're seeing in places like Arizona and Alabama. The federal government in the US has the responsibility for immigration policy. But neither Republican nor Democratic administrations have acted to pass legislation to legalize migrants, and this is the solution to the problem. They've done nothing. And during the current US administration we've seen a policy of deporting migrants, of imprisoning them unjustly. This doesn't accomplish anything. In IOAM we feel like we're shouting at a wall because we can't change any of this.

But I also don't believe that a program of guest workers or braceros will resolve the problems of migration. First, it perpetuates a dependence on remittances. We also know from our experience with the bracero program in the 1950s and '60s that these programs don't work. We have many former braceros who are still fighting to get the 10 percent of their wages that was withheld during those years. Current H2-A and H2-B programs give people a work visa, but the rights of workers in these programs are not respected. Often they aren't paid legal wages, they live in terrible conditions in substandard housing, and they have no right to organize or make demands on their employers. If we begin by talking about the right to organize, to sue their bosses, ensure their access to education and health care, maybe that would be a way forward. But if it's just "come sell your labor" with no respect for our rights, these programs are worthless. If people's rights are violated, if they're not paid adequately, if they can't earn Social Security to allow them to eventually retire, then this system is no good for us. It's just producing throwaway workers, whose labor gets used but who have no benefits.

When people have a green card, or residence visa, migrants have some security. That doesn't exist with a guest worker visa or crossing with a *coyote*. So why are we talking about more programs that fail to respect human and labor rights, and which don't guarantee housing, education, and health care? The governments of both Mexico and the US must prioritize human and labor rights, and even our state governments must include this in their agenda.

Next year we are going to focus on laws in Oaxaca for migrants, including one which would give migrants in the US political rights here. It would implement, not just the right to vote but also the right to representation in our state Congress. A migrant would take a seat as a deputy, after she or he was elected. We also need greater rights for migrants within Mexico itself, not just for those in the US. We're working with the deputies who are responsible for this, but as a migrant institution we want to pressure them to do more. These rights only exist at the federal level. We want to go way beyond that.

Our initiative includes the right of Oaxacans living outside the country, like those in California, to vote for governor. Any man or woman could run for deputy to represent migrants and could propose laws that would benefit migrants or proposals for economic development to implement the right to not migrate. And this would apply to Oaxacan migrants, not just in the US, but in other Mexican states as well. There are over three hundred thousand dispersed through Mexico, maybe more, and they have the same political rights as those in the US.

We have to talk about more than just the right to vote itself. I think the right is broader, and it's connected with the right to not migrate. The deputies pass the laws, and they have to pass ones, and also pass a budget, that will generate economic development in our communities. We get $1.29 billion every year in Oaxaca from remittances, but if we look at the budget of IOAM, it's only 8.5 million pesos, a minuscule part of what's received here. The state executive and the Chamber of Deputies have to give us a larger share of the budget. They have to pass more laws that benefit and strengthen programs for migrants. That's when we'll see a decline in forced migration.

People in transit through Oaxaca, who weren't born in Mexico, don't have political rights here. Nevertheless, we have to respect their human rights. We've reduced the number of rights violations for people passing through the Istmo de Tehuantepec, a region of Oaxaca near the coast traversed by many Central American migrants. They organized a Grupo Beta [a law enforcement unit focused on protecting migrants] and a permanent office for watching out for violations. Father Alejandro Solalinde has been very active, and the state government has supported him. I think there's a new vision of human rights. Still, it would be wrong to say that the rights of migrants are all protected now.

When Gabino Cue became governor, he said we were going to implement the right to not migrate. We have a commitment to put that into practice. We've had eighty years of the domination of one party, and we're all tired of it. Our previous governments were very repressive and authoritarian, and this new government is not. It respects human rights and is sensitive to the problems, not just of migrants, but of indigenous people and all Oaxacan society. It's important to recognize this, because before what we had were the events of 2006 and repression. A government born in fraud has to use force to make itself legitimate. Now we have a government of change. For sure we're not going to have miracles, but the government is closer to the people now. Governments before never had hearings about anything because they were afraid of the people. This government has gone to the people. I don't want Oaxaca to go back to authoritarianism, the arrogance of power, the lack of human rights, the disappearances and imprisonment. We have to respect the people's right of free expression, which is guaranteed in the state and federal constitution.

When I agreed to become director of IOAM I had to resign as an advisor to FIOB, which I'd been previously. I consider myself a member of the organization, but I can't be very active in it for obvious reasons, even though I was one of its founders and leaders. Now I'm wearing the hat of a government official. FIOB doesn't have to lose its character as part of the opposition, or as a critic of the government. Members of FIOB have the right to demonstrate, and they've exercised it, but always in a respectful, diplomatic way. But our critiques should also be accompanied by proposals, in other words, "I don't like what you're doing, and here's what I want you to do." That's been what FIOB has been doing, and I hope it doesn't stop. It's useless to criticize without making positive proposals. I've faced the criticisms of my own *compañeros* in FIOB, and we've talked in a respectful way. But when criticizing you also have to propose.

For me it's not easy to be here. Sometimes it feels like the whole world is beating up on me, and that's not good. When I got here I faced a lot of opposition, lots of criticism from the media controlled by the PRI. They said I had no experience, that I had no university degrees, and accused me of an endless list of things. That was a big challenge. So FIOB should stay in opposition and not lose its identity. I've never suggested that it should stop demonstrating, and I think it should keep on doing it. It shouldn't worry about me, because I know how to take care of myself here in the government.

In this binational assembly [October 2011], Sarahit Martinez was chosen as Women's Coordinator. She's someone I've known since she was young. I find it very inspiring, and it gives me a lot of hope for the future, that FIOB is giving responsibility to our youth and training them. Today wherever FIOB has a presence, you can see the work of our young people. If they want to know about my experiences, I'm happy to share what worked for me when I was leading FIOB. But they're the future of our organization. We have to continue helping our young men and women to develop so that they take over decision-making power. All the current leaders now are new blood. The only founders who are still around now are me and Gaspar. Maybe the rest got tired, or went off to do other things, but only the two of us remain. So now the leadership is actually the second and third generation. This doesn't invalidate our experiences. We can contribute and back up the skills they already have. But now there are new ideas, and we have to give credit to our young people, the new generation that's coming up.

In all the twenty years of FIOB, we were never able to hold our assemblies in a place as nice as the Mision San Felipe Hotel here. Maybe after twenty years we deserve it. And historically, in the past all the binational coordinators came from California. Therefore, considering the present political situation, and how it's improved in Oaxaca, we think it's a good time for Oaxaca to take over the binational leadership. Now we have a vice-coordinator in California to coordinate the activities there. This change is something we've needed to do for twenty years. It will be hard. But here we now have a government in Oaxaca that respects human rights and free expression, and that is our ally. FIOB needs to prioritize getting the government to create policies that give attention to migrants and indigenous people. If this doesn't work, I'm going to feel responsible, so I'm glad we have very capable leaders.

In some ways, it's just the geography that's changed. The ideals, the struggle, the strategy will all stay the same. The program adopted by this assembly is prioritizing the right to not migrate. I liked the resolution that declared that migration should be the last option for people. We need to combine forces with IOAM, which is working on the same thing. It doesn't mean FIOB is becoming part of the government, just that we try to coordinate all the efforts of organizations fighting for the right to not migrate. And not just these two organizations, but all of society should try to implement this right.

We also prioritize respect for the human and labor rights of migrants. We have the right to express our opinion about the anti-immigrant laws, which are unjust and inhuman, and which should not exist. IOAM is going to open an Oaxaca Center in Los Angeles, where we will network with agencies in charge of labor rights violations. That's the minimum we can do. The working conditions of Oaxacans are the worst. As a photographer [directing this comment to the interviewer] you know the housing conditions aren't fit for human beings.

There are only two Mexican consulates in the US that think about the fact that many of our people only speak indigenous languages, and that have hired translators. Without that language capacity, our people face yet another barrier and obstacle. Our consulates should play a much more active role in defending labor and human rights of Mexicans in the US, and consider the indigenous culture of many of them. Our Oaxaca Center will coordinate our efforts with the institutions of the Mexican government, as well as community organizations and legal programs in California. We want to follow up on the problems of Oaxacans and help them to resolve them.

We Want to Talk about the Right to Stay Home

The Story of Aldo Gonzalez

Aldo Gonzalez is an indigenous community leader from the Sierra Juarez region of Oaxaca, and today is the director of enforcement for indigenous rights in the state's Department of Indigenous Affairs.

In Guelatao, the town in the Sierra Juarez where I live, our main crop is corn. It's a very healthy life. We get up early and have coffee to get ready to work. Your machete has to be sharpened, and then you walk to your field. It can be twenty minutes or two hours away. There's no machinery for our farms, and the hillsides are very steep. When we need help, we ask for it from our neighbors, and when they need it, we give it to them. When we finish work in the field, we gather wood on the way home for cooking.

Our main problem is that the prices of agricultural products have fallen dramatically. The price for corn doesn't cover the costs of growing it anymore, so many people have chosen to leave to get the money they need to buy food. The prices for coffee have also fallen, and people have migrated for that reason too. [In May of 2011 coffee sold for about $2.90 per pound, and a year later, in June 2012, it had dropped to $1.55 per pound—almost in half.]

The services people need are in the bigger towns—the municipal seats. The surrounding communities don't have them. The roads going there are mostly dirt, so it's hard to travel there, especially in the rain, and takes a long time to get there. Most towns have no electricity, running water, or sewage services. There's a primary school in almost every town, but outside the municipalities they only go to the fourth or sixth grade. After that students have to leave, if their families can afford to send them. There are some clinics but no doctors—just nurses or recently graduated medical students.

In our schools there's a uniform national curriculum, so there's no distinction in what's taught from one school to another. But there's also no accounting for indigenous languages. In the Sierra Juarez students speak Zapoteco, but the classes are all in Spanish. We have been involved for years in fighting for indigenous rights, and we've visited Zapatista communities in Chiapas, to see how they put their ideas into practice. They have their own educational model, and their own teachers. We're trying to do the same thing, by developing our own materials and an educational model that preserves our cultural identity.

Here in Oaxaca, our teachers have been going through their own struggle, with the strike and events of 2006. But in our experience, they haven't focused much on the question of indigenous education.

Here in the Sierra Juarez we've started the Zapoteca Academy of Indigenous Rights. This grew out of the need for people in our communities to understand what's happening in the broader world outside them. Our people understand what's happening in their own communities, but when people arrive from outside, it's often difficult for them to understand who they are or what relation they have to the rest of the world.

This has been a problem especially in relation to mining projects. There are a lot of older mines in Oaxaca, most of which were inactive for many years. But recently the government has been promoting renewed activity, especially by Canadian companies. The promoters and investors from these projects come to communities and speak very highly about their plans. Local people don't know what the impact of mining projects has been in other parts of world. So in our academy we gather information about mining, so our people can make informed decisions.

In the Union of Organizations of the Sierra Juarez of Oaxaca (UNOSJO), we organize a lot of different activities, including seminars, forums, and training sessions. From the projects and their supporters we get a lot of unfriendly reactions. "Look at these troublemakers," they say. "Keep them quiet." We feel threatened and harassed, especially when we see the assassination of mine opponents in Central America, Chiapas, or even here in Oaxaca. One community here staged a sit-in to oppose a mine, and the government called in a thousand police to stop the demonstrators.

In the Sierra Juarez, land is held collectively. Decisions about land use must be made in a community assembly, which makes it more difficult for the projects. Still, some people get co-opted by the promises of the mine. Others are much more worried about the impacts. But in other parts of Oaxaca, the federal government has been looking for ways to convert land tenure into individual ownership. In these areas the mining companies arrive and start buying up land. By the time the community realizes what's happening, it's much harder for it to stop the project.

There are many problems in agriculture in the Sierra Juarez, especially economic ones. Many farmers have been forced to migrate to the US to look for work. We have been encouraging people to stay and continue farming. We've been promoting a sustainable form of agriculture that requires fewer inputs, and the ones it does require are local and organic.

Problems come when family members who have migrated send money back to their relatives at home. What is this money good for? Usually it's used to buy things that are not grown or produced in the community itself. We see stores and supermarkets popping up that sell primarily imported goods. We don't know where they come from or what their quality is. If the family members receiving the remittances use them to buy these products, then the money leaves, and just goes to whoever invested in these stores.

We've also seen that genetically modified corn has contaminated native varieties of corn in our region. This is a big problem. Mexico is the birthplace of corn, and it continues to be one of our staple foods. We can't survive without corn, so we're always looking for ways to preserve our native varieties. We have a saying in our organization: To sow and eat native seeds are political acts of resistance against globalization.

We want to talk about the right to stay home, the right to not migrate. We want to protect our native seeds, in order to stay on our land. We never expected globalization to come so close to communities that are so far from cities and from Western culture.

In 2006, when there was a lot of conflict in Oaxaca, a group of geographers arrived in our region from the University of Kansas, Carleton College, and the University of San Luis Potosi. They asked us to open our doors and give them access to our territory in order to do research on the PROCEDE program, the government program to certify land tenure. So we asked them to tell us more. They said they wanted to know more of local knowledge, of the local names for places in the territory. That sounded strange to us, because the names reveal many things.

The name *Oaxaca*, for instance, comes from the Nahuatl word *Oajaca*, which refers to a type of bean we grow and eat. [According to another source, the name *Oaxaca* comes from the Nahuatl word *huaxyacac*. *Huax* means gourd and *yacatl* means nose, so Oaxaca means "at the nose or top of the gourd." Another source says the name derives from the Nahuatl word for a tree, *guaje* (*Leucaena leucocephala*).] My community, Guelatao, comes from the Zapotec word *gelato*, which means enchanted lagoon. In our region of very steep hills and mountains it's very rare to find a lagoon, but there is in fact one here, which is why our community has its name.

In every community there are hundreds of names for local places like this. When people come in from the outside to document those names and map that biological and geographic knowledge, it can be used for things that won't necessarily benefit our own community.

Another thing they didn't tell us was that the financing for their project came from the Foreign Military Investigation Office of the US Army. That was another reason we decided we didn't want them to undertake that research. That office is based in Fort Livingston, which earlier was a prison where indigenous people of the United States were held before being relocated to Western reservations. It's now a repository of knowledge about indigenous people and territory, all over the world.

We know that some of this knowledge has been used for their Human Terrain System, which collects information about local people and passes it on to military commanders for use in military operations. They say the US wars must now be won by winning over the hearts and minds of people, and being less dependent on arms. But the objective of these wars is the same.

We're not saying we expect war in Oaxaca and Central America, but we are worried. We do see an increasing militarization of our area, associated with the Plan Merida, supposedly designed to combat drug trafficking. But when we see this military presence along the roads and highways, it does not make us feel safe or secure. On the contrary. We certainly have no plans to incite military conflict or overthrow the Mexican government. We are Mexicans. But we do see that the Mexican government does have an interest in inciting social conflict and violence.

In Mexico we're educated to think about our rights. In fact, there's a saying by Benito Juarez, who was born in my town of Guelatao: Respect for the rights of others is peace. In spite of that, policies like NAFTA represent a real aggression toward the Mexican people. Many of these policies are biased toward the interests of large corporations. I don't believe that it's the people of the United States who are aggressive toward Mexico, but many of the policies pursued by the government are very harmful.

Many policies of the US government don't just affect people who are in the United States. The have very harmful consequences for people all over the world. It's important for people in the United States to realize and be conscious of that.

THREE

THE RIGHT TO A UNION MEANS THE RIGHT TO STAY HOME

Mexican Miners Resist Repression and Poverty

Farmers and miners in Oaxaca are far from the only people in Mexico who assert the right to continue living in the towns and cities where they've resided for generations. When Mexican unions assert that right, even indirectly, they quickly come into conflict with the federal government, as they have in Sonora close to the US border, and in Mexico City itself. Nowhere is this result—displacement produced by the suppression of labor rights—as evident as it is in Cananea.

In 2010, Manny Armenta, a representative of the US union for metal miners, the United Steel Workers, led strikers' wives and children to safety in the middle of an armed assault by federal police on the miners' strike there. He'd just arrived from Arizona on one of his many trips bringing food and money to the strike. On the evening of June 7, the federal government sent two thousand police and soldiers into this small mining town—more than two for every striker. As darkness fell and helicopters clattered overhead, they charged the mine gate in riot shields and batons, filling the streets with tear gas. Miners retreated to the union hall with their families, and the police followed, barricading the doors and lobbing more tear gas inside. The union's leaders were already in hiding—the police had arrest warrants for them all. Armenta helped lead women and children down fire escapes and up through the basement to safety in the darkness.

Two months earlier the Arizona legislature had passed the notorious anti-immigrant law, SB 1070. Armenta, who's spent more time in Cananea than at home in Arizona over the last five years, was upset by what he viewed as the hypocrisy and cruelty in routing miners' families on one side of the border, and then criminalizing those who cross it on the other. "Especially in Arizona with the new law, all we hear about is illegal immigrants," he charged bitterly. "What do they think will happen here? Where do they think all the miners will have to go?"

That same day, police moved on the widows of sixty-five miners who died in an explosion on February 19, 2006, at the Pasta de Conchos coal mine in Coahuila. Five days after the explosion, Grupo Mexico, the mining and railroad giant that owns both the Pasta de Conchos and Cananea mines, abandoned rescue efforts. The company closed the coal mine for good, with the trapped miners still inside. Grupo Mexico and then Mexican labor secretary Francisco Salazar refused to make any further attempts to recover their bodies. Nevertheless, miners' widows camped at the gates for years afterward, asking for their husbands' remains. The same day that police fought copper miners in Cananea, other cops drove the women away from the closed coal-mine entrance in Nueva Rosita.

Both the Cananea strike and the widows' protests highlight extremely unsafe conditions in Mexican mines. At Cananea, silicosis-causing dust from crushed copper ore rises to miners' knees inside the buildings. Grupo Mexico disconnected the dust extractors several years before the strike, in retaliation for earlier protests. At Pasta de Conchos, dozens of uncorrected violations for dangerous methane buildup preceded the 2006 explosion.

The Cananea strike involves issues beyond health and safety, however. The Mexican Union of Mine, Metal, and Allied Workers, or Mineros, used to be a loyal ally of the old Institutional Revolutionary Party (PRI), which governed Mexico for seventy years. But Napoleon Gomez Urrutia, the Mineros' general secretary, took over the union in 2001 from his father, a PRI stalwart. Gomez Urrutia had much more militant and democratic ideas than his predecessor. He quickly forced employers, including Grupo Mexico, to concede much higher wage increases than those mandated by then-president Vicente Fox.

Gomez helped defeat Fox's reform of Mexico's labor laws, a proposal recommended by the World Bank. After the Pasta de Conchos explosion, he accused Grupo Mexico of "industrial homicide."

The government reacted violently. It accused Gomez of corruption, forcing him to flee to Canada to avoid arrest, where he's lived since, given sanctuary by the United Steel Workers. A government-backed effort to install a pro-company leader to head the union was twice rejected by workers, who reelected Gomez even while in exile. All the legal actions against him led instead to his exoneration, but the government still threatened to jail him if he returned to Mexico.

In June 2007, Section 65 of the Mineros went on strike at the Cananea mine over safety conditions. The following January, after police beat dozens of strikers in an attempt to break the strike, twenty-five thousand Mineros members struck in protest in ten mines and at the huge steel mill in Lazaro Cardenas, Michoacan, where two workers were shot and killed. In 2010, dozens more were beaten when they shut the mill down again and marched in the streets.

The government-dominated labor board (Junta Nacional de Conciliacion y Arbitraje, or JNCA) repeatedly declared the strike at Cananea legally "nonexistent," a decision allowing Grupo Mexico to fire the strikers and install a company union. The family of German Larrea, which owns Grupo Mexico, was a major contributor to the campaign of former president Felipe Calderon, and the president and his party control the labor board. After Calderon's election in 2006, the secretary of labor recognized a new, company-dominated union for miners. A rump election and the firing of fifteen hundred workers at another giant copper mine in nearby Nacozari allowed Grupo Mexico to sign a labor contract with this company union. This was followed by similar moves at several other mines.

Strikers at Cananea were trying to prevent a similar fate in their mine. "The government and the Larreas are making history, but backwards," the Mineros responded after the federal assault on Cananea, "trying to return to an era when we had no right to strike or right to industrial safety."

According to the Mineros, Calderon's labor secretary, Javier Lozano, held meetings with mine owners before bringing the police into Cananea. He offered them government recognition of the pro-company union as a way for them to get out of contracts with the Mineros. The Chamber of Mines, in turn, hosted a banquet in Calderon's honor.

In May 2010, just before the assault in Cananea, Calderon was also feted at a state dinner at the White House. Steel union leaders met with Obama administration officials, asking them to tell Calderon that the United States wouldn't tolerate an attack on the miners. AFL-CIO president Richard Trumka and Canadian Labour Congress president Ken Georgetti wrote to Washington and Ottawa with the same demand. According to Armenta, officials "assured us they were not turning their heads away. That was totally false." Seventeen days after the banquet, police attacked the copper strikers.

Armenta believes the assault on Cananea miners was the consequence, not just of Calderon's anti-labor policies but also of tacit US support for them. "Our government continues to give the Mexican government millions and millions of dollars, saying it will be used to fight drugs. But we see here clearly that this money is going to fight workers and progressive people. Our own government is creating this problem," Armenta says. "I condemn the Mexican government and Grupo Mexico. But I also condemn the US government for allowing this to happen, for not taking any action. "

Smashing the strike led to the same massive firings that followed an earlier lost strike in 1998, and the destruction of the union in Nacozari in 2006. Waves of desperate miners, unable to find other work in their tiny mining communities, crossed the border into the United States as undocumented workers. In both Nacozari and Cananea, displaced people from southern Mexico were used as a new migrant workforce to replace fired union members, while the miners who'd lived in those border communities for decades became displaced themselves.

The economic pressure on Mexican miners is evident in an agreement allowing the reopening of another mine, the old Boleo copper mine in Santa Rosalia, on the Baja California peninsula. About six hours south of the US border, Santa Rosalia lives on memories of its former mining heyday. On a bluff above the town, the buildings of the former French mine operators are a reminder of what life felt like when thousands of miners were employed there. Huge assemblies of rusting ore-crushing machinery tower over the north-south peninsular highway, skirting the water between downtown and the fishing harbor. One buff-colored edifice has been turned into a museum, but it's closed much of the time, since there's no money to staff it. Santa Rosalia instead attracts tourists who flock to see its church. Wealthy French managers a century ago imported its metal frame and embossed walls and ceiling from France, and assembled them according to a design reputedly by Gustav Eiffel, architect of Paris's famous iron tower.

Nostalgia doesn't interest Boleo's new owners, however. According to Tulio Ortiz, who edits the Baja California magazine La Tijereta, a Canadian investors group, Baja Mining Corporation, is spending $1.3 billion to restart production, expecting to recoup $10.5 billion by the end of its twenty-year concession. During that time the company promises it will hire a thousand residents, giving Santa Rosalia new life after twenty-eight years in which the mine has been closed.

Like other mining concessionaires, Baja Mining won't have to pay local or federal taxes on its operations for those two decades, however, according to Carlos Fernandez-Vega's column, Mexico SA. That's a slight improvement over the deal Porfirio Diaz struck with the French in 1904, when he gave the mine a fifty-year tax holiday. On the other hand, for the next half-century the mine's new owners won't pay any duties on its copper exports. And the government will rebuild Santa Rosalia's port facilities so that the mine's copper and cobalt ore and zinc sulfate can be efficiently loaded onto modern ships.

Fernandez-Vega quotes the former secretary of the economy, Bruno Ferrari, who claimed, "Mining has been synonymous with growth, dynamism and transformation for this country. We should continue making this sector a pillar of the economy and a spearhead for productivity." Jobs are surely an attraction in a town in which over half the adults never finished basic education and 6 percent are illiterate. Santa Rosalia shares the same poverty conditions as

Oaxaca—30 percent of its residents have no health care, 20 percent no drinking water, and 22 percent no connection to the sewer system. A third of Santa Rosalia's workers make less than 119 pesos ($10) a day, or twice the minimum wage of about 60 pesos a day.

According to the Mexican Department of Labor and Social Welfare, the average daily wage for miners in Mexico isn't much higher—150 pesos ($12.50). Falling wages in mining reflect the increased use of contract labor, in which workers employed by temp agencies have replaced thousands of people who worked directly for the mining companies. This is what has taken place in the huge Nacozari and Cananea copper mines in the wake of the smashing of the miners' union. Migrants from southern Mexico now labor for contractors. Consequently, weekly wages can be as low as 400 pesos ($33) for those contract workers. The use of migrant labor in the Boleo mine won't be new, however. The French imported workers from China and Japan, and brought in indigenous Yaqui people from Sonora.

The French prided themselves on building a then state-of-the-art hospital in Santa Rosalia. In 1925, five years after the end of the Revolution, they agreed to provide free medical care to the miners' families. Nevertheless, many of the migrant miners died from the terrible conditions in the shafts. Boleo's new owners won't have to do what the French did—build a hospital. The government's Social Security health-care system will provide what medical care the families will receive.

Low wages and bad conditions for miners reflect a general decline for workers throughout Mexico. As in the United States, the number of high-paying jobs is diminishing, while the number of low-paying jobs rises—those jobs paying twice the $5 daily minimum or less. Over the last six years of the Calderon administration, purchasing power declined by 32 percent. Labor authorities estimated that the economy would need 5.5 million additional jobs to fully employ those looking for work.

Miguel Reyes, director of the Wage Observatory of the Universidad Iberoamericana in Puebla, said that while jobs paying three to five times the minimum had become scarcer, those paying a "minisalary" of 60 to 120 pesos a day ($5 to $10) had gone up. A study by the Observatory found that "things have gone badly" for Mexican workers, while the country "has become a paradise for employers, who pay less and less for high-quality work, while they violate labor rights with impunity."

Labor Law Reform a Boss Could Love

That kind of impunity, and its implications for further declines in wages, has become a central argument Mexican unions make against a proposal for labor law reform sponsored by employers. Changing Mexico's labor law, they say, will transform the lives of millions of workers, cementing the power of a group of industrialists who have been on the political offensive for decades, and who now control Mexico's presidency and much of its national government. "Labor law reform will only benefit the country's oligarchs," claimed Andres Manuel Lopez Obrador, who most Mexicans think won the disputed presidential election in 2006, when he was candidate of the left-wing Party of the Democratic Revolution (PRD). Lopez Obrador was the PRD candidate again in 2012, in an election in which he lost to the PRI candidate, Enrique Peña Nieto. Napoleon Gomez Urrutia, head of the Mineros, says Mexico's old governing party, the PRI, which lost control of the presidency in 2000, wanted "to assure its return by making this gift to big business, putting an end to labor rights."

In part, the change is drastic because—on paper at least—the rights of Mexican workers are extensive, deriving from the Revolution that ended in 1920. At a time when workers in the United States still had no law that recognized the legality of unions, Article 123 of the Mexican Constitution, and later the Federal Labor Law, spelled out labor rights. Workers have the right to jobs and permanent status once they're hired. If they're laid off, they have the right to severance pay. They have rights to housing, health care, and training. In a legal strike, they can string flags across the doors of a factory or workplace, and even the owner can't enter until the dispute is settled. Strikebreaking is prohibited.

The new reform will change most of that. Companies would be

able to hire workers for a six-month probationary period, and then fire them at the end without penalty. Even firing workers with twenty or thirty years on the job would become much easier and cheaper, by limiting the penalty for unjust termination to one year's severance pay. "That's an open invitation to employers," according to Arturo Alcalde, past president of the National Association of Democratic Lawyers. "The bosses themselves say the PRI reform is the road to a 'paradise of firings.' It will make it much cheaper for companies to terminate workers."

The justification, of course, is that by reducing the number of workers at a worksite, while requiring those remaining to work harder, productivity increases and profits go up. For workers, though, a permanent job and a stable income become a dream. Instead, as the fear of firing grows, hours get longer and work gets faster, harder and more dangerous.

The labor law reform proposal accelerates those changes. The forty-hour workweek was written into the Federal Labor Law, which codified the rights in Article 123. That limit will end. Even the current 60-peso daily minimum wage would be undermined, as employers gain the unilateral right to set wages. The independent review of safe working conditions would be heavily restricted.

Mexican workers aren't passive. Work stoppages, strikes and protests are much more common in Mexico than in the United States. Greater activity by more angry workers, therefore, is not hard to predict. So the labor law reform takes this into account as well. Companies can subcontract work with no limit, giving employers the ability to find low-cost contractors with no union to replace unionized, higher-wage employees.

After the PRI regained the presidency in July 2012, in September a reform proposal passed through the Chamber of Deputies at breakneck speed, pushed by an alliance between the PAN and the PRI. Using the same arguments heard from employers and Republicans in the US presidential campaign, reform supporters argued that removing restrictions on employers would encourage them to hire more workers, producing more jobs. Rosalinda Velez Juarez, secretary of labor and social welfare, asserted that the reforms constituted "a watershed" that would generate an additional four hundred thousand jobs per year.

Critics pointed out, however, that nine hundred thousand young people enter the Mexican job market every year. But since the Calderon administration took office in 2006, only 1.54 million people have gained formal employment, according to the Social Security Institute—about 250,000 per year, or less than a third of those needing work. That is just one element of the economic pressure producing waves of migration to the United States. Evaluating the *reforma laboral*, the UN's Economic Commission for Latin America and the Caribbean found that it would not create any new jobs, but merely encourage contractors to hire workers already in the informal sector.

What the reform will also do, according to unions and other critics, is increase the productivity of the workforce by making workers more vulnerable to pressure by employers. A rise in productivity actually diminishes the need for new workers.

"The ultimate effect will be to impoverish workers even further," says Benedicto Martinez, general secretary of the Authentic Labor Front (FAT). "On the one hand, it makes it much easier to fire workers. On the other, the ability to subcontract workers paid by the hour gives employers a reason to fire permanent employees. This opens the doors of paradise for them." Unions will find it more difficult to organize workers who increasingly need better wages and conditions, but are even more frightened of losing the precarious jobs they have.

One provision added to the reform as it was debated would have given workers the right to elect the officers of their unions in direct, secret-ballot elections. That provision, however, was removed by deputies who are also leaders of unions affiliated with the PRI or minor parties backing the reform. Once the provision was removed, the PRI deputies who are leaders of the conservative, pro-PRI wing of Mexico's labor movement voted for the bill. "The supposed worker representatives in the Chamber of Deputies who approved this law betrayed their principles and their own members, and the whole Mexican people," Martinez fumed. "They handed workers over to the bosses on a silver platter."

The proposed labor law reform is the fourth in a series of basic changes to Mexico's economic, legal, and political framework made by the last two administrations of the conservative National Action Party (PAN). A fiscal reform began the process of privatizing the country's pension system, along the lines of the Social Security privatization plans proposed for the United States. Teachers charge that Mexican education reform is intended to impose a system of standardized testing for students and teachers, much like that in the United States, with control over curriculum even further centralized in the federal bureaucracy. In many cases, teachers say, the reform will allow the government to remove them from their jobs. President Calderon proposed an energy reform aimed at privatizing the national oil company, Pemex. Fierce opposition, however, was able to restrict it to some degree.

All the reforms have been part of a program of economic liberalization opening Mexico to private domestic—and especially foreign—capital. Lopez Obrador called the labor law reform "part of a series imposed on Mexico from outside over the last two decades, including the energy reform, fiscal reform, and education reform." In fact, the World Bank pressured Mexico to adopt an earlier labor law reform after the PRI lost the presidency in 2000, and Calderon's predecessor, Coca-Cola executive Vicente Fox, won it. Unions defeated that earlier proposal. While the two labor law reform proposals are not identical, they are very similar. Both reflect the surging power of corporate employers, and the way the PRI and PAN often trade places, pursuing the same political and economic agenda.

"At the same time," Lopez Obrador noted, "the fight against inequality and poverty is not on the national agenda." Changing labor law will make poverty more permanent, as well as rendering unions more impotent in challenging it. Conservative leaders insist Mexico's economic growth merits a seat in the "first world," and claim that the reforms bring it into line with wealthy countries. Juan Manuel Sandoval, a leader of the Mexican Action Network on Free Trade, predicts, "We will become part of the first world—the back yard."

The government's unemployment figures are low—5 to 6 percent—but a huge number of working-age Mexicans are part of the informal economy, selling goods on the street or working in jobs where the employer doesn't pay into government Social Security and housing funds (the basis for counting employed workers). Some estimate that there are more workers in the informal sector than in the formal one.

Even formal jobs often don't pay a wage capable of supporting a family. According to the Bank of Mexico, 95 percent of the eight hundred thousand jobs created in 2010 paid only $10 a day. Yet when a maquiladora worker buys a gallon of milk in a Tijuana or Juarez supermarket, she pays more than she would on the US side. That gallon costs a half-day's labor. Prices are a little lower further south, but not much. The price of that gallon of milk used to be fixed and subsidized, along with tortillas, bus fare, and other basic necessities. Previous waves of economic reforms decontrolled prices and ended consumer subsidies, as Mexico was pressured to create more favorable conditions for private investment.

Investors have done very well. In one of the diplomatic cables published by Wikileaks, the US government admitted, "The net wealth of the 10 richest people in Mexico—a country where more than 40 percent of the population lives in poverty—represents roughly 10 percent of the country's gross domestic product." Carlos Slim became the world's richest man when a previous PRI president, Carlos Salinas de Gortari, privatized the national telephone company and sold it to him. Ricardo Salinas Pliego, who owns TV Azteca, is now worth $8 billion, and Emilio Azcárraga Jean, who owns Televisa, is worth $2.3 billion. Both helped Calderon get elected in 2006.

Much of the PRI's labor law reform was a reality on the ground in Cananea, at other mines, and among maquiladora workers near the US-Mexico border long before the reform bill passed. For years the rights of workers in northern Mexico, and even the rule of law itself, have been undermined by the growing power of corporations.

Using labor contractors, for instance, was illegal in theory, but it became the employers' weapon of choice in the fierce labor battles of the past decade. After the strike by copper miners in Cananea was declared illegal, in 2010 Grupo Mexico, the huge corporation that owns mines on both sides of the border, brought in strikebreakers using contractors.

Humberto Montes de Oca, international secretary of the Mexican Electrical Workers Union (SME), notes bitterly that Cananea was the birthplace in Mexico of the fight for the eight-hour day, in the famous uprising of 1906 that heralded the beginning of the Mexican Revolution. "Now if you go to Cananea," he says, "you find subcontracted workers in the mine putting in twelve-hour days with no overtime pay. In the heart of the town where the eight-hour-day struggle started, workers now have a twelve-hour day."

Montes de Oca's own union suffered a similar fate. In 2009, Mexican president Felipe Calderón dissolved the state-owned Power and Light Company of central Mexico and declared that the union no longer existed. The SME, one of the country's oldest and most democratic unions, has been fighting ever since for the right of workers to return to their jobs and to regain its legal status.

"Our members were also replaced by subcontracted workers with no union," Montes de Oca says. "These new replacements had no training or experience, and as a result, there were countless accidents. Some of these workers died. This is the employment model promoted by the labor law reform. What happened to us anticipated the changes the reform will bring everywhere."

The corporate transformation of the Mexican economy began long ago moving the country away from nationalist ideas about development, which were dominant from the end of the Mexican Revolution through the 1970s. Nationalists advocated an economic system in which oil fields, copper mines, railroads, the telephone system, great tracts of land, and other key economic resources would be controlled by Mexicans and used for their benefit.

National ownership of oil, and later electrical generation, was written into the Constitution. Land redistribution and nationalization had a political as well as economic purpose—the creation of a class of workers and farmers who would defend the government and its political party, into which their unions and producer organizations were incorporated. Under President Lazaro Cardenas, in the late 1930s, Mexico established a corporatist system in which one political party, the PRI, controlled the main sectors of Mexican society—workers, farmers, the military and the "popular" sector. PRI governments administered a network of social services, providing health care and housing, at least for people in those organized sectors. Cardenas also nationalized Mexico's most important resource—oil—in a popular campaign.

After World War II, Mexico officially adopted a policy of industrialization through import substitution. Factories produced products for the domestic market, while imports of those products were restricted. The purpose was to develop a national industrial base, provide jobs, and increase the domestic market. Large state-owned enterprises eventually employed hundreds of thousands of Mexican industrial workers in mines, mills, transportation, and other strategic industries. Unions had their greatest strength in the public sector. Foreign investment was limited.

Enrique Davalos, professor and teachers' union activist at San Diego City College, calls the system "nationalism in rhetoric, selling out the country in practice." Under successive PRI administrations a vast gulf widened between the political and economic elite, who managed the state's assets and controlled government policy in their own interest, and workers and farmers, especially those not in the formal sector. To protect this elite, the country's political system became increasingly repressive. In the 1970s, to finance growth while the price of oil was high, Mexico opened up its financial system to foreign capital (mostly from the United States), and the country's foreign debt soared. Managers of state enterprises like the oil company ran private businesses on the side, along with politically connected union officials. Rackets and corruption proliferated while labor and *campesino* leaders who challenged the system were imprisoned or worse.

The debt and the hold it gave to foreign financial interests spelled the end of nationalist development. Oil prices fell, the US Treasury jacked up interest rates, and in 1982 the system collapsed when Mexico could no longer make debt payments. The government devalued the peso in a move still infamous as the great "peso shock." In the Constitution Mexicans still had the right to housing, health care, employment, and education, but millions of people went hungry, had no homes, were sick and unemployed, or couldn't read. The anger and cynicism felt by many Mexicans toward their

political system is in great part a product of the contradiction between the constitutional promises of the revolution a century ago,
plus the nationalist rhetoric that followed, and the reality of life for
most people.

In a desperate attempt to generate jobs and revenue for debt payments, the government encouraged the growth of maquiladoras, the
foreign-owned factories on the northern border. By 2005, more than
three thousand border plants employed more than two million workers making products for shoppers from Los Angeles to New York. In
1992 they already accounted for over half of Mexican exports, and
in the NAFTA era, became the main sector of the economy producing employment growth.

Maquiladora development undermined the legal rights of workers
in the border area, and any regulations were viewed as discourag-
ing investment. The government had a growing interest in keeping
wages low as an attraction to foreign investment, instead of high
enough that people could buy what they were making. The old official unions, including the Confederation of Mexican Workers, controlled restive workers rather than organizing them to win better
conditions. One of the most important methods of control is the protection contract. Corporatist unions sign agreements with factory
owners, who pay it "dues" for workers who often have no idea that
the union and contract even exist. They find out quickly, however,
when they try to organize any independent effort to raise wages or
improve conditions. The company and official union claim a contract already exists. If workers try to protest, they're forced into a
process before "tripartite" labor boards dominated by business owners, politicians dependent on them, and the official unions.

Labor history in Mexico for decades has been dominated by valiant battles fought by workers to organize independent unions and
rid themselves of protection contracts. Thousands have been fired,
and some even killed. Despite defeats, organizations like the Coalition for Justice in the Maquiladoras, the Border Committee of
Women Workers, Enlace, and the Workers Support Committee have
helped workers challenge this system. Some of these battles, fought
together with independent unions like the Authentic Labor Front,

have won union contracts, slowly building an independent and progressive sector of Mexican labor.

The Authentic Labor Front and the National Union of Workers, to which it belongs, made their own proposals for labor law reform. They suggested making all contracts public to let workers know what union they belong to, and to expose the corruption of the present system. They proposed reforming the labor boards that control union activity, making their process more usable to workers. Some proposed doing away with the boards, while removing the government controls used to punish independent unions. The reform bill didn't contain any of these progressive reforms, however. Instead, it takes direct aim at those independent unions.

New private businesses, often formed as a result of the privatization of former state enterprises, don't want to see independent unions spread. They therefore support restrictions to make it more difficult for them to organize their workers, as was the case for those formerly employed by the government-owned Mexicana Airlines. A new private carrier, Volaris, started airline service to the United States in 2007. Half the company belongs to the investment fund Discovery Americas and to Indigo Partners: Fund, led by former CEO of America West Airlines, Bill Franke. In 2010, after the government forced Mexicana into bankruptcy and laid off its workers, Volaris took over many of the old airline's routes.

What Volaris didn't want was the Mexicana union. As originally proposed, the PRI reform would have helped it accomplish the goal of remaining union-free, or weakening any union that might arise among its employees, by restricting unions to the one company or enterprise where they start. The union at Mexicana would not be able to spread to Volaris, and if one was organized there, it couldn't join forces with unions at other airlines. This kind of reform would make it impossible to organize industrial unions representing workers at many employers, a much stronger form of union than one confined to just one company. New private businesses like Volaris, then, would face no challenge by a union seeking to set a base wage for an entire industry. While it wasn't contained in the bill as it finally passed, nor were other restrictions on the right to strike, due to massive labor opposition, they have not fallen from the corporate agenda and will very likely reappear in new proposals during the Peña Nieto administration.

The state institutions enforcing Mexican labor law are already heavily stacked against progressive unions. The weakening of Mexico's labor law is making that struggle for survival into a desperate war.

Calderon Goes to War with the SME

The fight over the political direction represented by labor reform is at the heart of the Mexican government's attack on the Mexican Electrical Workers (SME). In October 2009, President Calderon declared Mexico's oldest and most progressive major union "nonexistent." He dissolved the state-owned Power and Light Company for central Mexico. And he fired all of the SME's forty-four thousand members who worked in the generation stations, serviced the transmission lines, and managed the distribution grid bringing power to businesses and homes. Most Mexicans believe this is a prelude to privatizing the electrical industry.

Since the peso shock of 1982, the International Monetary Fund and World Bank have used the leverage of foreign debt to require massive changes in economic priorities designed to encourage foreign investment, especially the privatization of Mexican state enterprises. Those put on the auction block include airlines, ports, railroads, banks, the phone system, and whole sections of formerly state-owned industries.

A majority of Mexican industrial workers worked for the government until the transformations started. The country's organized labor movement had its greatest strength in the state sector. While three-quarters of the workforce in Mexico belonged to unions four decades ago, less than 30 percent do so today. In the state-owned oil company, PEMEX, union membership still encompasses the vast majority of workers. But when the collateral petrochemical industry was privatized in the early 1990s, the unionization rate fell to 7 percent. New private owners reduced the membership of the railway workers union from ninety thousand workers to thirty-six thousand in the same period.

Resistance to privatization has often been fierce. Soldiers had to occupy the port of Veracruz at gunpoint in order to privatize it and fire its workforce. Mexico City's bus drivers fought the sell-off of the Route-100 company for three years, and their union leaders were imprisoned. Wildcat strikes hit the railroads when they were sold to Grupo Mexico, and copper miners fought a valiant battle against job reductions when the Cananea mine was bought by the same owners in the 1990s.

While these resistance efforts were defeated, one of the government's most important privatization schemes was consistently held at bay—the sell-off of the electrical system. In Mexico, two state-owned power companies provide electricity. The Federal Electrical Commission (CFE) brings power to all of the country except Mexico City and part of central Mexico. There it is supplied by Luz y Fuerza del Centro (Power and Light). Each entity has a separate union as well. The SME at Power and Light is one of the country's oldest and most democratic labor organizations. Under then general secretary Rafael Galvan, the union for workers at the CFE, the Sole Union for Electrical Workers of the Mexican Republic (SUTERM), led the movement to democratize the country's unions two decades ago. The government seized control of it, however, and since then it has remained a pillar of the main government-affiliated labor federation, the Congreso de Trabajo.

The electrical system was originally set up by private foreign investors, but in 1960 Power and Light was nationalized by President Adolfo Lopez Mateos. The then-private, foreign owners of Mexico's power system wanted a big rate hike and tried to pressure the government by threatening to stop bringing lines into rural areas and building new generating capacity. Article 27 of the Constitution was changed to make electrical power a national industry, including it with oil, which was nationalized by President Cardenas in 1938.

Popular opposition prevented the inclusion of the electrical and oil industries in the NAFTA negotiations, but while they were going on in 1992 President Carlos Salinas de Gortari opened the door to privatization. He announced that private companies, including foreign ones, could build and operate plants in Mexico so long as they consumed or exported all the energy they produced, or sold it to the Federal Electricity Commission. According to Jesus Navarrete, head of the movement opposing privatization in SUTERM, almost all new construction of power plants by the CFE and Power and Light was halted after 1992. Meanwhile, private plant construction surged ahead.

Ernesto Zedillo, Salinas de Gortari's successor as president, also proposed privatizing electricity in 1999. The SME formed the National Front of Resistance to the Privatization of the Electrical Industry, collected 2.3 million signatures on petitions in three weeks, and brought a million of Mexico City's angry *capitalinos* into the streets. Zedillo was defeated; it was the first time a privatization initiative in Mexico had not succeeded.

Zedillo's successor, Vicente Fox, was no more successful. A former Coca-Cola executive, Fox was allied with the industrialists of Monterrey and their US energy partners. His proposals carried the blessing of the World Bank and the IMF and were supported by US president George W. Bush. His plan looked very much like the plans for deregulating power in the United States. Most US proposals allowed large consumers like industry and commercial interests to generate their own power or buy it from private sources, while residential users remained with public or regulated utilities. In the United States, corporate forces steamrolled over ratepayers, unions and regulators in a successful effort to open power generation to the free market in state after state.

The SME warned that the Fox plan would bring about the immediate bankruptcy of both Power and Light and the CFE. Small users would have to shoulder all of the expenses of maintaining the transmission grid and the distribution system, while the existing companies would lose most of their revenue. The left-wing Democratic Revolutionary Party (PRD) predicted the CFE would lose 60 billion of its then 100 billion peso income. Adding fuel to the fire, Fox proposed to provide incentives to private companies to build generating plants, financing them by using the national pension fund.

Mexico's electrical rates are quite low by comparison with other countries, although much of its population is so poor they still can't afford them. In 1999, then-president Zedillo cut much of the subsidy that benefited the poor, and rates shot up 30 percent. The CFE runs in the black and is widely considered both honest and efficient. Power and Light, which had to contend with Mexico City's old infrastructure, was more strapped for cash. But the SME argued that the government was subsidizing large users, while cuts in Power and Light's budget undermined modernization of equipment. The SME also accused the government of draining the company's resources by forcing it to buy power at high prices from the CFE.

The most predictable result of privatization, opponents claimed, was that both national companies would be sold off once they were broke, or would be replaced in the market by foreign-owned ones. New owners would increase profits by raising rates for small customers while cutting wages, laying off workers, tearing up union contracts and holding down expenses on maintenance. These were not just doomsday predictions—they described the bitter experience of Mexico's railroads, copper mines, airlines, and other state-owned businesses.

US deregulation proposals not only influenced Mexican privatization plans, but some of their authors played a direct role in Mexico. As Jeffrey Skilling and Ken Lay were setting up shadow corporations to hide Enron's huge US losses in 2001, other Enron executives hobnobbed with Mexican politicians and designed projects in cooperation with that country's industrial elite. Enron created sixty-four subsidiaries to operate in the Mexican power market, headquartering most of them in Caribbean tax havens. The company already operated water systems in Quintana Roo state, and its executives advised Fox on energy policy in his transition to the presidency.

Following Fox's election, that alliance paid off for the Texans. On April 4, 2002, Enron Energia Industrial de Mexico received a license from Mexico's Electricity Regulatory Commission to build a 245-megawatt plant in partnership with two big glass makers, Vidreria Monterrey and Vidreria Guadalajara, Grupo IMSA (a steel and auto parts giant), Industrias Whirlpool, and other big Mexican companies.

Other familiar players in the California deregulation debacle also began building plants. Bechtel Enterprises, the multinational construction giant based in San Francisco, partnered with Shell Generating Ltd. to set up a company, Intergen Aztec Energy, to build a plant near Mexicali generating 750 megawatts, two-thirds of which would be sold in Mexico and a third exported to California. Sempra Energy Resources, a San Diego generator that figured in California's 2001 power meltdown, built another station near Mexicali, sending its power to the United States while burning US gas in a Sempra-built pipeline, making the plant the first true energy maquiladora. In addition to Enron, Sempra, and Intergen, twenty-three other foreign companies were granted licenses for plant construction.

The bitter California experience prompted San Diego-based US congressman Bob Filner to travel to Mexico City to denounce the deal. Filner was especially critical of the Sempra and InterGen border plants, which he predicted would produce three thousand tons of air pollution annually. Although US air-quality controls wouldn't apply to them, Imperial Valley residents a few miles north would wind up breathing the plants' effluents. "These are the same companies that robbed and defrauded people in the US," he told the daily *La Jornada*. "The question, therefore, is why should Mexicans trust them not to do the same here?"

One of Fox's principal arguments for his privatization plan was that the Constitution needed to be changed to legalize what already existed on the ground. Energy secretary Luis Tellez said Mexico needed to add twenty-two thousand megawatts to its then thirty-five-thousand-watt capacity, and that only foreign investors would come up with the necessary $50 billion. Navarrete and others, however, pointed out that cogeneration between the CFE and the oil monopoly PEMEX alone could generate nine thousand new megawatts.

"The industry could be self-financing if it weren't for the government's policy of disinvestment," said José Luis Hernandez of the SME. "What they really want to do is enrich some of their favorites by selling it off at deflated prices." A knowledgeable authority on the US side of the border agreed. Carl Wood, then a member of the California Public Utilities Commission, said, "It's crazy for Mexico to be doing this. Mexico is blessed with lots of energy resources. But this proposal accommodates the needs of the large consumers without meeting those of the public, and sticks the cost of old technology with consumers. That was always the root of California's deregulation problems."

Nevertheless, Fox's arguments swayed more than just his own party, the PAN. At first, early in 2002, the Mexican Congress passed a resolution opposing any changes in the Constitution to make privatization possible, and the PRI itself took a similar position at a national meeting. But then Fox invited PRI leaders Roberto Madrazo and Elba Esther Gordillo (head of the national teachers' union) to the presidential residence at Los Pinos for a late-night snack and talk. Afterward they announced they'd give his proposal serious consideration. Since the PRI had 40 percent of the votes in the Chamber of Deputies and the Senate, and Fox's PAN had another 40 percent, it looked like privatization was a done deal.

But national ownership of electricity is not just a matter of rates and jobs. It is a symbol of Mexico's independence from the United States, especially economic independence. "We don't just look at this as workers, but as Mexicans," said the SME's secretary for external relations in 2002, Ramon Pacheco. "Yes, we'd lose our contract and jobs, and the company would go bankrupt. But this is about more than that—it's about the direction our country is taking."

Privatization proposals provoked splits in the other electrical union, SUTERM. On May 22, 2002, some three thousand members defied their national leaders and marched in the capitol, openly allying themselves with the SME. Another demonstration in August brought out five thousand, and a national coordinating committee was set up representing fifteen thousand workers. "We have seen the consequences of deregulation in the electrical sector in the state of California, which has been detrimental to the interests of the electrical workers and of the population," said a statement signed by leaders of both Mexican electrical unions. "In Mexico, the people rightly think that the electrical industry and the petroleum industry should be public property and that such public property is the fundamental basis for their nation's existence and of their national sovereignty."

At the end of September 2002, the SME and its allies brought fifty thousand people into Mexico City's main square, the zocalo. The union distributed ten million leaflets nationwide urging opposition to privatization. Even some of the PRI's most conservative but nationalist leaders, including its former chair Manuel Bartlett, organized vocal opposition. "Look at the energy chaos in California," he declared. "Do they want to sell the American failure to us?"

The battle was internationalized by a conference in Mexico City that featured delegations from many Latin American countries. Further conferences brought together the Worker's University of Mexico, the National Association of Democratic Lawyers, and the PRD, along with union representatives, academics, nongovernmental organizations, and other political parties. An alliance of the SME, Mexico's independent National Union of Workers, the PRD, and nationalist elements in the PRI all vowed to cooperate in mass protest. In the end, Fox was unable to overcome the opposition, and his proposal was abandoned for the rest of his six-year term.

But the political forces that sought privatization had seen that the SME stood at the center of a broad alliance of opposition to free-market neoliberal policies in general. Restructuring the Mexican economy, and changing its political and legal structure accordingly, would become much easier if the SME could no longer organize opposition. Doing away with Power and Light, therefore, achieved two goals: setting the stage for privatization, and dealing a major defeat to those organizations in Mexico calling for a change in direction—in essence for an alternative to poverty and forced migration.

That attack began with a public relations offensive. After successive administrations had starved the company of the capital it needed to modernize electrical service, the Calderon administration attacked it for being inefficient, blaming the workers and their union. This was the same scenario used by administrations since Salinas de Gortari to justify privatizing other state enterprises—mobilizing public anger over corruption and inefficiency against workers and unions, who in many cases had been allies of the PRI for decades. In the case of the SME, however, the union had been a critic and a thorn rather than an ally. Nevertheless, the government claimed its contract made its workers a privileged elite, in a city where the average income is much less than that of a union electrical worker.

Then, on October 9, 2009, Calderon called in twenty-seven thousand police and army units, and at gunpoint threw the workers out of the generating stations, workshops, distribution centers, and offices. It declared the company, and therefore the union, nonexistent.

The union responded by organizing huge protest marches to the Zocalo, some with more than a hundred thousand *capitalinos* marching with the fired workers. Despite the propaganda barrage, many people knew the SME's history of supporting left-wing and neighborhood social movements and worried that the union's disappearance would hurt more than just its own ranks. Over the next two years, the SME organized plantons, or tent encampments, not just in the zocalo, where they're traditionally held, but also on the Reforma in front of the electrical commission and even at busy intersections in other parts of the city. At one point, several of its members went on a hunger strike in the zocalo, and only ended it when they were close to death.

Along the way the union won legal decisions restoring its legal status and returning its building in downtown Mexico City. Deputies in the national Congress proposed various solutions to end the conflict. The SME negotiated with the government, winning an agreement that Calderon's administration then renounced after the man who negotiated it, Interior Secretary Francisco Blade Mora, died in a plane crash.

The SME also won much more international support, especially from US unions, than it had in its previous confrontations with the Mexican government. US unions stayed out of previous fights over privatization, especially around electrical generation, in part because the SME is still affiliated to the World Federation of Trade Unions (WFTU). The WFTU was organized when the United Nations was founded, originally with the participation of one US union federation—the Congress of Industrial Organizations (the CIO—later part of the AFL-CIO). But almost all US unions later abandoned the WFTU at the beginning of the Cold War, and it became the rival of the AFL-CIO–dominated International Confederation of Free Trade

Unions. During the Cold War, the leadership of the AFL-CIO called unions that belonged to the WFTU "communist" and said they were too radical and too opposed to US foreign policy.

In Mexico, that Cold War hostility began to soften after the leadership of the AFL-CIO changed and John Sweeney became president in 1995. "There's more discussion with the SME," said Stan Gacek, a staffer at the AFL-CIO's International Affairs Department in the early 2000s. "It's on a de facto basis, although not on any grand scale. But a number of WFTU affiliates are talking to us because they've gotten over the Cold War and so have we. There are broader and more important common objectives."

As the Mexico-US labor solidarity movement grew, so did the number of US activists who saw the important role the SME plays in Mexican politics. They respected its democratic structure and strong contract. In earlier confrontations with Mexican administrations, unions like the United Electrical Workers (UE), whose relationship with the SME goes back decades, mobilized US support.

When Calderon launched his attack in 2009, that network was mobilized. The UE's website, Mexican Labor News and Analysis, became a source of news as the SME fought to maintain picket lines at installations and launched the hunger strike in the zocalo. News also came from the Solidarity Center's Ben Davis, who was already putting out daily bulletins for the Mineros. Progressive journalists began covering the fight, in the complete absence of any mainstream US media coverage. Delegations of SME leaders came to the United States, hosted by the San Francisco chapter of the Labor Council for Latin American Advancement and local labor councils. Their efforts led eventually to press conferences and meetings between SME and AFL-CIO leaders in Washington DC, and complaints at the ILO and under NAFTA's labor side agreement. Los Angeles unionists sent a delegation to the Mexican consulate.

In 2011, five international union bodies—the International Metalworkers' Federation; International Federation of Chemical, Energy, Mine, and General Workers' Unions; International Transport Workers' Federation; UNI Global Union; and International Trade Union Confederation—cooperated in organizing actions in forty countries.

Over fifty thousand workers, students, and human rights activists demonstrated at Mexican consulates, and twenty-seven actions took place in Mexico itself. The international federations and Mexican unions formed a coalition, which agreed to press the government to abolish the protection contract system and to stop the use of force against strikers at the Cananea mine, at Power and Light, and in similar situations. To win US labor support, solidarity activists argued that the destruction of SME and privatization of generation would lead eventually to Mexican power exports to the United States, using low wages and a lack of unions to undercut US production costs.

Migration and Cross-Border Labor Solidarity

As miners and electrical workers lose their jobs in Mexico, many migrate to the United States. The SME's Humberto Montes de Oca says, "We're exporting the struggle and the workers who experienced it." These labor veterans have a strong interest in aiding the movement for social change in Mexico, since the suppression of labor rights and growing power of corporations is the chief reason they've had to leave home. Montes de Oca notes that some come back for events organized by the SME in its continuing resistance, and others undoubtedly send money. He also predicts that they will have an important impact as migrants in the United States: "We're also exporting the experience of resistance and class consciousness."

This continues a process that is almost as old as the labor movements on both sides of the border. They both began in the decades after the seizure of Mexican territory in the War of 1848, its incorporation into the territory of the United States, and the unequal relationship cemented by the Treaty of Guadalupe Hidalgo.

After the turn of the century, cross-border solidarity became an important political movement as Mexicans began migrating to the United States as railroad workers, miners, and farm laborers. Ricardo and Enrique Flores Magon, on the run from the regime of Porfirio Diaz, began organizing what became the uprising in Cananea of 1906, and the Mexican Liberal Party, in the communities of railroad workers in Los Angeles, St. Louis, and elsewhere north of the border.

The two were active participants in the radical socialist and anarchist movements of the day and were associated with the Industrial Workers of the World. During the Mexican Revolution, IWW members went to Mexico and fought. J. Edgar Hoover, later head of the FBI, pursued the Flores Magon brothers on behalf of both the United States and the Mexican governments. In 1917, Ricardo was caught, tried, and sent to Leavenworth Federal Prison, where he died in 1922.

During the 1930s, strong cross-border relationships continued to develop between workers on both sides of the line. In Mexico and the United States, the challenge facing them was the same—to organize the vast bulk of workers in the largest enterprises, especially the basic industries. And a similar, although far from identical, political process took place in both countries at the same time.

Through the presidency of Lazaro Cardenas, the Mexican government depended on a strong, albeit politically controlled, union movement. Communists and socialists organized the Confederation of Mexican Workers (CTM) and began supporting the beginnings of labor movements in other countries through the Confederation of Workers of Latin America, headed by Vicente Lombardo Toledano. In the United States, a popular upsurge against unemployment and economic crisis, led by left-wing parties and workers, created a favorable environment for labor organizing. The large industrial unions created as a result of that upsurge became the organized base for the New Deal reforms.

The growth of left-wing unions and parties in both countries led to greater cooperation across the border as well. At the beginning, the strongest relationships existed between industrial workers—miners, railroad workers, factory workers, farmworkers, longshore workers, and others. According to historians Zaragoza Vargas and Juan Gomez-Quiñones, during the period of the labor upsurge of the 1930s and '40s, most solidarity activity was organized by Mexican unions in support of workers in the United States. Mexican unions saw Mexicans and Mexican Americans, especially along the border, as their own constituency. They sought to protect and defend the interests of people they viewed as their own fellow countrymen, linked by bonds of language, migration, and history.

In 1937, five thousand workers marched to the bridge in Laredo during an onion strike in the Rio Grande Valley. The major working-class organizations of the border states were present—the Congreso de Trabajo, the railroad union, and the Mexican Communist Party. Vicente Lombardo Toledano came from Mexico City to speak. Together with grassroots unions organized by left-wing workers on the US side, they set up the Asociacion de Jornaleros (the Agricultural Workers Union) in Laredo, Texas. In the following years, Mexican unions increased their organizing activity there. The CTM held a Convention of Mexican Workers in Dallas in 1938, in San Antonio in 1940, and in Austin in 1941. The program of these gatherings emphasized the fight for civil rights for Mexican Americans in the Southwest. Other demands included stopping local authorities from dropping Mexicans from the relief rolls during times of high unemployment, a situation that still faces undocumented Mexican immigrants today in their exclusion from almost all forms of social welfare benefits.

As the Congress of Industrial Organizations began to grow in the United States, Mexican unions and organizers helped organize Mexican workers on the US side. The CTM set up committees among Mexican workers in the Southwest. After Lombardo Toledano and others established the Universidad Obrera in Mexico City, Mexicans living in the United States were sent for training. Emma Tenayuca, the young Communist who led the most famous strike of Mexican women of the time, the pecan strike in San Antonio, was trained as an organizer at the Universidad Obrera.

In US copper mines, 60 percent of the workers were Mexican or Mexican American. The Mine Mill and Smelter Workers Union, with roots in the Western Federation of Miners and the IWW, used border alliances to build union locals in mining towns. This was a logical and necessary step, since the same families worked in mines on both sides of the border. They shared a similar union history, in which the fight against the inferior Mexican wage was a central demand in both Mexican and US mines, which belonged to the same companies. On May Day in 1942, five hundred Mine Mill members marched with ten thousand Mexican workers in Ciudad Juarez. Humberto Silex, Mine Mill's leading organizer, established Local

509, which became the union's most important local. Silex addressed the rally. The following July 4, Toledano traveled from Mexico City to speak at El Paso's Independence Day celebration. Solidarity went beyond speeches and conventions. CTM organizers coordinated with US organizers during the first strikes by Mine Mill in El Paso, especially during the key battle to organize its giant smelter. In 1946, Mine Mill struck at fourteen ASARCO plants to gain national bargaining. The CTM donated money and pledged to stop Mexicans from crossing the border to break the strike.

In Los Angeles, the International Longshore and Warehouse Union established Local 26 for southern California warehouse and light manufacturing workers. The union employed Mexican organizers, including Jess Armenta and Bert Corona. Corona, a left-wing labor and civil rights activist born in Ciudad Juarez, became local president. Later, Humberto Camacho, a Mexican organizer for the United Electrical Workers, helped establish UE Local 1421.

Corona and Camacho became the two most influential leaders of the immigrant rights movement through the 1970s, not just in Los Angeles but nationally. Their labor and solidarity activity created a core of activists and organizers. Their militant program called for defending the rights of undocumented workers. With the contribution of other left-wing organizations, like the Committee for the Protection of the Foreign Born, they made the modern immigrant rights movement possible. Corona, Camacho, and their generation of labor activists believed that unions in both countries had a common interest. Labor, they preached, should try to raise the standard of living in both countries and stop the use of immigrants as a vulnerable labor supply for employers.

Immigration laws in the United States were constantly used against strikes by Mexican workers. From 1930 to 1935, more than 345,000 Mexicans were deported from the United States. As the Cold War started, deportations were used to try to break this cross-border labor movement. The Immigration and Naturalization Service (predecessor of today's Immigration and Customs Enforcement, or ICE) arrested and tried to deport Humberto Silex. He became one of the most famous anti-deportation cases of the postwar period.

Luisa Moreno, an organizer of garment workers in Los Angeles, was deported to Guatemala. Another political deportee was Refugio Martinez, a leader of the United Packinghouse Workers in Chicago. Martinez helped build community organizations in Mexican barrios, including El Frente Popular Mexicano, the Toledano Club, and the Asociacion Nacional Mexicano Americano. Armando Davila, of the United Furniture Workers in Los Angeles, was also deported. The government tried to deport Lucio Bernabe, a leader of the Food, Tobacco, and Agricultural Workers who led organizing drives in canneries in San Jose, California. His deportation was stopped. But Rosaura Revueltas, the Mexican movie actress, was deported after playing a role in *Salt of the Earth*, the movie written by blacklisted Hollywood screenwriters documenting the role of women in the strike by Mine Mill at the Empire Zinc mine.

Many of the deportations were fought by the Committee for the Protection of the Foreign Born, a left-wing immigrant rights organization based in Los Angeles. Political deportations marked the rise of Cold War hysteria and were part of a wave of deportations of Mexican immigrants generally. As a political weapon, deportations were part of a general wave of repression that included firings, and even prison, for left-wing and labor activists. During the same period, the labor movements in both the United States and Mexico were purged of left-wing leaders. In the United States, the Congress of Industrial Organizations expelled nine unions, charging they were communist-dominated. In Mexico, independent movements like that of the railroad workers were crushed, and its leaders Demetrio Vallejo and Valentin Campa, also accused of being communists, were sent to prison.

The people who had organized the solidarity movement of the 1930s and '40s had to fight for survival. Unions that were the most involved in cross-border activity, like the miners and farmworkers, were attacked and, in some cases, destroyed. The labor movements in both countries became more nationalistic. In the United States, a Cold War labor leadership defended US foreign policy goals, especially anti-communism. Anti-communism provided a common ground with the conservative leadership of the CTM and other Mexican unions, who feared any independent movement challenging them from the Left. The American Institute for Free Labor Development, funded by the Central Intelligence Agency, had an office in Mexico City—but not to organize efforts to defend workers against US corporations and the military interventions that supported them. Instead, US labor-intelligence agents helped in the suppression, imprisonment and even murder of militant unionists throughout Latin America. When solidarity efforts began again years later, the distrust and suspicion engendered by that era took years to overcome. Some still exists today.

Even during the worst times, however, relationships continued among some progressive activists and union locals. When miners went on strike in Cananea in the 1960s, a Mine Mill leader, Maclovio Barrajas, organized food and money for them from the US side. When Mine Mill went on strike later, the Cananea miners reciprocated. During the 1960s, as the introduction of container technology transformed work on the waterfront, the International Longshore and Warehouse Union (ILWU) invited Mexican longshore workers to work in the Los Angeles harbor area and learn to drive the giant cranes. Today some retired members of the Federation of Stevedores in Mexican Pacific coast ports still remember that experience of worker-to-worker solidarity.

Corona and Camacho, and ILWU Local 26 and UE Local 1421, supported some of the first efforts in Tijuana to organize independent unions in the maquiladoras, as factories started to mushroom along the border in the late 1960s. A critical strike at Solidev and Solitron in the late 1970s was supported both by Tijuana's left, including veteran Communist Blas Manriquez, and a network of activists on the US side led by Camacho.

After the repression of the student movement in Tlatelolco in 1968, and especially in the years just before the Mexican Communist Party became the Unified Socialist Party of Mexico and eventually the Party of the Democratic Revolution, left-wing worker activists moved from Mexico City to Los Angeles to organize what had become a huge population of Mexican workers living there. Some became organizers for the UE and eventually other unions as well, helping to spark the city's labor upsurge of the 1980s and '90s.

Corona helped organize the Centro de Accion Social Autonoma (CASA) with other Mexican exiles and radical Chicano activists. CASA single-mindedly fought for the rights of undocumented workers, urging them to join unions while fighting to get unions to defend them. When unions were unresponsive, CASA activists tried to organize workers on their own.

The movement for solidarity between workers and unions in the United States and Mexico is an integral part of the history of the labor movements of both countries. The efforts of these earlier eras are an important reservoir of experience—a store of knowledge of tactics, strategy, and, above all, politics. They are a reminder that solidarity has always gone in both directions. Mexican unions played a key role in the organization of US unions, some of which would not exist today without that early support, particularly in the Southwest. Today the strikers in Cananea acknowledge that support from US miners and their union has helped to keep their own strike and union alive.

The solidarity efforts of the 1930s and '40s met success by concentrating on the key role of Mexican workers in the United States. Today's circumstances are different, but the migration of people is just as important to solidarity today as it was eighty years ago, and the number of people migrating between the two countries is much greater.

Oaxacan migrants have become an especially important and growing community in the United States. During the 2006 teachers' strike in Oaxaca, members of Section 22 of the teachers' union, Sindicato Nacional de Trabajadores de Educacion, traveled to California and spoke at the convention of the California Federation of Teachers. Solidarity efforts between US and Mexican teachers have barely started, but with the vast number of Mexican students in California schools, and with many immigrants themselves now working as teachers, the basis is growing for much closer relationships. Where Mexican teachers have won control of their state federations through the left-wing caucus, the Coordinadora Nacional de Trabajadores de Educacion (CNTE), relations with US union activists are growing. Teachers in the CNTE have controlled Oaxaca's Section 22 for many years. Now some teachers' union activists in California are cooperating with Rufino Dominguez and the IOAM to train teachers in Oaxaca to work in California schools.

The FIOB is one of many organizations Oaxacans have organized as migrants. Many of its founders were strike organizers and social activists in Oaxaca and the fields of north Mexico. Years ago they saw the organizing possibilities among people dispersed as a result of displacement, whose communities now exist in many places in both Mexico and the United States. FIOB's ability to organize binationally complements efforts by unions. It has a strong base among communities on both sides of the borders, and a carefully worked-out program for advocating the rights of migrants and their home communities. It sees the system as the problem, not just the bad actions of employers or government officials.

FIOB's base makes it a good partner for US farmworker unions trying to organize a new generation of mostly indigenous migrant workers, and there have been several attempts to forge an alliance especially between FIOB and the United Farm Workers. Though the UFW had very little activity in Mexico for most of its history, today it has begun to explore organizing H-2A guest workers and even programs for recruiting workers in Mexico into H-2A guest worker programs. The UFW and the Farm Labor Organizing Committee argue that they can organize these workers to win contracts, better conditions, and protection for their rights. Historically, however, FIOB has rejected those programs, calling them "slave labor" and arguing that if unions become the contractors, they won't be able to strike or use jobsite actions against the employers.

While these groups disagree about guest worker programs, however, they do agree about the rights of workers, especially their rights as migrants. And increasingly they talk about their right to stay home as well.

We're Fighting for Our Right to Keep on Living in Cananea

The Story of Jacinto Martinez

Jacinto Martinez is a copper miner in Cananea, a tiny mining town in the Sonora mountains fifty miles south of the Arizona border. He has been on strike for five years.

I'm secretary for work of Section 65 of the Mineros, the miner's union in Cananea. Our town is where the Mexican Revolution began in 1906, at a time when miners there were virtually enslaved. The mine was eventually taken over by the government, which ran it for many years. Nevertheless, over the last hundred years there were many strikes in this mine over wages and working conditions.

Finally, in 1989, the government stopped all operations at the mine, and President Carlos Salinas de Gortari declared that the mine was bankrupt. In August of that year, the government sent in federal troops. The miners were expelled from the mine, and the mine was closed for three months. Then Salinas sold it to private owners, Grupo Mexico, the company run by the Larrea family. Really, it was basically given away. The government had just invested 400 million pesos in the ore concentrator alone. Grupo Mexico bought the whole mine for 650 million.

After the Larrea family took over, we've had nothing but battle after battle with them. They are one of the largest mining companies in the world, and one of the richest families in Mexico. The company was forced to make certain commitments in order to take over the mine, but they've never fulfilled any of them. One was to share with the workers five percent of the price they'd paid for the mine. Because of their failure [to do so], in 2004 we went on strike, to force the company to pay what had become by that time a debt of 55 million pesos.

After that things became even more difficult. Before, the government was at least a little concerned for our welfare. Now all dialogue with the government has been cut off, and they give total support to Grupo Mexico.

We went on strike again on June 30, 2007, because of the deteriorating conditions in the mine. Once the strike started, the federal government, through the labor board, declared it illegal several times. Each time we've gone to court, and the courts have overruled the board and restored the strike's legal status. According to the Inter-American Commission on Human Rights, we have a right to return to our jobs.

Once again, on April 14, 2010, the strike was declared legal. Nevertheless, at 10 p.m. the same day, the company withdrew recognition from our union and broke off its employer-union relationship with us. That was completely illegal. But the government has brought in police and troops, and allowed the company to reopen the mine.

At the time we went on strike, there were about 1,200 members of our union. Now there are still 850 people on strike, five years later. The company has tried to buy people off by offering them severance pay if they'll give up any claim to their jobs. In my case, after twenty-three years working in the mine, they've offered me 1,007,000 pesos. They've said that in addition, they'd give me 830,000 pesos to try to buy me out.

We don't have Social Security medical insurance, however. The medical care we get comes from the company as part of our employment. So if we take their offer, we lose all our medical care. The 850 strikers have been fighting for this too. To make matters worse, on Mother's Day in 2008, the company gave us an additional gift by closing the hospital where we received our care. Counting children and retirees, an additional 1,200 people lost their medical care because of that.

The government stepped in to provide some services, but even though we can see a doctor again, we have no money to buy medicine. This has hurt our retirees especially, because now they'll have to pay for medicine, where in the past the company had to provide it. Some of us have severe problems because of working in the mine, like silicosis and high blood pressure.

So to protest government support for the company, about fifty miners have gone to Hermosillo, the state capitol, where they are occupying a site near the government building. When they come back to Cananea, other workers go to take their place.

We are not the only local union of miners on strike. Section 17 has been on strike in Taxco and Section 201 in Zacatecas. We are all facing Grupo Mexico. We are also protesting over what happened at Pasta de Conchos in 2006. The union made many requests to the labor secretary, asking that the government conduct inspections of that mine. But there were none, and finally there was a terrible explosion in which sixty-five miners were trapped inside and died. The only thing they did was close the mine. The company and government claimed it was an accident. But the president of our union, Napoleon Gomez Urrutia, held a press conference and called it industrial homicide. After that, the government tried to arrest him and he had to flee to Canada.

Since we've been fighting Grupo Mexico, we've had the financial support of the United Steel Workers in the US. That's how we've been able to survive. Over eighty thousand workers are contributing to our ability to go on fighting. And we are also receiving contributions from our own members in Mexico who are still working. So our situation in Cananea isn't good, but we've been able to continue for five years. Our members still support the strike totally.

The company has been able to restart production, using about three thousand workers who are employed by contractors. There are about two thousand federal soldiers guarding them. They've turned Cananea into an armed camp. They have towers with machine guns watching over people, and you can't even pass through certain streets in the center of town. This is why, like the SME, we're supporting Andres Manuel Lopez Obrador in his campaign for President. He's promised that if he's elected, he'll defend us.

Grupo Mexico is really destroying Cananea. The mine pumps water from about seventy wells. Cananea, with a population of thirty thousand, only has two or three. The mine is buying up land throughout this area, and now has more land than the town itself. They use it to dump the mine tailings, which have already buried part of the old town.

Meanwhile, of the three hundred members of our union who betrayed us and went back to work, only about fifty are left. So the only way they've been able to make the mine run is by bringing in three thousand people from outside, from Oaxaca, Puebla, and other states in the South. The reality in these states is worse. There's no work, no jobs there.

Grupo Mexico has built special housing for many of the strikebreakers on the mine property, called *colectivos*. They're like barracks. For others, the company rents big houses in town, where a lot of them are housed together. The company then picks them up in buses in the morning and brings them back at night. That way it controls them. And the whole economy of Cananea has collapsed because these workers aren't living in the area like normal residents. Many of them actually come here because we're close to the US border, and they're thinking about jumping the fence. The reality is that the economy here is pretty dead.

Grupo Mexico mistreats these workers too. It's gone back to the same conditions people rose up against in 1906, when miners went on strike for the eight-hour day. The strikebreakers are working twelve hours a day. They all have to belong to a protection union, part of the CTM. Then, after working four or five months, the company fires them. They only get 1,300 pesos a week [about $100], so when people want to go home, they don't have enough money to get back. Some of the fired workers wander through the streets, begging for help from other workers so they can get home.

With people brought in from outside to work the mine, the only solution for the people of Cananea itself is to leave, to migrate. There's no other work here. Some go to other states, or to other cities in northern Mexico. They leave by themselves to look for work. Then, right after they get paid on Friday, they send or bring the money home to their families. But most go to the US. That's logical, because the border is only a half hour away, and Tucson's only three hours from here. And that's where the work is. Sometimes people just go to work for two or three weeks, and then come back, trying to find a way to keep on living here. They try to use the work in the US to build up their reserves. This also happened after the three-month strike in 1998.

The people who are on strike are all people who live here, and most of us have been living here for generations. The head of our strike committee, Jesus Verdugo, is the third generation in his family to work in the mine. Now his children are old enough to work. But if we don't win the strike, they'll never work here. We're losing our traditions; we're losing the whole history of Cananea. And this is because of what Grupo Mexico and the federal government are doing to us.

You could say we're fighting for our right to keep on living in Cananea.

No Matter What the Result, We Will Continue to Resist

The Story of Humberto Montes de Oca

Humberto Montes de Oca is a fired electrical worker and the secretary for external relations for the Mexican Electrical Workers Union (SME).

Our organization is the oldest democratic union in Mexico. The Mexican Electrical Workers Union [SME] was founded in 1914 when the armies of Emiliano Zapata took Mexico City. Our founders saw that the peasant insurrection would finally create the conditions for their efforts to organize to succeed. They'd already made many attempts to set up the union in underground conditions and endured repression because of it.

In 1916, we organized Mexico's first general strike. Our leaders were imprisoned and condemned to death, but their lives were saved by huge demonstrations. In 1936, we went on strike against the Mexican Power and Light Company, which at that time had US, British, and Canadian owners. Mexico City went without electricity for ninety days, except for emergency medical services. The strike was successful and led to the negotiation of one of the most important labor contracts in Latin America. That strike helped set the stage for the nationalization of oil and created the political conditions that made the expropriation possible.

Then, in 1960, we were one of the organizations that pushed for the nationalization of electrical power. President Adolfo Lopez Mateos modified Article 27 of the Mexican Constitution and added a paragraph that says the Mexican government has the exclusive right to provide electricity to the country. Since then, under the Constitution public electrical service can be provided only by the state.

In 1992, President Carlos Salinas de Gortari changed the regulations to take some kinds of electrical generation out of the public sphere, and since then a lot has been in private hands. This started a process of privatizing electricity through secondary laws. In 1994, the Power and Light Company was decentralized, and it was closed in 2009, putting its forty-four thousand workers out in the streets.

For the previous ten years these workers, members of the SME, had resisted the privatization of electricity. In 1999, then-president Ernesto Zedillo launched an effort to privatize it through constitutional reform, by eliminating the sixth paragraph of Article 27, which made the industry the exclusive property of our nation. Zedillo tried to dismantle it. He proposed allowing the creation of private companies for the generating, transmission, distribution, and sale of power.

The union reacted quickly to stop it. We formed a front of resistance, and we succeeded because we were able to bring together many social movements that were opposed to privatization. Zedillo's proposal was defeated.

Later, President Vicente Fox made another attempt at privatization. This time he didn't try to change the Constitution. He tried to change the Public Law for Providing Electricity, a secondary law. He wanted the public enterprises to supply electricity only to homes. Private enterprises would provide it to large-scale consumers, like commercial and industrial users. This initiative was also defeated. In the same way, the union organized a front of organizations against it.

The experience of the past privatizations, including even those in the US, is that private owners invest their money to make a profit, not to provide a service. That affects the users of services, because the rates they pay go up while the quality of the services provided goes down. Investors only care about their profits. They don't invest in maintenance or in the means by which the service is provided. High rates and deficient service, in other words.

For workers, it means losing what we've achieved over decades of struggle. Things start going backwards. What we have now isn't some kind of privilege but rights that cost a lot to win. They are the minimum, which allow us to work with dignity and support our families and ourselves.

One important aspect of our contract is called the agreement among different parties. This requires the company management to consult with the union about changes they want to make that affect our work. In other words, they can't make unilateral changes. Few other unions have this, and we've used it to protect users and ratepayers.

The contract covers benefits as well. We have strong protections for health and safety that force the company to maintain a safe workplace, as well as changing rooms and showers. We have vacations and sick leave, and we can take leaves of absence. We have a fund that helps workers find adequate housing. If you've worked there a long time, the company will help you build or buy a home. We have the *aguinaldo* [an extra month's salary distributed at the end of the year] and a savings fund in which the company matches what workers contribute. Basically, our contract means that we have the minimum conditions you need for a decent life.

Really, the only effort to privatize electricity that succeeded was that of 1992. Eventually, 50 percent of the power in Mexico was produced by private generators in a process that was known as "hidden generation." After the subsequent privatization efforts were defeated, the right-wing governments, with their neoliberal policies, decided to use force to privatize through action rather than legislation. We say they tried to take the fish out of the fishbowl, and when that didn't work, to break the bowl.

Before taking action, the government mounted a campaign for months to discredit the company, the workers and our union. It intervened directly in the life of our union, in violation of the law, seeking to divide workers and buy off some of the union's leaders. The government refused to recognize our elected leadership, as a way of denying our union its legal right to exist and function.

The government sought to turn public opinion against us. To ratepayers, it said the company wasn't productive, that it was inefficient and had become a public charge. The workers were privileged, and their contract was expensive and a burden on the Mexican people. The union was inflexible and corrupt, they said, and the workers were lazy. All this was on radio, on TV, and in the movies— everywhere, creating the preconditions for action.

Then, on October 9, 2009, President Felipe Calderon issued a decree to end the existence of Power and Light and brought in twenty-seven thousand soldiers and federal police to expel our members from their workplaces. This was a military assault on workers. Many of us were injured in the violence. Since then, the Federal Preventive Police have continued an occupation of our worksites. They've stolen tools and equipment. They're looting the company.

There was no judicial order, and the action violated the Constitution and Mexican law. Immediately after, the government published a decree against the union and launched a campaign to defend its use of the military against workers. The closing of the company was portrayed as justified and in the best interest of the Mexican people. Calderon went on TV and said that with the closing of the company the electrical rates would go down and the quality of service would improve. There would be more generation and we'd have thousands of new jobs. That justified his authoritarian and illegal action.

But the president has no authority to close a national public enterprise that has a strategic value to the nation. Only Congress can take such an action and end the existence of a company. The government violated the labor and human rights of the workers, without even a hearing about these issues. There was no warning about the firings, which violates the labor law. There was no notice to the labor board that a conflict existed—without it, the workers have a right to stay in their jobs. The decree dissolving the company was clearly illegal. It had no right to cancel our labor contract or dissolve our union either.

The government had a secret document that was recently declassified. In it, they analyze the possible effects of destroying our union and predict that we wouldn't last more than three months. It predicted we'd be violent and that we'd try to reenter our workplaces by force. That's why they brought in thousands of police and soldiers. One high military officer revealed that it wasn't the police that took control of our workplace, but the army. They were prepared to repel any action by workers and stop any sabotage of our workplaces. But we never would do that. We have a historical memory, and we've resisted the government before.

The government tried to bribe the workers, promising them

twice the normal severance pay if they resigned their jobs. They took out full-page ads in the papers and said the first ten thousand who resigned would get jobs in the Federal Electricity Commission. They promised loans to help people start businesses. They promised training for jobs out of the industry, even classes to learn English in case people wanted to come to the United States.

So, twenty-eight thousand workers gave up their jobs. The government said they weren't fired—they'd quit. And those who quit couldn't find jobs anywhere. But sixteen thousand people refused to quit, and for two years we have been resisting. There's been no legal solution for us.

We've been organizing support among users and ratepayers. In their effort to keep the system going, the government has brought in workers with no experience. They have no training in providing uninterrupted service. As a result, in central Mexico, especially in Mexico City, there have been constant blackouts. The lights go out, leaving people sitting in the dark. These workers have not been able to reestablish the service as we provided it before.

We've proposed a legislative solution to create a new employer, to take the place of Power and Light, which would employ the workers and keep the union contract. We also tried to negotiate a solution with the secretary of labor. In 2011, we occupied the zocalo, the main plaza, for six months. We were the first Occupy. On the thirteenth of September, before our national anniversary, we negotiated an agreement with the government. They said they'd reemploy our members and free the twelve leaders who are still in jail. We said we'd leave the plaza. But right after we made the agreement with Interior Minister Francisco Blade Mora, his plane crashed—the second interior minister to die in a plane crash in the last six years.

The new interior minister refused to recognize the agreement. So the route of negotiations was closed. Now we're pursuing a fourth road. We won legally, in the legislature and through negotiations, but nothing changed. The next route is political and electoral. At present there is no political party that represents our interests. In 2010 and 2011, we launched a political organization for people and workers. We're working especially with SNTE

[Sindicato Nacional de Trabajadores de Educacion] Section 18, the teachers union in Michoacan.

At the same time, we are supporting Andres Manuel Lopez Obrador as candidate for president because he's promised that if he's elected he will revive the Power and Light Company, and reinstate the sixteen thousand workers with their SME union contract. This is not a corporatist effort. We made the decision in a general meeting, but no one is obligated to support Andres Manuel. No matter what the result, we will continue resisting until we win. [Lopez Obrador lost the election in July 2012.]

Certain rights are written into the Mexican Constitution. Every person has the right to work, to Social Security, to public free education, to culture, to health. These are social rights that the free trade regime is pulling apart. This is the effect that free trade agreements have had throughout the world. There's a ferocious competition for markets, in terms of money, for labor markets, for energy, even now markets in terms of environmental protections or the lack of them.

The expansion of free trade comes with a wave of violence against society and against social and democratic rights. This generates the expulsion of citizens from one country to another and produces the phenomenon of migration, as people seek opportunity and access to the minimum they need to survive.

This is what's happened in Mexico. Mexico is exporting its labor force—people who are expelled from their land and communities and jobs. So they leave for another country, in our case, for the United States.

The government uses the remittances that come back to Mexico, like the income from the oil, to compensate somewhat for the fact that the social budget in this country keeps shrinking. The money has helped to soften some of the sharp contradictions. But the amount of money available for this purpose keeps shrinking all the time, because the economic crisis is hitting so hard. It's not a sustainable model for economic development. It keeps economic activity going to some degree in the communities where people are sending back money, but in the long run, this can't be sustained.

The labor law reform will push this process further along, because it exacerbates the flexibility of labor, and jobs become unstable and wages go down. It generates a greater and greater desperation among people being pushed out. These are people who can't find a place in the labor market any longer.

In the case of the SME, which suffered the termination of forty-four thousand workers, we're now finding that we have coworkers who were fired, who never accepted the severance bribe, living in the United States. These are workers who belong to the resistance and who went there to survive. We also have *compañeros* who've gone to Canada to survive.

We've tried to maintain contact with many of them. On certain important events, such as the anniversary of the founding of the union this past fourteenth of December, some fly back from Tucson and San Antonio to Mexico City to participate. So our fight in Mexico is making a contribution to the labor movement in the US too. We're exporting the struggle and the workers who experienced it. The expulsion of militant activists to other places means that we're also exporting the experience of resistance and class consciousness.

FOUR

DEFENDING THE HUMAN RIGHTS OF MIGRANTS

Special Courtrooms for Immigrants

For the fired miners from Cananea, crossing the border to find work in Tucson is more dangerous than ever. The Coalición de Derechos Humanos (Coalition for Human Rights) in Tucson has counted 2,381 people who've perished just in this stretch of the border between Sonora and Arizona and estimates that 8,000 might have died on the border's entire length since 1994.

The treatment of those caught by the Border Patrol has changed over the past eighteen years as well. Now, a special federal district court convenes every day at 1 p.m. in Tucson's new federal courthouse. In the courtroom all the benches, even the jury box, are filled with young people whose dark brown skin, black hair, and indigenous features are common in hundreds of tiny towns in Oaxaca or Guatemala. Their jeans, tee shirts, and cheap tennis shoes show the dirt and wear from the long trek through north Mexico. Most have spent three nights walking across the desert and then more nights sleeping at the immigration detention center on the Davis Monthan Air Base, just inside Tucson's city limits.

Presiding over one court session in June 2008, Judge Jennifer Guerin called defendants in groups of eight to come stand before her. They got up and walked in tiny waddling steps, heavy chains binding their ankles together and their wrists to their waists. Judge Guerin recited a litany of questions, translated into Spanish through headphones. "You've been charged with illegal entry, a criminal offense . . . at trial you would have the subpoena power of the court . . . you have certain rights," she intoned. At the end, she asked if they'd understood what she'd said. No one responded. She then asked if they pleaded guilty. After a moment in which her question was translated, seventy voices mumbled, "Si."

Leaving the courtroom one young woman stumbled, eyes streaked with tears. A public defender told the judge her feet were covered with blisters from walking through the wilderness. A boy looking no older than thirteen or fourteen searched the room with his eyes as he was led away, perhaps seeking a friend or relative. No one seemed older than thirty, and most were much younger. After they all pleaded guilty to a federal criminal charge, they received sentences that ran from time already served to six months in a federal lockup run by the Corrections Corporation of America or the Geo Corporation, the two largest operators of privately run detention centers for immigrants.

Eighteen years after NAFTA took effect these are the border crossers—mostly indigenous youth from southern Mexico and Central America. According to the Spanish news agency EFE, this court process, dubbed Operation Streamline, convicted 5,187 migrants from January 14 to June 10 of 2008. The number of people processed in the years since then hasn't slackened off. Isabel Garcia, who heads Derechos Humanos, a leading immigrant rights organization in southern Arizona, said the daily quota could rise to one hundred by trying fifty on one shift and fifty on another. Meanwhile new federal prosecutors have been hired, with detention facilities expanding to house the prisoners.

This new bureaucracy has grown rapidly to meet the surge in deportations and the criminal prosecution of immigrants, thanks to drastic changes in immigration enforcement. In past decades, migrants were treated very differently when caught without papers. They were allowed to leave voluntarily, or deported after being found guilty of an administrative infraction, the equivalent of a parking ticket. Today's migrants have become criminals. The features pioneered in Tucson's courtroom—serious federal criminal charges, mass trials of defendants in chains, and incarceration—became standard features of immigration raids during the Bush administration.

State laws now supplement federal statutes, and federal, state, and local authorities cooperate closely to bring a large variety of criminal charges against migrants.

The number of deportations increased under the Obama administration, as the Department of Homeland Security sought to implement a quota of four hundred thousand deportations per year. New enforcement programs, like Secure Communities, pressed local law enforcement authorities into service as immigration agents.

Isabel Garcia's public denunciations of Operation Streamline and the deportations have made her a target of right-wing talk-radio hosts, who routinely urge listeners to call the county executive to get her fired from her job as a public defender. According to Garcia, each day's defendants in the Operation Streamline court are less than 10 percent of those picked up on the Arizona border. "They're making an example of them to create a climate of fear," she charged. "We are a laboratory. The model they're developing in Arizona is coming everywhere."

In Postville, Iowa, Tucson's assembly-line justice was transplanted virtually intact. On May 12, 2008, Immigration and Customs Enforcement (ICE) agents swooped down on workers at the Agriprocessors meatpacking plant. Twenty minutes after the shift started, Maria Rosala Mejia Marroquin saw people running past the line where she stood cutting up chicken breasts, shouting that the *migra* was in the plant. She ran too, and in a dark warehouse tried to squeeze between huge boxes. "Men came in with flashlights. One pointed a gun in my face, shouting, 'No one will escape!'" she remembered. When she was interrogated, she told agents she had a daughter in child care, but lied to keep them from knowing where the babysitter lived, fearing she'd be picked up as well. Agents finally strapped an electronic monitoring device onto her ankle, letting her leave but telling her she had to stay in Postville to wait for a hearing.

Her brother Luz Eduardo was taken with 388 others to the National Cattle Congress, a livestock showground in Waterloo, two hours away. In a makeshift courtroom they went in chains before a judge who'd helped prosecutors design Tucson-style plea agreements five months before the raid took place. In order to get a job at Agriprocessors, workers had given the company Social Security numbers that were either invented, or belonged to someone else. The judge and prosecutor told workers they'd be charged with aggravated identity theft, which carries a two-year prison term, and held without bail. If they pleaded guilty to misusing a Social Security number, however, they would serve just five months and be deported immediately afterward.

"They told [my brother] if he signed the papers they'd deport him, but it was a lie," Mejia said after the raid. "He didn't know he was agreeing to criminal charges, and now he's been in prison in Kansas for months." Translation into Spanish was provided, but according to Elida Tuchan, who was also arrested, about half the detainees speak only Kaqchiquel, an indigenous language from San Miguel Dueñas, their Guatemalan hometown. "They felt terrorized, that everything was against them. They didn't understand anything about the process or their rights."

To the workers, deportation became desirable. Anacleta Tajtaj was also braceleted, while her husband was deported and three brothers went to prison. "Our family in Guatemala was eating because of us. Now they'll go hungry," she lamented. It cost them each 33,000 quetazales (about $4,000) to get to the United States, a huge sum in San Miguel Dueñas. "Now we just want to go back. Everything here is a crime—all the normal things like working." Tajtaj and the other women couldn't go home right away, however. Three months after the raid they didn't even have dates for their first hearing.

"They can't work, they have no way to pay rent or buy food, their husbands or brothers are in prison or deported, and they're being held up to ostracism in this tiny town," said Luz Maria Ramirez, who headed the support network for forty-eight braceleted women at Postville's St. Bridget's Catholic Church. "This is a form of psychological punishment." If it hadn't been for the help of Ramirez and St. Brigit's parishioners, who found the women a house to live in, as well as money and food, they would have been homeless, along with their children.

Bush Ties Workplace Raids to Immigration Reform

According to Bush administration Homeland Security secretary Michael Chertoff, arrests in worksite cases jumped from 850 in 2004 to 4,940 in President Bush's last year in office. In the first five months of 2008 alone, ICE had arrested 3,000 people for immigration violations and 875 more on criminal charges.

April 2008 saw raids detaining twenty-eight landscapers in El Paso, twenty-four construction workers in Little Rock, sixty-three taco makers at El Balazo restaurants in the San Francisco Bay Area, twenty-two restaurant workers on Maui, thirty-three laborers on the federal courthouse project in Richmond, Virginia, twenty workers at Shipley's Do-Nuts in Texas, and forty-five workers at a Mexican restaurant chain in several states. In May, "cops and guns and badges and everything" were used to detain sixteen workers at San Diego's French Gourmet bakery, according to Rod Coon, company vice president. The same month, twenty-five construction laborers were picked up in Florida working on the Lee County Jail. In June, among those arrested were a hundred sixty workers at Action Rags in Houston, thirty-two farmworkers for Boss 4 Packing in Heber, California, and nine workers at water parks in Arizona.

Bush officials were proud of their statistics and claimed that worksite enforcement hardly existed before its own sweeps. Massive workplace raids, however, also took place during Bill Clinton's presidency. In the mid-1990s, thousands of workers were forced from meatpacking jobs in Nebraska during Operation Vanguard. More traditional raids seized workers for deportation at Nebraska Beef, Montfort Packing, and Tyson plants, among others.

Following the attacks of September 11, 2001, however, worksite enforcement actions did accelerate. Raids dubbed Operation Tarmac targeted airports around the country, leading to the firing and deportation of hundreds of mostly food-service workers. After the creation of the Department of Homeland Security, the new ICE bureau took over from the old Immigration and Naturalization Service, and more raids followed.

Immigrant rights activists charge that some raids were timed to respond to rising protests by immigrants themselves. On April 10, 2006, in a huge immigrant rights march, a million people filled the streets of downtown Los Angeles. They denounced House passage of HR 4437 the previous December, which would have made undocumented status a federal felony. A week later, on April 19, 1,187 workers were arrested at plants of IFCO Systems North America Inc. in New York, Texas, Wisconsin, and Massachusetts—one of the largest raids up to that time.

The administration also used worksite enforcement actions to dramatize its call for comprehensive immigration reform legislation in Congress. In December, after the Senate passed an immigration bill more in line with administration proposals, ICE mounted probably the largest workplace raid in US history. Some 1,282 workers were detained by hundreds of heavily armed ICE agents in military garb at six Swift and Company packinghouses. Afterward, Homeland Security secretary Michael Chertoff openly linked the raid to the administration's reform proposals. At a Washington, DC, press conference he told reporters that raids would show Congress the need for "stronger border security, effective interior enforcement and a temporary-worker program." Bush wants, he said, "a program that would allow businesses that need foreign workers, because they can't otherwise satisfy their labor needs, to be able to get those workers in a regulated program."

The Bush administration's drive was dramatized by other large-scale, highly publicized worksite sweeps. They included the arrest of 81 plastics workers at Iridium Industries in Poconos, Pennsylvania, 136 chicken workers at George's Processing in Missouri, 165 workers at Portland, Oregon's Fresh Del Monte produce plant, 327 workers at the Michael Bianco leather factory in New Bedford, Massachusetts, and 200 janitors for Rosenbaum-Cunningham International in seventeen states.

Once the comprehensive reform proposals died in Congress in June 2007, more major raids followed, including two at the Smithfield pork slaughterhouse in Tar Heel, North Carolina. In addition, 130 immigrants were arrested at Micro Solutions in Van Nuys, dozens at a Fresh Direct produce warehouse in New York City, and 161 poultry workers at Koch Foods in Ohio. Just before the Postville raid, 311 workers were detained at Pilgrim's Pride plants, where they had been cutting up chickens for KFC.

As early as the IFCO raid, some workers and low-level supervisors were charged with criminal violations, not just with being in the country illegally. In the Swift packinghouse raids, the administration employed a strategy of substituting criminal charges for status violations. Some sixty-five of the workers arrested were charged with identity theft or other criminal offenses, as were workers picked up at Smithfield. Barbara Gonzalez, an ICE spokesperson, told reporters outside one Swift slaughterhouse, "We have been investigating a large identity theft scheme that has victimized many US citizens and lawful residents." ICE head Julie Myers told other reporters in Washington, DC, that "those who steal identities of US citizens will not escape enforcement."

Criminalizing work for the undocumented is a result of the Immigration Reform and Control Act (IRCA), passed in 1986. Prior to that, workers could be detained for being in the United States without a visa, but hiring undocumented workers was not a crime, nor was working itself. The then-INS conducted some workplace raids, but immigrants were either forced to leave the country voluntarily or deported. They could make bail while in detention, prior to deportation.

In the late 1970s, the INS and its political allies began to argue that if undocumented immigrants could not work legally, they would leave the country and others could take their jobs. The INS campaigned for passage of the Simpson-Mazzoli and Simpson-Rodino bills, which embodied this logic, with a wave of raids called Operation Jobs. Agents would arrest workers in a factory raid, as they did at the Solectron and Levi Strauss plants in Silicon Valley in the early 1980s. Then they'd go to the local unemployment office to hold a press conference. With reporters and unemployed workers in tow, they'd return to the raided factory, claiming they'd "created" jobs. They then would demand that Congress pass the legislation that sought to penalize, or sanction, employers for hiring the undocumented. This concept was called "employer sanctions."

But raids became more difficult after the INS was sued by Molders Union Local 164 and the Mexican American Legal Defense and Education Fund. Afterward, agents had to stop their practice of locking workers in a factory and interrogating foreign-looking people about their legal status. Instead, agents were required to have warrants in advance naming specific individuals.

President Reagan signed IRCA into law, making it a federal offense for an employer to hire someone without immigration papers. It set up a procedure in which job applicants had to provide two pieces of identification to show their immigration or citizenship status and provide a Social Security number. By inspecting employer hiring records, INS agents then could come up with the names of workers to put on warrants for a raid.

Despite the law's announced intention, however, immigrants didn't go home. Defenders of sanctions ignored the ongoing displacement of people and their subsequent migration, caused by structural adjustment programs in Mexico and other developing countries and reinforced by the passage of the North American Free Trade Agreement. In the NAFTA years, over eight million Mexicans came to live in the United States, and since relatively few visas were available for legal immigration, over half came without them. Officials of the George W. Bush administration often claimed immigration continued because the Clinton administration never enforced employer sanctions. But while few employers were fined under IRCA, thousands of immigrant workers were fired, while yet more people came to the United States.

One widely used technique of sanctions enforcement was the no-match check. During the Clinton administration the Social Security Administration began sending letters to employers listing employees' names and numbers that didn't match SSA records. Employers were then left free (and often encouraged) to assume that the reason for the mismatch was that the workers were undocumented and had made the numbers up or were using ones belonging to other people. After many employers used the letters to fire activist workers during union organizing campaigns, unions and immigrant advocates convinced SSA to include language in the letters warning employers not to construe a mismatch as evidence of the lack of immigration status. Although no count was ever made, thousands of undocumented workers likely lost their jobs because of the letters.

During Operation Vanguard, INS agents used Social Security number mismatches to sift through the names of 24,310 workers in forty Nebraska meatpacking plants in 1999. They then sent letters to 4,762 demanding that they report to INS agents at their jobs. A thousand did, of whom thirty-four were arrested and deported. The rest, more than 3,500 people, were forced to find new jobs. Social Security grew so uncomfortable with this use of their database that they refused to make it available for similar operations in other states. Nevertheless, one of Operation Vanguard's architects, INS Dallas district director Mark Reed, claimed it was a great success, saying the operation was really intended to pressure Congress and employer groups to support guest worker legislation. "We depend on foreign labor," he declared. "If we don't have illegal immigration anymore, we'll have the political support for guest workers."

The point wasn't lost on the meatpacking industry. In 1999 the American Meat Institute and a group of corporate trade associations made up of industries employing large numbers of immigrant workers formed the Essential Worker Immigration Coalition (EWIC) and began lobbying for new guest worker programs. Industry faced a huge labor shortage, EWIC announced, and "part of the solution involves allowing companies to hire foreign workers to fill the essential worker shortages." The group, headed by the US Chamber of Commerce, included the National Association of Chain Drug Stores (Walmart, among others), the American Health Care Association, the American Hotel and Lodging Association, the National Council of Chain Restaurants, the National Restaurant Association, the National Retail Federation, the rabidly anti-union Associated Builders and Contractors, and its more union-friendly cousin, the Associated General Contractors.

EWIC guest worker proposals were circulated to Congress through a Cato Institute report authored by Daniel T. Griswold in 2002. "The experience of the bracero program," he alleged, "demonstrates that workers prefer the legal channel." A temporary work visa "should be created that would allow Mexican nationals to re-main in the United States to work for a limited period." When the Bush administration issued its own proposals a year and a half later, they were identical to those contained in the report. Cato's ties to the media helped guest worker proposals achieve greater legitimacy. When the Institute asserted that industries face a tremendous labor shortage rather than a corporate unwillingness to pay higher wages to attract workers, much of the media treated it as fact. Cato and EWIC members shared an aversion to minimum wages. Rob Ro-sado, director of legislative affairs for the American Meat Institute, said, "We don't want the government setting wages. The market de-termines wages."

EWIC's ideas were embraced by Democrats as well as Republi-cans. A much more liberal immigration bill, sponsored by Congress-woman Sheila Jackson Lee (D-TX) and members of the Congressional Black Caucus, was dismissed as "politically unrealistic" because it contained no new guest worker program. Meanwhile, John Gay, representing the National Restaurant Association at EWIC, became board chair of the National Immigration Forum, a powerful main-stream immigrant advocacy group in Washington.

The comprehensive immigration reform bills introduced into Congress from 2005 onward, with crucial input from EWIC, sought to make guest worker programs the only option for migrants by linking them to heavy enforcement. The McCain-Kennedy, Hegel-Martinez, and STRIVE bills all shared a similar architecture. They established large guest worker programs, allowing corporations and contractors to recruit hundreds of thousands of workers a year out-side the country, on temporary visas that would force them to leave if they became unemployed. To force workers to come only as guest workers, and to stay in the program once they were in the United States, the bills all mandated a tighter border to make crossing with-out papers more difficult and beefed-up employer sanctions to make it impossible to hold a job without a guest worker visa. The combina-tion of guest worker programs, increased enforcement, and legaliza-tion for the undocumented already in the United States was called comprehensive immigration reform.

In the bracero program of the 1950s and early 1960s, many work-ers simply remained in the United States, working under the table until they found a way to get a permanent visa. Many workers in current guest worker programs also stay in the country as undocu-mented immigrants, even though getting permanent status has be-come almost impossible. The enforcement provisions sought to cut off that option. "Enforcement is not an issue you can separate from guest worker programs," said Mary Bauer, director of the Immigrant Justice Project at the Southern Poverty Law Center (SPLC). A 2007 SPLC report cited earlier, *Close to Slavery*, documented not only the extensive abuse of workers in current programs but also the ben-efit to employers of a workforce with few rights whose vulnerable status makes organizing to raise wages and improve conditions dif-ficult. "Immigration enforcement is structurally necessary for these programs, to drive both workers and employers into them," Bauer explained.

Most comprehensive bills also contained legalization provisions for currently undocumented people, but would have imposed fines and long waiting periods from eleven to eighteen years, during which time applicants would be as vulnerable as ever. Employers, however, would be immune to fines or punishment for employing them, while at the same time they recruited new workers through guest worker programs.

Citing the failure of Congress to pass a guest worker, enforcement and legalization package, the Bush administration began to imple-ment many of the enforcement proposals through increased raids. "Even in the immigrant rights community, people say the reason for the raids is that Congress failed," said Marielena Hincapie, executive director of the National Immigration Law Center. "But we would have had the raids with those bills too, because of their enforcement and funding provisions."

The administration also used the bills' failure as a pretext for re-laxing restrictions on current guest worker programs. ICE director Julie Myers told the Detroit Economic Club after the Swift packing-house raids, "The administration has both streamlined the H-2A [agricultural guest worker visa] application process and has given

US employers more flexibility. . . . These changes will make it easier for agricultural employers to hire foreign temporary or seasonal labor to harvest crops." It also allowed employers seeking H2-B guest workers to simply "attest" that they'd tried to find local workers rather than have the Department of Labor certify that they'd made a real effort. The SPLC, the AFL-CIO, and immigrant rights groups bitterly opposed these changes.

"We see employers on the Hill all the time, saying they have to have guest workers. At one hearing on the H2-B program they had to open extra rooms to accommodate all the lobbyists," Bauer fumed. "And support came, not just from Republicans, but from Democrats like Barbara Mikulski, Zoe Lofgren, Ted Kennedy, and even John Conyers."

While complaining about the impact of raids on hiring, employers generally supported the administration's positions. In a *New York Times* interview, Homeland Security Secretary Chertoff said, "We are not going to be able to satisfy the American people on a legal temporary worker program until they are convinced that we will have a stick as well as a carrot." Chertoff's carrot was the prospect of massive contract labor programs for business. The sticks were the chains in the Tucson courtroom and the mass trials and the ankle bracelets worn by women in Postville. Immigrants were paying the price for gaining guest worker programs.

Myths and Realities of Enforcement

ICE, and the INS before it, historically has tried to win public support for workplace raids by claiming they were protecting wages and labor standards against employers' use of undocumented labor. A week after the Postville raid, ICE director Julie Myers told a legal conference, "Our goal is not to shatter the hopes of people coming to America in search of a better life. We are prying those people . . . from predatory criminals who are turning the search for the American dream into a living nightmare." In another speech, she claimed ICE was targeting "unscrupulous criminals who use illegal workers to cut costs and gain a competitive advantage." An ICE

Worksite Enforcement Advisory claimed "unscrupulous employers are likely to pay illegal workers substandard wages or force them to endure intolerable working conditions. . . . ICE's Worksite Enforcement Unit also helps employers improve worksite enforcement of employment regulations."

In reality, the Bush administration had little commitment to the agencies actually charged with enforcing labor standards. At a House hearing in 2007, representatives of the Government Accounting Office charged that inspectors working for the Wage and Hour Division of the Department of Labor routinely didn't investigate many complaints and closed half of those they did after short calls to employers. From 1997 to 2007, the number of inspectors dropped from 942 to 732, and the number of cases went from 47,000 to 30,000. Kim Bobo, testifying for the Interfaith Center for Worker Justice, charged that the division made fewer investigations than it did in 1941, the year it was founded, when it made 48,000.

The affidavit supporting ICE's warrant authorizing the Postville raid stated, "In February, Source #7 told ICE agents he or she observed a Jewish floor supervisor duct-tape the eyes of an undocumented Guatemalan worker shut and hit the Guatemalan with a meat hook, apparently not causing serious injuries. The Guatemalan did not want to report the incident because 'it would not do any good and could jeopardize his job.' The company fired illegal immigrants on occasion with no explanation." Yet at the end of ICE's enforcement operation, the beaten worker was undoubtedly in federal prison, while the supervisor remained at work.

Similarly, the Iowa Labor Commissioner documented fifty-seven cases of child labor at Agriprocessors, including complaints of exceeding allowable hours, exposure to hazardous chemicals, and other violations. (The company said that in 2007 it fired four for being underage.) Some of the fifty-seven most likely went to prison, while others were among the women wearing the bracelets. Desperate families in Guatemala who took loans out on their homes to send their children to work in the United States probably lost those homes.

ICE's claim it was defending labor standards was an appeal to US citizen and legal resident workers, who worry employers will pit them against undocumented immigrants in hiring and use that competition to lower wages. Yet ICE often attacked the actual efforts made by undocumented workers to organize and raise wages, as it did during the Smithfield organizing drive. After the first Smithfield raid, in January 2007, Mark Lauritsen, United Food and Commercial Workers (UFCW) packinghouse director, said the Department of Homeland Security and the company "were worried about people organizing a union, and the government said, 'Here are the tools to take care of them.'" The National Immigration Law Center's Marielena Hincapie explained that "enforcement drives wages down because it intimidates workers, even citizens and legal residents. The employer brings in another batch of workers and continues business as usual, while people who protest get targeted and workers get deported. Raids really demonstrate the employers' power."

To tighten the net on the undocumented and to create an atmosphere in which its proposals become politically palatable, the Bush administration and later the Obama administration have encouraged local and state authorities to play a part in enforcement. Tucson's new courtroom was set up, and the contract for federal detention facilities was given to Corrections Corporation of America, at the same time Arizona passed bills requiring state employers to use the E-Verify system, an error-prone database, to ensure they were not hiring the undocumented. The original bill would have punished any employer with an undocumented employee, but after employers protested the law was changed so that they would be fined only for future hiring. Arizona's E-Verify bill was signed by then-governor Janet Napolitano, who was appointed secretary of Homeland Security once the Obama administration took office.

In practice, E-Verify made undocumented workers even more vulnerable. One woman employed in a Tucson bakery, who withheld her name for obvious reasons, explained that she was getting only $10 an hour for tending the oven, while legal residents were getting $16 an hour for the same job. "If I leave or get fired, how will I find another job with a bad Social Security number?" she wondered. "Even though it's very unfair, I accept this situation without question, because I'm afraid to leave."

A Tucson union organizer, also unwilling to be identified, added that construction workers told her contractors lowered their wages from $18 to $10 an hour after the law passed and told them to bring their own tools to the job. "'What else can we do?' they asked me," the organizer recounted. She described rising unemployment in the Tucson barrio, with workers leaving for other states. "It's not going to stop us from organizing the union," she said, "but it will certainly make it harder."

Arizona employers, however, even ones with a good record toward their own workers, seemed willing to accept E-Verify and a greater enforcement regime. Nan Walden, a former Democratic congressional aide who owns a large pecan ranch south of Tucson, said that "removing 9 to 12 percent of the workforce will be a disaster." She criticized the state's sanctions law for its "piecemeal approach" and helped organize Arizona Employers for Immigration Reform. She advocated comprehensive immigration reform that includes a humane guest worker program, a verifiable identification and verification system, a path to citizenship for undocumented people, and "market-based" quotas for future migration. "I'm very disturbed by the hatred stirred up by opponents of immigration," Walden cautioned, but warned that without a reform like the one she described, employers would move operations out of the state and country. "Raising wages isn't the answer, because our costs are all going up, and we still have to be competitive."

The American Meat Institute also supports employee verification and employer sanctions, according to chair and Tyson Foods CEO Dick Bondhas. He told industry newsletter *Meatingplace* that the enforcement plan was "a good one, because it included some of the provisions that AMI and the industry really want: a path to legalization, a guest worker program and a better employee verification program."

Criminalizing work has become a tactic to gain the involvement of state and local authorities. In Tucson, the Arizona state police were given the names of fourteen employees at a Panda Express restaurant, whose Social Security numbers didn't match the SSA database. They then carried out a raid on their own, arresting workers for using the numbers. Except for one, all were denied bail under another Arizona law passed just prior to the raid, which made undocumented immigrants ineligible. The state prosecutor threatened the workers with felony identity theft charges, which carry long prison sentences under yet another statute. They finally pleaded guilty to a lesser charge and were sentenced to time served. Nevertheless, they were still in jail four months after the raid, waiting to be turned over to ICE for deportation. As in Postville, deportation became a desirable outcome that would at least free them from incarceration.

Francisco Mondaca, a Panda Express employee with a valid border-crossing visa but without work authorization, was trying to earn enough money at $9.25 an hour to get married and transfer from Pima Community College to the University of Arizona. He pleaded guilty to the trumped-up charge of "impersonating a Panda worker," he explained. "I didn't hurt anyone. I filed W-2s and paid taxes. All I did was go to work." After the raid, Panda Express management fired all its Arizona workers and brought in a new workforce from Las Vegas, according to one terminated worker. "The company knew we didn't have papers," he said. "Managers would all talk about it." No action was ever taken against Panda Express management.

In Phoenix, county sheriff Joe Arpaio became a hero to the extreme anti-immigrant vigilante group the Minutemen, the equally anti-immigrant Federation for American Immigration Reform, and other nativist groups. His deputies and supporters invaded immigrant communities, accompanied by helicopters and the media, arrested people on the street for minor violations, and then held them for lack of immigration status. When the local Pruitt's Furniture Store hired six people to arrest day laborers on a nearby street corner, Arpaio came to the store's defense. For three months, day laborers, churches, and immigrant rights groups organized demonstrations twice a week, accompanied by a boycott of the store. "In the first one," says Pablo Alvarado, director of the National Day Laborer Organizing Network, "there were only sixty workers and supporters, and the sheriff arrived with all 150 deputies, plus fifty Minutemen. But workers kept the line going every week, which eventually grew to a thousand people. Even the Phoenix Police Department came out to protect us. The mayor had to criticize Arpaio and the Minutemen, and called for an FBI investigation." After the Obama administration took office, Arpaio was investigated by the Justice Department.

The Bush administration's enforcement program had one effect it undoubtedly did not anticipate—demonstrations and lawsuits. Immigrant rights organizations and unions, who were badly split over the comprehensive immigration reform bills, united in opposition. The UFCW campaigned against the meatpacking raids, organizing five hearings to investigate the mistreatment of workers by ICE. In September 2007, the UFCW filed a lawsuit to stop ICE from using warrants naming a few individuals as a pretext for pulling in thousands of people in mass raids, as it did in the Swift packinghouses. It also organized a National Commission on ICE Misconduct and Violations of Fourth Amendment Rights. "Showing up for work should not subject workers to being detained," said UFCW president Joe Hansen. "Work is not a crime. Workers are not criminals. We do not leave our constitutional rights at the plant gate."

In California, the AFL-CIO, two central labor councils, and one building-trades council, the National Immigration Law Center, and the ACLU filed suit in September 2007 to stop ICE from issuing a new regulation that would have led to mass firings. Homeland security secretary Chertoff sought to require Social Security to send out letters to over 160,000 employers, listing the names of at least eight million workers whose numbers did not match SSA records. Workers would have had ninety days to come up with new numbers, after which employers would have had to fire anyone without a verifiable number. The order was blocked by US District Judge Maxine Chesney.

Mississippi Resists Political Raids and Anti-Immigrant Bills

Over a dozen states now have some state version of employer sanctions. On March 17, 2008, Mississippi governor Haley Barbour signed SB 2988, which requires that state's employers to use E-Verify and gives them immunity for hiring undocumented workers if they do. An undocumented worker holding a job, however, faces felony charges carrying one to five years in prison and fines up to $10,000. Undocumented workers are ineligible for bail, as in Arizona. At roadblocks near local chicken plants in Laurel, Mississippi, according to one worker who asked that her name be withheld, "They take us away in handcuffs. We have to pay over $1,000 to get out of jail and get our cars back."

On August 25, five months after the state sanctions bill was signed, ICE agents raided Howard Industries, a Mississippi electrical equipment factory in Laurel. They took 481 workers to a privately run detention center in Jena, Louisiana, while 106 women were released wearing electronic monitoring devices strapped to their ankles. Eight workers were taken to federal court in Hattiesburg and charged with aggravated identity theft. For two weeks the workers in Jena had no idea where they were. They were not charged, had no access to attorneys, and could not get released on bail. "They were rounded up and just dumped in a privately run detention center," said Patricia Ice, attorney for the Mississippi Immigrants Rights Alliance (MIRA). "We heard reports that there weren't even enough beds and that people were sleeping on the floor."

She charged that the raid had a political agenda—undermining a growing political coalition that threatens the state's conservative Republican establishment. The raid also took place during union contract negotiations, and helped the company resist demands for better wages and conditions. Jim Evans, a national AFL-CIO staff member in Mississippi and a leading member of the state legislature's Black Caucus, said, "This raid is an effort to drive immigrants out of Mississippi. It is also an attempt to drive a wedge between immigrants, African Americans, white people, and unions—all those who want political change here."

Patricia Ice agreed, "This is political. They want a mass exodus of immigrants out of the state, the kind we've seen in Arizona and Oklahoma. The political establishment here is threatened by Mississippi's changing demographics and what the electorate might look like in twenty years." Evans added that the state's employer sanctions law and the Howard Industries raid served the same objectives: "They both just make it easier to exploit workers. The people who profit from Mississippi's low-wage system want to keep it the way it is."

In the week before the raid, MIRA organizers received reports of a growing number of ICE agents in southern Mississippi. They began leafleting immigrant communities, warning people and explaining their rights should they be questioned about their immigration status. When agents finally showed up at the Howard Industries plant, many workers said they tried to invoke those rights and warn others that a raid was in progress. One woman, later detained and then released to care for her child, began to call workers who had not yet come to the factory on her cell phone, warning them to stay away. "She first called her brother, and then began calling anyone else she could think of," explained her mother, who worked in a local chicken plant. "An agent grabbed her arm, and asked her what she was doing, so she went into the bathroom, and kept calling people until they took her phone away."

The raid had an impact on the union in the plant as well. Howard Industries, like most Mississippi employers, has a long record of opposing unions. Nevertheless, workers there chose representation by the International Brotherhood of Electrical Workers in 2000. The company manufactures electrical ballasts and transformers, and in 2002 it received a $31.5 million state subsidy for expansion. "The company is very well-connected politically," said Evans, who noted that its owners donated to the campaigns of former Democratic governor Ronnie Musgrove and then to his successor, Republican Haley Barbour.

MIRA director Bill Chandler said that earlier election campaigns set up the conditions for the raid. "Barbour and Republicans campaigned against immigrants to get elected," he explained. "But so did all the Democratic statewide candidates except Attorney General Jim Hood. Now the raid will make the climate even worse."

After the election, employment grew at Howard Industries to over four thousand workers at several locations. As it grew, the company hired many immigrant Mexican and Central American workers, diversifying a workforce that was originally primarily African American and white. Following the raid, the company released a press statement disclaiming knowledge of their lack of immigration status. It said, "Howard Industries runs every check allowed to ascertain the immigration status of all applicants for jobs. It is company policy that it hires only US citizens and legal immigrants."

Tension between the company and union increased when the union contract expired. According to workers, the union was asking for a raise of $1.50 an hour, better vacation benefits, and changes to medical benefits that were costing workers over $100 a week, putting it out of reach for most. Mississippi is a right-to-work state, and labor contracts cannot require that workers belong to the union. Instead, unions must continually try to sign workers up as members. In past years, according to other union sources, IBEW Local 1317 had a reputation as a union that did not offer much support to its immigrant members.

According to one worker, there were just a few hundred members at one plant, and in negotiations the company used that low membership as a reason not to sign a new agreement. Then Local 1317 brought in a Spanish-speaking organizer, Maria Gonzalez, to sign up immigrant workers. Many began to join, and IBEW's national newspaper, *Electrical Worker*, ran an article about it. Local 1317's African American business manager, Clarence Larkin, said, "Supervisors yell at people a lot—not just immigrants, but at everyone. Howard has always been an anti-employee company, and treats workers with no respect."

Three days after the raid, while many immigrants hid in their homes in fear, Vicky Cintra, then a MIRA organizer, and over a hundred raid victims and family members marched down to the plant to demand withheld paychecks. Company managers called the police, who tried to arrest Cintra, and the immigrants began shouting "Let her go!" As news reporters arrived on the scene, the police backed off. Seventy families got paychecks. The following day, Cintra and the women returned to the plant, seeking pay for other unpaid workers. They sat on the grass across the street from the factory in a silent protest. "When the shift changed, African American workers poured out of the gate," she recalled. "They went up to these Latina women and began hugging them. They said things like, 'We're with you. Do you need any food for your kids? How can we help? You need to assert your rights. We're glad you're here.' There's a lot of support inside the factory for the workers who were caught up in the raid."

Three months after the Laurel raid, voters elected Barack Obama president. Voting took place as millions of people were losing their jobs and homes. Lou Dobbs and talk-show hysteria-mongers tried to scapegoat immigrants for the economic crisis, but most voters did not drink the Kool-Aid. Instead, they voted for change, or the promise of it. This included the hope for a change in immigration policy. In its last year, the Bush administration had deported 349,041 people. Candidate Obama promised he would try to pass immigration reform, although a close look at his website revealed that the proposals he favored were those of the comprehensive immigration reform bills of previous years. Still, he visited the border during the campaign and called for a more cooperative relationship between border communities rather than the militarization that makes the area seem like a war zone. It was a brave moment that symbolized for many immigrant rights activists the potential for a different direction.

The political coalition that put Obama into office—African Americans, Latinos, Asian Americans, women, and union families— expected change. Immigrant rights activists around the country made lists of actions the president could take administratively, without confronting the problems of negotiating a bill through Congress. Stopping the raids was at the top of every list. Other hoped-for actions included a moratorium on criminal charges for using bad Social Security numbers and closing the burgeoning private detention centers. Obama was urged to beef up labor standards enforcement as an alternative to workplace raids, and to end the Bush program requiring local police to cooperate in immigration enforcement. Arizona activists, in particular, urged him to disband the Operation Streamline court and bring civil rights charges against Sheriff Joe Arpaio.

Over the next two years, Obama gave those supporters somewhat less than half a loaf. Workers no longer went to prison after being caught in military-style raids, but mass firings took their place. The Operation Streamline court continued. The number of detention centers increased to house deportees, whose numbers swelled beyond even the Bush-era statistics to almost four hundred thousand a year. Obama appointed Hilda Solis, a Los Angeles–based congress-woman with a long record of support for workers and unions, as labor secretary, and she began rebuilding the labor standards en-forcement apparatus. But he also appointed Arizona governor Janet Napolitano secretary of homeland security. Cooperation between lo-cal police and ICE increased, and the administration developed new programs, like Secure Communities, to require such cooperation.

Illinois congressman Rahm Emanuel, famous for calling im-migration the "third rail" of American politics, became the presi-dent's chief of staff and one of his closest White House advisors. No proposal for immigration reform, even a pro-corporate one, came from the administration. Congressional Black Caucus members like Houston's Sheila Jackson Lee and Oakland's Barbara Lee suggested federal jobs programs to meet the crisis of growing unemployment, tied to increased rights and legal status for immigrants without pa-pers. Emanuel treated these progressive proposals as politically un-realistic and unworthy of discussion.

At the same time, the right wing of the Republican Party took advantage of anger against the economic crisis and cynicism over the lack of effective federal jobs programs. In the Republican cal-culation, economic insecurity hooked to anti-immigrant hysteria could win seats in the congressional elections of 2010. Arizona then became a battleground on which this strategy unfolded, much as Isabel Garcia had predicted two years earlier. Kris Kobach, a profes-sor at the University of Missouri–Kansas City School of Law, who'd worked for Bush's attorney general, John Ashcroft, drafted a bill. He presented it to Arizona state senator Russell Pearce, who had introduced previous anti-immigrant bills in the state's legislature. In a December 2009 meeting, the American Legislative Exchange Council took Kobach's draft and began circulating it to other states as well. ALEC is one of a constellation of far-right groups, including the Moral Majority and the Heritage Foundation, founded by Repub-lican Party strategist Paul Weyrich in the 1970s. Its board includes Walmart, Exxon-Mobil, the Koch brothers oil firm (which supplied much of ALEC's financing), and other large corporations.

The Arizona bill, SB 1070, made it a state crime for immigrants not to carry their immigration documents and required police and other law enforcement officers to question the people they stopped about their immigration status. No person arrested could be released unless they could prove legal immigration status. The bill made it a crime to seek work on the sidewalk, a direct nod to Sheriff Arpaio, who'd been conducting street sweeps against Phoenix day laborers for years. Giving a ride to an undocumented person could be considered a crime, as could encouraging an undocumented person to come to Arizona. In the middle of a national storm of protest, the Arizona legislature passed the bill in April 2010, and Napolitano's replacement as governor, Jan Brewer, signed it. Numerous organizations, including the federal Department of Justice, filed suit to stop its implementation, arguing that only the federal government has the authority to regulate immigration.

Most suits did not, however, challenge the racism or anti-immigrant bias inherent in the law. The hysteria SB 1070 encouraged eventually even led to the banning of Chicano Studies in the state schools, a measure directed against one of the most successful such programs in the country, in Tucson high schools. The Latino community nationally, as well as students, unions and immigrant rights activists made SB 1070 a household word synonymous with racism and promoted an economic boycott of the state announced by Tucson Congress member Raul Grijalva.

Defense of SB 1070, however, also became a litmus test for candidates in the Republican Party, where the Tea Party led a successful right-wing offensive to gain control over its electoral apparatus. In the November election that followed, anti-immigrant hysteria, promoted by the law's supporters, helped lead to landslide victories by Republican candidates.

After the election, ALEC moved the push for SB 1070 look-alike laws to other states. Thirty-six states introduced them in 2011, and five passed them: Utah, Indiana, Georgia, Alabama, and South Carolina. Georgia passed HB 87 that May, and Alabama and South Carolina signed their bills into law in June. Of them all, Alabama's was the most extreme. In addition to adopting SB 1070's provisions, it also prohibited undocumented immigrants from receiving any benefits from the state, barring them from public universities or even checking books out of libraries. The law required teachers to question students in public schools about their immigration status, and said each school had to report the number of its undocumented students to the state. Giving a ride, renting an apartment, or offering a job to an undocumented immigrant all became illegal. It was also a crime for an undocumented person to apply for a job, and employers had to use the E-Verify database to detect them. Any contract signed by an undocumented person was considered null and void. And all voters had to show proof of citizenship when registering.

Then, in April 2012, an anti-immigrant bill like those that swept through legislatures in Alabama, Georgia, and South Carolina was stopped cold in Mississippi. By that time, Tea Party Republicans were confident they'd roll over any opposition, and they had brought Kris Kobach, the Kansas City School of Law professor involved in drafting Arizona's SB 1070, into Jackson to push for their bill. He was seen huddled with the state representative from Brookhaven, Becky Currie, who introduced it. ALEC had its agents on the scene.

Their timing seemed unbeatable. In November 2011, Republicans took control of Mississippi's state House of Representatives for the first time since Reconstruction. Mississippi was one of the last Southern states in which Democrats controlled the legislature, and the turnover was a final triumph for Richard Nixon's and Ronald Reagan's Southern Strategy. And the Republicans who took power weren't just any Republicans. Haley Barbour, now considered a "moderate Republican," had stepped down as governor. Voters replaced him with an anti-immigrant successor, Phil Bryant, whose venom toward the foreign-born rivaled that of Lou Dobbs.

Yet the seemingly inevitable didn't happen. Instead, from the opening of the legislative session just after New Year's, the state's legislative Black Caucus fought a dogged rearguard war in the House. Over the last decade the caucus had acquired hard-won expertise on immigration, defeating over two hundred anti-immigrant measures. After the election, though, they lost the crucial committee chairmanships that made it possible for them to kill those earlier bills. But they did not lose their voice. "We forced a great debate in the

House, until one thirty in the morning," said Evans, caucus leader and MIRA chair. "When you have a prolonged debate like that, it shows the widespread concern and disagreement. People began to see the ugliness in this measure."

Like all of Kobach's and ALEC's bills, HB 488 stated its intent in its first section: "to make attrition through enforcement the public policy of all state agencies and local governments." In other words, to make life so difficult and unpleasant for undocumented people that they'd leave the state. And to that end, it said people without papers wouldn't be able to get as much as a bicycle license or library card, and that schools would have to inform on the immigration status of their students. Following its Arizona model, it mandated that police verify the immigration status of anyone they arrested, an open invitation to racial profiling.

"The night HB 488 came to the floor, many black legislators spoke against it," reported MIRA director Bill Chandler, "including some who'd never spoken out on immigration before. One objected to the use of the term 'illegal alien' in its language, while others said it justified breaking up families and ethnic cleansing. Even many white legislators were inspired to speak against it." Nevertheless, the bill was rammed through the House. Then it reached the Republican-controlled Senate, presided over by a more moderate Republican, Lieutenant Governor Tate Reeves. Reeves could see the widespread opposition, and was less in lockstep with the Tea Party's anti-immigrant agenda. Although Democrats had just lost all their committee chairmanships in the House, Reeves appointed a rural Democrat, Hob Bryan, to chair one of the Senate's two judiciary committees. He then sent HR 488 to that committee, and Bryan killed it.

On the surface, it appeared that fissures inside the Republican Party facilitated the bill's defeat. But they were not the cause of that defeat. As the debate and maneuvering played out in the Capitol building, its halls were filled with angry protests, while noisy demonstrations went on for days, up until the bill's final hour. That grassroots upsurge produced political alliances that cut deeply into the bill's support, including calls for rejection by the state's sheriffs' and county supervisors associations, the Mississippi Economic Council (the state's chamber of commerce), and employer groups from farms to poultry packers.

That upsurge was neither spontaneous nor the last-minute product of emergency mobilizations. "We wouldn't have had a chance against this without twelve years of organizing work," Evans explained. "We worked on the conscience of people night and day and built coalition after coalition. Over time, people have come around. The way people think about immigration in Mississippi today is nothing like the way they thought when we started."

At the end of the 1990s, Evans, Chandler, attorney Patricia Ice, Father Jerry Tobin, activist Kathy Sykes, union organizer Frank Curiel, and other veterans of Mississippi's social movements came together to build political power. Their vehicle was the Mississippi Immigrants Rights Alliance and a partnership with the Legislative Black Caucus, along with other coalitions fighting on most of the progressive issues facing the state. Their strategy was based on the state's changing demographics. Over the last two decades, the percentage of African Americans in Mississippi's population has been rising. Black families driven from jobs by factory closings and unemployment in the North have been moving back south, reversing the movement of the decades of the Great Migration. Today, at least 37 percent of Mississippi's people are African Americans, the highest percentage of any state in the country.

Then, starting with the boom in casino construction in the early 1990s, immigrants from Mexico and Central America, displaced by NAFTA and CAFTA, began migrating into the state as well. Poultry plants, farms, and factories hired them. Guest workers were brought to work in Gulf Coast reconstruction and shipyards. "Today we have established Latino communities," Chandler explained. "The children of the first immigrants are now arriving at voting age."

In MIRA's political calculation, blacks and immigrants, plus unions, are the potential pillars of a powerful political coalition. HB 488's intent to drive immigrants from Mississippi was an effort to make that coalition impossible. MIRA has not just focused on defeating bad bills, however. It built a grassroots base by fighting immigration raids at Howard Industries and other worksites, while helping families survive sweeps in apartment houses and trailer parks. Its organizers brought together black workers suspicious of the Latino influx and immigrant families worried about settling in a hostile community. Political unity, based in neighborhoods, protects both groups, they urged.

MIRA became a resource for unions organizing poultry plants, factories, and casinos, helping to win over immigrant workers. It brought labor violation cases against Gulf employers in the wake of Hurricane Katrina. Yet despite fighting on opposing sides in legal battles and union drives, some employers and MIRA recognized they had a mutual interest in defeating HB 488. Both opposed workplace immigration raids and enforcement, based on the "attrition through enforcement" justification.

"They violate the human rights of working people to feed their families," Chandler argued. "For employers, that opposition was a meeting point. They didn't like workplace enforcement either. All their associations claimed they didn't hire undocumented workers, but we all know who's working in the plants. We wanted people to stay as much as the employers did. Forcing people from their jobs was an attempt to force them to leave—an ethnic cleansing tactic." During the protests, Ice, Sykes, and others underlined the point by handing legislators sweet potatoes with labels saying, "I was picked by immigrant workers who together contribute $82 million to the state's economy."

Over the last decade, when Congress debated proposals for comprehensive immigration reform that called for strengthening workplace enforcement, MIRA opposed them. "They would have led to more raids and firings," Chandler said. "That's why we didn't support those bills." MIRA also fought the bills because they contained expanded guest worker programs, like those used by Mississippi casinos and shipyards to recruit workers with few labor rights. "When it came to HB 488, employers were tactical allies," Chandler cautioned, "not permanent strategic ones. We basically want opposite things."

Unions, on the other hand, are members of the MIRA coalition. While MIRA and employers saw a mutual interest in opposing

HB 488, MIRA sees unions as an important part of a coalition to win political power. When unions have sought to organize the workers of those same employers, MIRA has helped them, as well as assisting rank-and-file workers to defend themselves when employers violate their rights. When HB 488 hit, buses brought in members of United Food and Commercial Workers Local 1529 from poultry plants in Scott County, the Laborers union from Laurel, Retail and Wholesale union members from Carthage, African American workers from catfish processing plants in Indianola, and electrical union members from Crystal Spring. The black labor mobilization was largely organized by the new pro-immigrant leadership of the state chapter of the A. Philip Randolph Institute, the AFL-CIO constituency group for black union members.

Catholic congregations, Methodists, Episcopalians, Presbyterians, Evangelical Lutherans, Muslims, and Jews also brought people to protest HB 488, as did the Mississippi Human Services Coalition—all of whom had a long history of working on immigrant issues. And groups around MIRA and the Black Caucus not only fought the immigration bill, but others introduced by Tea Party Republicans. One bill sought to ban abortions if a fetal heartbeat is detected. Another promoted charter schools. A third would have restricted access to workers compensation benefits, while another would have stripped civil service protection from state employees.

Dr. Ivory Phillips, a MIRA director and a member of the Board of Trustees of the Jackson Public Schools, explained that charter school proposals, voter ID bills and anti-immigrant measures are all linked. "Because white supremacists fear losing their status as the dominant group in this country, there is a war against brown people today, just as there has long been a war against Black people," he says. "In all three cases—charter schools, 'immigration reform' and voter ID—what we are witnessing is an anti-democratic surge, a rise in overt racism, and a refusal to provide opportunities to all."

"Because of our history we had a relationship with our allies," Chandler concluded. "We need political alliances that mean something in the long term—permanent alliances, and a strategy for winning political power. That includes targeted voter registration that focuses on specific towns, neighborhoods and precincts." Despite the national importance of stopping the southern march of the anti-immigrant bills, however, the resources for the Mississippi effort were almost all local. MIRA emptied its bank account fighting HB 488, and additional money came mostly from local unions and the Muslim Association. "The resources of the national immigrant rights movement should prioritize preventing bills from passing as much as fighting them after the fact," Chandler warned.

On the surface, the fight in Jackson was a defensive battle waged in the wake of the Republican legislative takeover of the legislature. Yet Evans believes that time is on the side of social change. "We're worried about redistricting, and a Texas-style stacking of the deck," he cautioned. "But in the end, we still believe our same strategy will build power in Mississippi. We don't see last November as a defeat, but as the last stand of the Confederacy."

Some in Arizona drew the same lesson. Reaction to SB 1070 resulted in the recall of State Senator Russell Pearce. His replacement, Jerry Lewis, a more moderate Republican, said, "We need to consider the humane aspects . . . of keeping families together."

Utah's Immigration Bills: A Blast from the Past

In March of 2011, the Utah legislature passed three new laws hailed in the media as a new, more reasonable approach to immigration policy—reasonable, that is, compared to Arizona's SB 1070. Utah's bills were even called "the anti-Arizona" by Frank Sharry, head of America's Voice, a Washington, DC, immigration lobbying firm. According to Lee Hockstader of the *Washington Post*, Utah's laws are "the nation's most liberal—and most reality-based—policy on illegal immigration." The Utah laws, however, were not new and certainly not liberal, at least toward immigrants and workers. Their main provisions—labor supply programs for employers, with deportations and diminished rights for immigrants—have marked US immigration policy for more than a hundred years.

One Utah bill would have established a state system to allow employers to bring people from the Mexican state of Nuevo Leon as "guest workers." Under this program, workers would have to remain employed to stay in the country, and would not have the labor and social rights of people living in the communities around them. Another bill would have given undocumented workers now living in Utah a similar guest worker status, lasting two years. The National Immigration Law Center said the third bill, the Arizona look-alike, "requires police to interrogate individuals and verify their immigration status in a wide array of situations, promoting harmful and costly incentives for law enforcement to racially profile."

Utah has been down this road before. Even given the growth in population, federal deportations are higher now than they were during the Depression-era wave. In the 1930s, "the climate of scathing anti-Mexican sentiment created intense polarization, producing a sweeping suspicion of foreigners . . . which linked housing congestion, strained relief services and social ills to the large presence of Mexicans," recounts Zaragosa Vargas in his history of Chicano labor, *Labor Rights Are Civil Rights*. Most immigrants in Utah at that time were farmworkers, many laboring in sugar-beet fields for the Mormon-backed Utah-Idaho Sugar Company. Their wages were so low that families went hungry even when they were working. When beet workers in nearby Colorado tried to organize a union and went on strike, Vargas says their communities were targeted with deportations.

Then World War II created a labor shortage. To supply workers to growers at low wages, the government started the bracero contract labor program, bringing immigrants first into the beet fields of Stockton, California, and then into the rest of the country in 1942. During World War II, Utah-Idaho Sugar first used labor from the Japanese internment camps in Minidoka, Idaho; Topaz, Utah; and Heart Mountain, Wyoming. When that wasn't enough, they brought in braceros.

Braceros were treated as disposable, dirty and cheap. Herminio Quezada Durán, who came to Utah from Chihuahua, says ranchers often had agreements between each other to exchange or trade braceros as necessary for work. Jose Ezequiel Acevedo Perez, who came from Jerez, Zacatecas, remembers the humiliation of physical exams that treated Mexicans as louse-ridden. "We were stripped naked in front of everyone," he remembers, and sprayed with DDT, now an outlawed pesticide. Men in some camps were victims of criminals and pimps. Juan Contreras, from Tuxtla Gutierrez, Chiapas, recalls that "in Utah, women often went to the camps, and they were rumored to be especially fond of Mexican men."

In the 1950s, at the height of the Cold War, the combination of enforcement and contract labor reached a peak. In 1954, nearly 1.1 million Mexicans were deported from the United States. And from 1956 to 1959, between 432,491 and 445,197 braceros were brought in each year.

The civil rights movement ended the bracero program and created an alternative to the deportation regime. Chicano activists of the 1960s—Ernesto Galarza, Cesar Chavez, Bert Corona, Dolores Huerta, and others—convinced Congress to repeal Public Law 78, the law authorizing the bracero program, in 1964. Farmworkers went on strike in Delano, California, the year after the program ended, and the United Farm Workers was born. In 1965, the same activists also helped convince Congress to pass immigration legislation that established new pathways for legal immigration—the family preference system. People could reunite their families in the United States. Migrants received permanent residency visas, allowing them to live normal lives and enjoy basic human and labor rights. Essentially, a family- and community-oriented system replaced the old labor supply and deportation program.

For the past decade, however, Congress, and now the states, have been sliding back into the Cold War labor supply framework. Congress has debated, and almost passed, bills that sought to accomplish the same goal—vastly increase immigration enforcement and set up huge new guest worker programs. Some undocumented people might have been able to gain legal status under those bills, but most proposals would have forced them into a temporary status, à la Utah. In the end Congress never passed those "comprehensive immigration reform" bills, but that became increasingly irrelevant. Many of their provisions became the reality on the ground—implemented by

administrative action despite Congress' inaction. The number of deportations has grown. Thousands of undocumented workers have
been fired from their jobs as part of the same enforcement policy.
And in California, for instance, where only one grower historically
used the federal H-2A guest worker program for farmworkers, dozens more began using its provisions to bring in contract labor.

Utah's bills follow the same "comprehensive" pattern. Its guest
worker bill was written by a dairy farmer. "The root of this discussion is productivity," said the bill's sponsor, State Representative
Bill Wright. To this conservative Republican, no one, including citizens, has a right to a job. "People think because you're born here . . .
'I have a right to that job, I'm going to charge what I want for my labor even if I'm not productive.' Wrong." Immigrants don't have any
rights to jobs either. If they try to organize and get more expensive,
or they're just lazy and don't work, he warns, they "need to go."

The Utah bills were the product of negotiations, called the Utah
Compact, between the Salt Lake Chamber, a statewide business
group, and the Salt Lake City Police Department and mayor's office.
The Mormon Church of Latter Day Saints and the Catholic Church
signed off on it, as did some local immigrant advocates. The National
Immigration Law Center's Marielena Hincapie, however, called the
Utah laws "fundamentally unconstitutional. Taken together, they
signify an even more sweeping state takeover of federal immigration regulation." Her group supports legislation legalizing undocumented people, and believes it must pass at a federal level.

Some anti-immigrant nativists agreed about the bills' uncon-
stitutionality, but for different reasons. Dan Stein, president of the
anti-immigrant Federation for American Immigration Reform, said,
"States do not have the constitutional authority to write their own
immigration policies." The group wants the federal government to
stop virtually all immigration and deport the twelve million undocumented people living in the United States. It saw the Utah bills as a
weak distraction. On the other hand, it supported Arizona's SB 1070,
despite the fact that it's a state law.

One prominent Washington, DC, immigration think tank, the
Immigration Policy Center, also questioned the constitutionality

of state immigration bills. The think tank, however, supported the labor supply–enforcement tradeoff when it was contained in the federal bills of the last few years. According to the IPC, "Enforcement strategies must be coupled with reform of our legal system of immigration in order to meet legitimate labor force needs." This declaration by one of the most powerful voices in Washington on immigration went beyond questioning the right of states to set immigration policy. It restated the purpose of immigration policy itself, tying enforcement (firings and deportations) to labor supply schemes (work visa programs). The problem of the Utah bills, therefore, was not that they ran counter to that purpose. It was simply that they were state bills, not federal ones.

Some immigration reformers, however, believe that the purpose itself is wrong and argue for a different system, as Chicano and Asian activists did in the 1960s. For them, the purpose of immigration policy should be to give immigrants a way to come to the US with social equality and rights. Among these groups are the Binational Front of Indigenous Organizations in California and Oaxaca, Derechos Humanos in Tucson, Arizona, the Mississippi Immigrants Rights Alliance, and the AFL-CIO's constituency group for Latino workers, the Labor Council for Latin American Advancement.

Utah's laws, especially their guest worker provisions, are not capable of implementation without changes in federal law. In a Republican-controlled Congress in which the Tea Party holds power, political movement toward immigration reform has been deadlocked. No legislation in Salt Lake City can change that. But the purpose of the Utah bills has more to do with popularizing a labor supply–based immigration policy, one with strong corporate support and deep historical roots, in one of the most conservative Republican states in the country. The bills' passage shows clear progress toward that goal.

In the meantime, workplace raids and firings have become part of an overall program for increasing immigration enforcement. One of its most bitterly fought elements is the growing connection between police departments and immigration authorities. Under President Bush, the federal government began implementing "287g" agreements, under which local police departments shared information and turned over to immigration agents people arrested for even minor traffic violations. In a federal program called "Secure Communities," ICE began signing agreements with state and local law enforcement bodies, requiring them to turn over the fingerprints of anyone with whom they came into contact. The Obama administration claimed that it was only seeking criminals for deportation, and that participation in the program was voluntary. But when New York state and Massachusetts formally refused to participate, DHS announced that participation in Secure Communities was mandatory and implemented the program everywhere.

In practice, this increased cooperation led to the detention of hundreds of thousands of immigrants with no criminal record, who were held simply because they were undocumented. Deportations skyrocketed to over a million people in the first two and a half years of the Obama administration. A rising wave of protest met this wave of deportations. In response, the administration called for the passage of "comprehensive immigration reform" as its alternative to criminalization and mass removals—essentially using repression to advance a corporate immigration reform program.

Increased cooperation in the end led to the loss of the government's own suit against Arizona's SB 1070, when in June 2012 the Supreme Court struck down some sections of the law but upheld the provision that encourages racial profiling. The court struck down those sections that make it a state crime for an immigrant not to carry a visa, and a crime for an undocumented person to apply for work. But the court upheld the law's most controversial section, which directs police to question any person they stop about their immigration status if they think the person appears undocumented, as well as any person they arrest.

The court said that while federal authority over immigration law invalidated the measures it overturned, the federal government itself had invited local law enforcement to question people about their status. The court cited the 287g agreements and the Secure Communities program. Familia Latina Unida in Chicago, an organization close to Representative Luis Gutierrez, angrily blamed the Obama administration for sabotaging its own case: "We lost that challenge to the law because the Obama administration had provided federal cover for what they [the Arizona state legislature] were doing." In other words, it was impossible for the federal government to protest a policy that it was mandating itself, other than by claiming that it had sole power to implement such discriminatory measures.

Gabriel Camacho of the American Friends Service Committee said the application of the law "means speaking with an accent, or being a person of color—or any other form of racial profiling—can trigger a profound violation of human rights. Most troubling is this decision undermines the moral fiber of the US Constitution, and can be used by other states to enact laws that also enable racial profiling."

They Pay Us a Wage That Barely Allows Us to Make a Living

The Story of Lucrecia Camacho

Lucrecia Camacho, born in the Mixteca region of Oaxaca, spent her life working in the fields of northern Mexico and California.

I was born in a little town called San Francisco Higos, Oaxaca. I've worked all of my life. I started to work in Baja California when I was a little girl. I've worked in the fields all of my life, because I don't know how to read or write. I never had an opportunity to go to school. I didn't even know what my own name was until I needed my birth certificate for the immigration amnesty paperwork after I'd come to the US.

When I was seven, my mother, stepfather and I hitchhiked from Oaxaca to Mexicali, and I lived there for two years. I spent my childhood in Mexicali during the bracero years. I would see the braceros pass through on their way to Calexico, on the US side. I would beg in the streets of Calexico and they would throw me bread and canned beans on their way back home. I also begged in Tijuana. I'm not ashamed to share that because that is how I grew up.

I began working when I was nine years old. In Culiacan I picked cotton, then I went to work in Ciudad Obregon, Hermosillo, and Baja California. I would get three pesos a day. From that time on, I have spent my entire life working.

When I was thirteen, my mother sold me to a young man, and I was with him for eight months. I soon was pregnant. After I started having children, they were always with me. In Culiacan I would tie my young children to a stake in the dirt while I worked. I tried to work very fast, so that the foreman would give me an opportunity to nurse my child. After I came to the US I did the same thing. I took them to the fields with me and built them a little shaded tent on the side of the field. Every time I completed a row, I would move them closer to me and watch them while I worked. I nursed them during lunch and they would fall asleep while I worked. It was always like that.

In Baja California we didn't even have a home. But my mother also was always with me. It was like I was the man and she was the woman. I gave her all my wages. In Mexico my children struggled in school, because we never stayed in one place too long. I would take them out of school one or two months and them put them back in when we returned. It wasn't until we arrived here in Oxnard that they went to school regularly. So not all of them were able to go to school. My oldest son never did.

I come from a Mixteco town in Oaxaca, but I didn't know how to speak Mixteco when I was young. I learned it later. As a child I spoke Spanish. Two years after my father passed away I came to the US, in 1985. I'd borrowed a lot of money for my father's burial and couldn't pay it back. I didn't want to come to the US because I didn't want to leave my children, but my mother convinced me. I left the kids with her. I became a legal resident in the amnesty program. My employers in Arizona and Gilroy gave me the employment proof I needed, and my two youngest children and I were able to file our paperwork. They became legal residents first and I completed my paperwork in 1989.

I didn't want to leave my mother alone, so I brought her in 1994. My mother died seven years ago, but she was always with me in good times and bad. I had children and she cared for them. She wanted to die in her hometown, so I had to grant her that last wish. I even have great-grandchildren now.

I began working here in the fields in Oxnard when I first arrived in 1985 and worked until last year. I already had seven children by the time I got here. At first they stayed behind with my mother in our little town. Then I brought them in 1989 by paying a *coyote*. I have a sister who lives in Tijuana, and first I brought them from Oaxaca to her home. I'd go to Tijuana every week or two to take them money for food. From there I brought each of them across, one by one. In those times, it cost $1,600 for each one.

Now they charge $7,000, which is nearly impossible to pay because we don't make that much money. It's a sad situation. We want a better life, so we come here. We earn a living, but with a lot of hard work and sweat. It was very hard for me because I have ten children and have always been their mother and father.

I've always been alone, a single mother of ten children. When I got here I traveled with other illegal workers just like myself. I came here because people said money was literally for the taking, but it wasn't true. It was hard to find work in 1985, and immigration authorities picked me up sometimes twice a week. But it was easier to cross the border back then. We were dropped off in San Ysidro, but we just crossed the border again, and were back at work in three days. It wasn't very expensive either. It became more expensive to cross the border in 1987 and 1988.

I first began to work illegally, but I couldn't get steady work. I earned $80 a week in those days. It was difficult to find a place to live. We lived in a small trailer that was rented by many of us, so we literally slept side by side. We would bathe outside, wherever we could find water.

From Oxnard I went to work in Arizona in 1986 because we heard work was bountiful. We struggled a lot, because we didn't have food and lived out of our old car in the orchards where we were working. I earned $7 a day then, but was charged $3 for rent and 50 cents for drinks. We cut asparagus in bunches of thirty-two and placed them in boxes. If the boxes weren't the required weight, they told us to do them again. They hardly paid us anything.

From there I went to work in the green onions. I had to go to work at 2:00 a.m., but we couldn't begin to pick until the dew on the plants had dried, which often meant we didn't start work until 11:00. But we still had to leave at 2:00 a.m., or others would be hired in our place. If we arrived later, we wouldn't get a job. So we'd get in line and build a fire to keep warm and wait for 11:00. I'd work from 11:00 until 1:30, and only earn $3 a day. What am I going to do with $3? Nothing. I sometimes earned $2.

I came back to work in Oxnard after that, in January of 1987, and I couldn't find work. I went to Gilroy, where I was lucky to find a good boss, who rented us a small house. There we harvested bell peppers.

He took good care of us, because immigration officials were everywhere. We began work at 5:00 a.m. and worked until 9:00, which is when they usually came around. We came back to work at two in the afternoon, once they were gone. We were able to work a lot, and didn't go to bed hungry.

I've always worked the strawberry harvest here in Oxnard. I'd finish that in July and go to Gilroy to work the jalapeño peppers, bell peppers, and cherry tomatoes in July. I brought my oldest daughter and son with me, and the three of us worked there. They would get out of school in June and worked July and August with me to earn money for their school clothes. They went back to school the fifteenth of September, so they worked with me forty days. I would bring them back to Oxnard to start school, which is why I couldn't just leave my Oxnard apartment. I'd pay $775 rent for my children to stay in Oxnard, and then $600 for myself in Gilroy. I never had any money left after that, but I had to do it.

I'd take my kids back to Oxnard for school, and return to Gilroy to work all of September and October. I lived in a large room that was divided into smaller rooms. It had a stove and outdoor bathroom. We were paid piece rate, not by the hour. They paid 80 cents for a bucket of jalapeños. Jalapeños with the stem were paid at $1.10 a bucket. I was able to fill thirty-eight to forty a day. I'd get back to Oxnard in the middle of November, rest a bit, and then start the strawberry harvest again about January twentieth. I worked a long time in Gilroy, starting in 1985. It's been six to eight years that I haven't gone. I couldn't find housing one year, and after that they wouldn't hire me anymore.

In the strawberries they also paid piece rate in April, May, and June. The other months they paid by the hour. When I first started, it was $3 an hour and the piece rate was eighty cents a box. The year before last I was paid $8.25 an hour. The regular box rate was $1.25, the little box was $1, and the two-pound box was $1.50. If I was able to fill forty boxes, it was a good day. The younger faster men can pick seventy or eighty boxes a day.

The strawberry harvest looks easy enough, but once you try it, it's hard. I don't wish that kind of work on my worst enemy. When you're young, you work hard and get tired, but once you get home and take a shower you're fine. Now that I'm old, I deal with arthritis and osteoporosis. My feet hurt and they swell. Many workers have been permanently injured. I have a nephew who hurt his back working in the strawberries, and a cousin who died of pneumonia because we work in the mud when it's raining.

We ate bean, potato, and egg tacos. No beef or chicken. We couldn't afford to buy meat. At times we ate vegetables from the fields that had been sprayed with pesticides. We just washed them and ate them anyway. When I was working in the pepper harvest, I would make delicious salsas for my potato and egg tacos.

The fruit that brings the most money here is the strawberry crop, but they pay us a wage that barely allows us to make a living. Then they turn around and sell each box of strawberries for $18 or $20. If we pick eighty boxes, how much do you think they make from that? You'd think the owners would have enough money to pay workers higher wages, but they pay it to the foreman instead. The foreman has a brand new car every year and the worker doesn't get anything. Every year I see foremen driving around in those brand new cars, and I ask myself why.

The foremen now choose workers who can pick 100 to 130 boxes per day. I know one who only hires immigrants without papers because she says legal residents complain too much. They tell the ones without papers they're going to call immigration officials or fire them if they complain. These workers try and stay on the foreman's good side by bringing her homemade tortillas, mole, and even Chinese food. I'm not going to bring her anything, I don't get paid enough.

If the foreman doesn't like you, he makes you redo the work. In the strawberry fields you're always worried that the foreman is going to send you back and tell you to redo your box because it's not full enough. In the morning, as soon as I get to the field, I pick four boxes so that I can have extras in case they tell me I have to redo some of the boxes during the day.

It's always based on if they like you or not. We just have to put our heads down and work quietly. There were many times I stayed quiet and didn't defend a fellow coworker, but one time I did speak up. I had a woman foreman who spoke to us disrespectfully. When

I asked her why she told me to give her my tools and fired me. I told her I didn't understand why I was being treated that way, but the other foreman grabbed me by the arm and told me to leave.

Our work and life is hard here, and we don't see many benefits. When the cost of living was low, our wages were low. When our wages went up, it was only because of the increased cost of living. Have you seen the current gas prices? Before we had to work an hour to cover our cost of gas, and now we have to work two hours. We don't have anything left. The more we earn, the more they take away. We can't move forward.

If you want to get ahead here, you have to live in cramped quarters. Here, the rich even have rooms for their pets, but we have no room for ourselves. When we first moved here, there were about twenty people living in this house. Now that my kids have moved on, there are ten. . . . We needed to share the cost of rent as much as we could. We can pay more now because some of us get decent wages. My daughter gets $12 an hour. She speaks English, Spanish, and other languages.

I tell my kids how much I've struggled. When I worked the strawberry harvest, if I didn't work fast I was fired immediately. I'm old now, so the last four years I was told I worked too slowly. But it's difficult to work in the rain and mud. At times you're lucky and find a good foreman who gives you waterproof ponchos. Other places charge for them, $25 for ponchos and $25 for rain boots.

All my life I've worked in the fields, but the work is harder for me now. I felt so strong when I was younger. I could work twenty-four hours. I don't know if it's old age or my diabetes, but I work a lot slower now. The machine in the strawberry fields goes very fast and it's frustrating to get left behind. I can't fill the amount of boxes I used to. I feel nauseous and get headaches.

They won't give me a job anymore. If the foreman doesn't like you, then you aren't hired. They always choose the pretty women and family members first. As a woman working in the fields, if you didn't have a good foreman, you were treated badly. You had to ask for permission to take a day off, but you were given a ticket. After accumulating three tickets, you were fired. I've also heard complaints of sexual harassment from women. Sometimes women don't want to speak up. There are a lot who have lived through it, but are afraid to say something for fear that they'll be reported to immigration officials.

In Culiacan, when I was young, I had a foreman who always sought out women to be alone with. He told me he liked me, but I told him I knew he had a wife and mistress. He told me that if I let him do what he wanted to me, I would still have a job. If not, I needed to look for another job. I told him he would not see me there the next morning. Some of us women don't take that kind of abuse, but many do what they feel necessary to keep their jobs, even if it means being in the hands of the foreman. My daughter tells me of her factory job and how that still happens there. The women that let the foremen do what they want move up in position. Those that don't stay in their same position.

As long as women accept this, there isn't much that can be done. We need someone to help us and provide us with support. There are only a few of us in Lideres Campesinas [a grassroots organization in California of women farmworkers]. If I had a hidden camera, it would be so easy to show others what we face. Without that, people don't believe what we're saying. When I worked in a plastics factory, a coworker had a doctor's note saying she needed to work in a sitting position. The foreman fired her and then fired me for speaking up and defending her. I think a union would help, but it's been difficult for one to get organized in the Oxnard area. When I began to wear my Lideres Campesinas t-shirt, I was told there wasn't work for me anymore. I've been working here for many years and all of a sudden there wasn't work for me. I've been looking for work ever since.

When I came here I didn't expect a better life. I knew I would have to earn my living with physical labor. I was happy living in Mexico, but I didn't have money even to clothe my children. Here I live better. I have the basics and I thank this country for giving me that. I hope to retire soon and go back to Mexico. I don't plan on staying here. I'll leave neither rich nor poor. The only thing I'll take with me is aches and pains, because it' s not like I have any money to take with me.

We Made Them Millions of Dollars

The Story of Lupe Chavez

I was born in Santa Tecla, near San Salvador. My father was a big rig driver and my mother was a stay-at-home mom. We had a big family—four brothers and two sisters. When I was old enough, I worked in the Armando Araujo coffee and soap factory. We Salvadoreños are hard-working people.

From the time I was twelve, my aunts took me with them whenever they had a demonstration. They were teachers and taught me that we have to fight for what we need, because that's the only way to achieve anything. Even before the war, it was dangerous to be involved with a union. After the war started, many died protesting.

I was nineteen years old when I came to the US to care for an elderly woman. My family was very poor and when the opportunity came I didn't hesitate. The woman eventually returned to El Salvador, but I stayed on with her family. I thought I was going to earn money and help my family, but they didn't pay me for an entire year. They told me I had to repay the transportation fee and all the money they'd spent on me.

A friend of my grandmother told me I was being treated as a slave. She said she'd rescue me, so I found my passport where they'd hidden it, grabbed my bag and left. But my rescuer took me to another home, to care of another elderly woman. They hardly paid me anything—just $100 a month. When I said I wanted to go to school, they told me immigration officers would get me.

Finally I met my husband—a carpenter who'd come to put in new windows. He rescued me and we got married. That was 1974, and we've been married ever since. When I married him I no longer felt like a slave.

I already had a Social Security number—it wasn't so hard to get a number back then—and in 1986 I got my green card through the amnesty. I brought my brothers here too, but I told them that they would never suffer like I did.

In those years we could live in San Francisco because the rent was only $150 for a one-bedroom apartment. Now living in San Francisco is almost impossible, and we moved to the East Bay.

After my first daughter was three I told my husband I wanted to go back to work. I found good daycare and applied at the Hilton. They hired me right away as a housekeeper, the same job I've been doing for 29 years.

Since I've been here for so long I work on only one floor. It's a very big hotel, with three buildings. At the beginning of the day I fill my cart with new linens, towels, pens and everything I'll need. We carry everything from toilet paper to a vacuum cleaner, and the cart easily weighs 100 pounds.

When I get to a room I first organize the hangers in the closet, and make sure it has one pillow and blanket. Then I empty the garbage cans and make the beds. I continue on to the bathroom, clean the tub and toilet, and restock the toilet paper, towels and Kleenex. I clean the mirror, sink, and counter—they have to be spotless. It's hard work to clean the mirrors and shower doors because you have to stretch so much to do it.

Making the beds is backbreaking because they're a lot larger now and you have to lift up the mattress. You have to put three sheets on—the fitted sheet, flat sheet and down comforter. Work wasn't as hard when I first started there because the beds were small with one pillow per bed. Now beds are bigger and some have four pillows. Sometimes guests even ask for four more.

They switched accessories from plastic to silver, which weigh a lot more. We have to lift the ice bucket with both hands to clean it with Windex, soap, or sometimes hot water. The garbage cans are also silver. They warn us that they don't want any fingerprints on them, and managers follow us into the rooms to check. It takes an extra half an hour everyday just to clean the silver accessories.

We have to finish all fourteen assigned rooms by the end of the day. Some of us don't go on breaks or take shorter lunch breaks in order to finish. Recently I had a room with a big family, but in a room with only one bed. I wasted an extra forty minutes because the room was so messy. At the end of the day I was exhausted. When I got home I just wanted to sleep.

Like it or not, there is pressure to have the room spotless. I've seen other workers weep because the job is so hard. It's never good enough and managers want more. I've heard them tell housekeepers that they came to the US to work, so they should work harder. They call them crybabies. I tell them it's not right to make women cry—it just makes it harder to do the work. Because I've been there for so long and I'm very outspoken, they don't follow me around, but I feel pressured too.

In the long run you end up with permanent problems working this way. I now have to wear a brace on my arm. When I don't have it on my arms hurt tremendously. I had to go on disability because my tendons hurt so much. When I returned to work I couldn't take a morning or afternoon break because my legs hurt too much for me to walk down to the break room. I simply stayed up on the floor.

My hands tingle and ache, and my fingers go numb. Sometimes my arms start to hurt during the night and I can't sleep. The pain starts about 3 a.m., and I can't stand it. The doctor said I have carpal tunnel syndrome and gave me two braces, one for each hand. My hands now feel better, but I still use them during the day. I take a Motrin pill before leaving for work in the morning and another one in the afternoon and before going to bed. I don't want to be dependent on them, but it's hard. My doctor told me many housekeepers have the same problem. It's very difficult to work in pain. It's something I cannot get used to.

I have to continue working because I need the insurance. If I don't work, I'm not accumulating hours, and my insurance stops. I had to return to work because I had no insurance left. My husband, daughter and myself depend on it. My daughter's nineteen, and she needs medical checkups and to go to the dentist. My husband has high blood pressure and clogged arteries so he needs expensive medication daily.

My back and knees hurt from moving the heavy cart every day. I don't want to get even more injured than I already am because I'll be replaced. There are many workers still working with disabilities right now. It's like a circus in there when we're changing into uniforms. We all smell like Bengay and have braces all over. We all have medical conditions. They say it's the handicap room, because we're all injured.

With the union at least we feel we have someone who will back us up. I was suspended a few years ago. The manager was upset because I had criticized her during a meeting. The other workers were in an uproar. My union representative told the general manager they were going to protest in the lobby. They called me that afternoon to say I could return to work the next morning. We all fight for each other.

Medical insurance is the most important issue for us this year. They're talking of increasing the hours needed to qualify for health benefits. That is what we're trying to avoid. I just have a few years left until I can retire. I've lost my health at the hotel, and all they think about is money. We made them millions of dollars, and they complain about paying insurance.

FIVE

FIGHTING THE FIRINGS

Mass Firings: The Obama Administration's Workplace Enforcement Policy

Ana Contreras would have been a competitor for the national tae kwon do championship team in 2009, when she was fourteen. For six years she'd gone to practice instead of birthday parties, giving up the friendships most teenagers live for. Then disaster struck. Her mother, Dolores, lost her job. The money for classes was gone, and not just that. "I only bought clothes for her once a year, when my tax refund check came," Dolores Contreras explained. "Now she needs shoes, and I had to tell her we didn't have any money. I stopped the cable and the Internet she needs for school. When my cell phone contract is up next month, I'll stop that too. I've never had enough money for a car, and now we've gone three months without paying the light bill."

Contreras shared her misery with 1,800 other families. All lost their jobs when their employer, American Apparel, fired them for lacking immigration status. She still has the letter from the Department of Homeland Security, handed to her by the company lawyer. It said the documents she provided when she was hired were no good, and without work authorization, her work life there was over. Of course, Contreras still had to keep working if she and her daughter were to eat and pay rent. So instead of a job that barely paid her bills, she had to find another one that wouldn't even do that.

Contreras is a skilled sewing-machine operator. She came to the United States in 1996, after working many years in the garment factories of Tehuacan, Puebla. There companies like Levi Strauss make so many pairs of stonewashed jeans that the town's water has turned blue. In Los Angeles, Contreras hoped to find the money to send home for her sister's weekly dialysis treatments and to pay the living and school expenses for four other siblings. For five years, she moved from shop to shop. Like most garment workers, she didn't get paid for overtime, her paychecks were often short, and sometimes her employer disappeared overnight, owing weeks in back pay.

Finally Contreras got a job at American Apparel, famous for its sexy clothing, made in Los Angeles instead of overseas. She still had to work like a demon. Her team of ten experienced seamstresses turned out thirty dozen tee shirts an hour. After dividing the piece rate evenly among them, she'd come home with $400 for a four-day week, after taxes. She paid Social Security too, although she'll never see a dime in benefits because her contributions were credited to an invented number.

After being fired, Contreras started working again in a sweat-shop at half what she'd earned before. Meanwhile, American Apparel replaced those who were fired. Contreras says the replace-ments are mostly older women with documents, who can't work as fast. "Maybe they sew ten dozen a day apiece," she claimed. "The only operators with papers are the older ones." Younger, faster workers either have no papers, or if they have them, they find better-paying jobs doing something easier. "President Obama is responsible for putting us in this situation," she charged angrily. "This is worse than an immigration raid. They want to keep us from working at all."

Contreras may be angry, but she's not wrong. During the period of her firing the White House website said, "President Obama will remove incentives to enter the country illegally by preventing em-ployers from hiring undocumented workers and enforcing the law." On June 24, 2009, he told Congress that the government was "crack-ing down on employers who are using illegal workers in order to drive down wages—and oftentimes mistreat those workers."

The law Obama is enforcing is the 1986 Immigration Reform and Control Act. Its employer sanctions provision is the legal basis for all the workplace immigration raids and enforcement of the last twenty-three years. "Sanctions pretend to punish employers," says

Bill Ong Hing, law professor at the University of San Francisco. "In reality, they punish workers."

The audit at American Apparel actually began in 2007, under President George W. Bush. In Minneapolis, another Bush-era audit examined the records of janitors employed by American Building Maintenance (ABM). After the election, enforcement actions continued unabated. In May 2009, ABM and Immigration and Customs Enforcement (ICE) told twelve hundred workers that if they didn't provide new documents that showed they could legally work, they would be fired. Weekly firings in groups of three hundred began in October. The janitors belong to Service Employees Local 26 and work at union wages. The terminations took place as the union was negotiating a new contract.

In Los Angeles, 254 workers at Overhill Farms were fired in May of the same year. The company, with over eight hundred employees, was audited by the Internal Revenue Service. According to John Grant, packinghouse division director for Local 770 of the United Food and Commercial Workers, which represents production employees at the food processing plant, "they found discrepancies in the Social Security numbers of many workers. Overhill then sent a letter to 254 people—all members of our union—giving them thirty days to reconcile their numbers."

Then the company stopped the production lines and sent everyone home, saying, according to worker Isela Hernandez, that "there would be no work until they called us to come back." For 254 people, that call never came. According to Alex Auerbach, spokesperson for Overhill Farms, "The company was required by federal law to terminate these employees because they had invalid Social Security numbers. To do otherwise would have exposed both the employees and the company to criminal and civil prosecution."

"We asked to see the IRS letter or any other documents related to this," Grant responded. "We've never heard of the IRS demanding the termination of a worker. They never showed us any letter." Some of the terminated workers actually had valid Social Security numbers, but were fired anyway. Workers accused the company of hiring replacements, classified as "part-timers," who didn't receive the benefits in the union contract. "By getting rid of the regular workers, to whom they have to pay benefits, they're saving a lot of money," worker Lucia Vasquez charged. Auerbach said the replacements were paid at the same rate, although he acknowledged they lacked benefits.

In the fall of 2010 Chipotle restaurants, a chain that made its fortune selling Mexican food made by Mexican workers, fired hundreds of those workers throughout Minnesota. One was Alejandro Juarez, who'd spent five years at the Calhoun Lake Chipotle in Minneapolis. Juarez came to the United States nine years earlier, leaving two daughters and a wife at home in Mexico. Once he arrived, he couldn't risk going back, not even once, to see them grow up. Crossing back over the border to return to work would have cost more than $2,500, he said, a prohibitive expense for a fast-food worker. Over the years Juarez learned how to fix stoves, grills, refrigerators, and hot tables, for which he was paid $9.42 an hour. He worked hard, sent money home, put his girls through school, and knew their voices only from the telephone.

In the restaurant, he said, you couldn't think about that because the company had a rule that you had to smile all the time. "People would come to work leaving sick kids at home, not able to get enough hours to pay the rent, and then had to smile for fear of losing their job," he recalled. "It was humiliating."

In December of 2010, he and coworkers all over the state were called in by managers. ICE had audited the company records, they said, and told Chipotle to fire them. After losing their jobs, the workers got in touch with the Center for Workers United in Struggle, a local workers' center, and the Minnesota Immigrant Rights Action Committee. They formed an alliance with SEIU Local 26 to fight for back wages and vacation pay. Supporters were even arrested in civil disobedience at a Chipotle restaurant.

Almost none of the displaced farmers and workers coming north and crossing the US-Mexico border, like Alejandro Juarez, can get visas. They therefore can't get Social Security cards or "work authorization" either. Hungry migrants invent or borrow numbers, give them to managers at Chipotle and thousands of other employers, and go to work for the lowest wages in the US economy. Social Security payments are deducted from their paychecks, but since they're working with bad numbers, they'll never collect benefits when they get old or sick. The money stays in the Social Security fund. In essence, it subsidizes the payments to every person collecting retirement or disability benefits.

ICE says it punishes employers who "force [workers] to endure intolerable working conditions." Curing intolerable conditions by firing or deporting the workers who endure them doesn't help the workers or change the conditions, however—and that's not who ICE targets anyway. Workers at Smithfield were trying to organize a union to improve conditions. Overhill Farms has a union. American Apparel pays better than most garment factories. In Minneapolis, the twelve hundred fired janitors got a higher wage than non-union workers—and they had to strike to win it. The history of workplace immigration enforcement is filled with examples of employers who use audits and discrepancies as pretexts to discharge union militants or discourage worker organization.

ICE's campaign of audits and firings, which SEIU Local 26 president Javier Murillo called "the Obama enforcement policy," targets the same set of employers the Bush raids went after—union companies or those with organizing drives. If anything, ICE seems intent on punishing undocumented workers who earn too much, or who become too visible by demanding higher wages and organizing unions. At American Apparel in Los Angeles, and at ABM, the janitorial employer in Minneapolis, the companies were rewarded for cooperation by being immunized from prosecution. ICE threatened to fine Dov Charney, American Apparel's owner, but then withdrew the threat, according to attorney Peter Schey. Murillo says, "The promise made during the audit is that if the company cooperates and complies, they won't be fined." If the employer does have to pay a fine, it's treated as another cost of doing business. "So this policy really only hurts workers," Murillo charges.

The justification implicit in the policy announced on the White House site—"remove incentives to enter the country illegally"—was the original justification for employer sanctions in 1986. If migrants can't work, they won't come. It is also the justification for SB 1070 and written into the preamble for all the ALEC-sponsored laws: to make "attrition through enforcement" public policy. It is difficult for the Justice Department to challenge the discriminatory intent of SB 1070 in a lawsuit because it endorses the same idea as the principle behind federal immigration enforcement in the workplace.

In reality, no one in the Obama or Bush administrations, or in the Clinton administration before them, has wanted to stop migration to the United States or imagined that this could be done without catastrophic consequences. The very industries they target for enforcement are so dependent on the labor of migrants they would collapse without it. Instead, immigration policy and enforcement consign migrants in those industries to an "illegal" status, and this undermines the price of their labor. Enforcement becomes a means for managing the flow of migrants, and making their labor available to employers at a price they want to pay.

Bush's secretary of homeland security, Michael Chertoff, explained this apparent contradiction in policy by saying the purpose of enforcement was to "close the back door and open the front door." The intent of that policy was clear when ICE agents did an audit of the I-9 forms in 2010 at Gebbers Farms, an apple grower in remote eastern Washington. At ICE's insistence, Gebbers fired five hundred workers, some of whom had worked at the ranch for years. In the tiny town of Brewster (population 2,100), 90 percent of the school students were Mexican. After the firings, Gebbers applied for twelve hundred H-2A visas, allowing it to bring workers from other countries (including three hundred from Jamaica) to pick its crops. Their visas were tied to their jobs, and these "guest workers" had to leave once the work was done.

Enforcement didn't do away with immigrant labor at Gebbers Farms. It allowed a grower to bring in workers under even more exploitative conditions. Their children will never be with them in the United States, much less see the inside of that Brewster school. "We have to look at the whole picture," urged Renee Saucedo, former director of San Francisco's day labor program. "So long as we have trade agreements like NAFTA that create poverty in countries like Mexico, people will continue to come here, no matter how many walls we build. But instead of turning some into guest workers, while firing and even jailing others who don't have papers, we need to help people get legal status and repeal the laws that make work a crime."

That is not the Obama administration's policy, however. Homeland Security secretary Janet Napolitano has called on employers to screen new hires using E-Verify, and said those who do so will be entitled to put a special logo on their products stating "I E-Verify." John T. Morton, assistant secretary for ICE, told the *New York Times* in November 2009 that the 654 companies audited in 2008 and early 2009 were just a beginning, and that audits would be expanded to an additional 1,000 companies. "All manner of companies face the very real possibility that the government . . . is going to come knocking on the door," he warned. Since President Obama took office, thousands of workers have been fired. No one, except perhaps ICE, knows exactly how many. But by 2010, Morton announced, ICE had audited more than 2,900 companies.

This growing wave of firings has provoked sharp debate in unions, especially those with large immigrant memberships. Many of the food processing workers at Overhill Farms or janitors at ABM have been dues-paying members for years. They expected the union to defend them when the company fired them for lack of status. "The union should try to stop people from losing their jobs," demanded Erlinda Silerio, an Overhill Farms worker. "It should try to get the company to hire us back, and pay compensation for the time we've been out."

At American Apparel, although there was no union, some workers had actively tried to form one in past years. Jose Covarrubias got a job as a cleaner when the garment union was helping them. "I'd worked with the International Ladies' Garment Workers and the Garment Workers Center before," he recalled, "in sweatshops where we sued the owners when they disappeared without paying us. When I got to American Apparel, I joined right away. I debated with the non-union workers, trying to convince them the union would defend us."

The twelve million undocumented workers in the United States include lots of people like Covarrubias. Many are aware of their rights and anxious to improve their lives. National union organizing campaigns, like Justice for Janitors and Hotel Workers Rising, depend on the determination and activism of immigrants, documented and undocumented alike. That reality finally convinced the AFL-CIO in 1999 to reject the federation's former support for employer sanctions and call for their repeal. Unions recognized that workplace immigration enforcement made it much more difficult for workers to defend their rights, organize unions, and raise wages.

Opposing sanctions, however, put labor in opposition to the Obama administration, which it helped elect. Some Washington, DC, lobbying groups decided to support the administration policy of sanctions enforcement instead of fighting it. One of them, Reform Immigration for America, announced on its website that "any employment verification system should determine employment authorization accurately and efficiently." Verification of authorization is exactly what happened at American Apparel and ABM. It inevitably leads to firings. In 2009, the AFL-CIO and the Change to Win labor federations also agreed to support a "secure and effective worker authorization mechanism . . . one that determines employment authorization accurately while providing maximum protection for workers."

But if the "authorization mechanism" means that Covarrubias gets fired, no "maximum protection" will put him back to work. Instead, Covarrubias urged, "we need the unity of workers. There are fifteen million people in the AFL-CIO. They have a lot of economic and political power. Why don't they oppose these firings and defend us? We've contributed to this movement for twenty years, and we're not leaving. We're going to stay and fight for a more just immigration reform."

The Firings Spread, along with Resistance

In the fall of 2010, federal immigration authorities pressured one of San Francisco's major building service companies, ABM, into firing hundreds of its own workers. Some 475 janitors were told that unless they could show legal immigration status, they would lose their jobs. ABM has been a union company for decades, and many of the workers had been there for a good part of their lives. "They've been working in the buildings downtown for fifteen, twenty, some as many as twenty-seven years," said Olga Miranda, president of Service Employees Local 87. "They've built homes. They've provided for their families. They've sent their kids to college. They're not new workers. They didn't just get here a year ago."

ABM is one of the largest building service companies in the country, and it appeared that union janitorial companies had become targets of the Obama administration's immigration enforcement program. "Homeland Security is going after employers that are union," Miranda charged. "They're going after employers that give benefits and are paying above the average."

The San Francisco janitors were faced with an agonizing dilemma. Should they turn themselves in to Homeland Security, who might charge them with providing a bad Social Security number to their employer and hold them for deportation? For workers with families, homes and deep roots in a community, it wasn't possible to just walk away and disappear. "I have a lot of members who are single mothers whose children were born here," Miranda said. "I have a member whose child has leukemia. What are they supposed to do? Leave their children here and go back to Mexico and wait? And wait for what?"

Union leaders like Miranda see a conflict between the rhetoric used by the president and other Washington, DC, politicians and lobbyists in condemning Arizona law SB 1070 and these immigration enforcement actions. "There's a huge contradiction here," she said. "You can't tell one state that what they're doing is criminalizing people and at the same time go after employers paying more than a living wage and the workers who have fought for that wage."

In July 2011, over 1,400 Los Angeles janitors, members of United Service Workers West SEIU, protested more firings by Able Building Maintenance, another janitorial services company. The company fired workers whose immigration status it suddenly questioned, even though the workers had been cleaning office buildings in downtown

Los Angeles for years. In protest, workers marched through the financial district at lunch hour, stopping in front of buildings where Able had the cleaning contract. They finally sat down in an intersection, stopping traffic.

These mass firings were called "silent raids" in the press, because they relied on cooperation between employers and immigration officials and removed workers from the workplace by firing them, instead of through the highly publicized raids by armed agents in black uniforms that took place during the Bush administration. Paraphrasing Woody Guthrie's "Ballad of Pretty Boy Floyd," one organizer commented bitterly, "They used to rob workers of their jobs with a gun—now they do it with a fountain pen." Silence also described the lack of outcry on behalf of workers losing their jobs. No delegations of immigrant rights activists traveled to Washington, DC, to protest. Unions said little, even as their own members were fired. And undocumented workers themselves were afraid. Those working feared losing their jobs. Those already terminated worried that immigration agents might come knocking on their doors at night. As the raids hit West Coast janitors, however, protests began to break that silence.

Labor and immigrant rights activists accused Obama administration officials of targeting union employers. In non-union garment sweatshops and small restaurants, they charged, finding and inspecting the I-9 immigration forms in personnel records is difficult, time-consuming and laborious. On the other hand, unions generally force employers to keep records in good order to ensure they adhere to the pay levels, benefits, and worker rights in labor agreements. In those companies, immigration agents easily sweep in and build their case for firings.

Employers also often found advantages in demanding that their workers re-verify their immigration status. At Able Building Maintenance in Los Angeles, the company used the process to lower its labor costs. Every time Able took over a new building from another janitorial contractor, it demanded that the workers provide new proof of their legal status. When some couldn't, the company fired them and replaced them with new hires at much lower wages and benefit levels. These actions violated the intent of the union's master janitorial contract. That agreement says that when one building service company is brought in to replace another to clean a downtown building, it must continue to employ the workers who have always done that work. The agreement provides workers some job security in an industry where contractors change constantly. Although companies compete fiercely against each other, they can't gain advantage by firing high-wage workers and replacing them with low-wage ones.

But Able was able to use immigration status as a pretext to terminate longtime janitors in Los Angeles high-rises. The thousand workers who marched among those same buildings in protest not only feared Able would continue to fire them, but that other companies would use the same tactic to lower costs in order to compete. Workers at Stanford University made similar accusations, after one union janitorial contractor was replaced by another. When the new contractor demanded that longtime employees re-verify their immigration status, nineteen were fired.

At Pacific Steel Castings in Berkeley, the largest steel foundry west of the Mississippi River, ICE gained access to the company's I-9 and other personnel records in February 2011 and began its audit. Union contract negotiations had begun just weeks before. In March the foundry's workers struck for a week, successfully defending their medical benefits. Conducting an audit in the middle of a labor dispute violates an internal operating procedure dating from the Clinton administration, in which ICE is barred from workplace enforcement actions during labor disputes. In May, therefore, the union filed an unfair labor practice charge against the company and ICE, accusing them of violating the instruction in order to punish union activity.

To win support for workers threatened with termination, Glass, Molders, Pottery, and Plastics Workers (or GMP) Local 164B and other local unions pointed to the disastrous effect firings would have on the community. "If these skilled workers are removed from the foundry, the operation of the business will suffer greatly," said Josie Camacho, executive secretary of the Alameda Labor Council. "If the foundry were to close as a consequence, it would be an economic disaster for the Bay Area. The company and the workers pay taxes that support local schools and services, which cannot afford to lose money desperately needed in these challenging economic times."

In addition to city council resolutions, many elected officials, churches and immigrant rights organizations wrote to the Department of Homeland Security voicing opposition to the immigration audit. "These audits affect workers in many other workplaces beyond Pacific Steel," added Camacho. "They could deepen unemployment and make recovery from the current recession more difficult. That should concern the administration as it faces a national election in 2012." Mike Garcia, president of United Service Workers West, SEIU, which represents the Able janitors, suggested that every labor council survey unions in its area to find out where the audits and firings were taking place. In its effort to encourage worker participation in their own defense, Local 164B organized an immigration clinic in which a dozen attorneys from legal aid organizations talked to employees one on one to help them resolve their status questions. And as undocumented students did in their campaign to pass the Dream Act, some workers began to speak out publicly.

The Pacific Steel and Able protests marked rising opposition in unions to the I-9 audits. "The union is responsible for representing and protecting union members against any violation of human rights," said Ignacio DeLaFuente, international vice president of the GMP. The audits also began to cause some unions to question support for key elements of the comprehensive immigration reform (CIR) bills that Congress had been debating, especially the proposals for beefed-up workplace enforcement.

When employer sanctions were passed as part of the Immigration Reform and Control Act in 1986, the AFL-CIO supported them, despite significant local opposition. Sanctions were justified as a means to force undocumented workers to leave the country and to discourage others from coming, a justification still used today by some supporters. Over the following thirteen years, however, unions saw sanctions used by employers to threaten and fire workers when they tried to organize or enforce minimum wages and labor standards. After a growing outcry, the AFL-CIO then reversed its position at its 1999 convention in Los Angeles. Its new position called for the repeal of employer sanctions, legalization of the undocumented, and enforcing labor rights for all workers.

Under the Bush administration, however, as CIR bills were introduced with massive employer support, parts of the labor movement began to call for the "fair enforcement" of sanctions. Some unions saw sanctions as a means to get rid of workers viewed as "low-wage competitors," while others saw support for sanctions as a tradeoff that could lead to legalization for the undocumented. Almost all the CIR bills would have increased audits and penalties on employers for hiring undocumented workers. Many included mandating use of the E-Verify database and a national ID program to make it easier for ICE to find and fire people. The Obama administration not only supported the CIR approach but also implemented many of the enforcement measures those bills proposed. As a result, firings skyrocketed, while deportations rose to almost four hundred thousand per year in each year of the administration's first term.

Renee Saucedo, attorney for La Raza Centro Legal and former director of the San Francisco Day Labor Program, was critical of the support given to the CIR proposals. "Those bills, which were presented as ones to help some people get legal status, would actually have made things much worse," she charged. Because the White House is essentially implementing by administrative action many of their enforcement provisions, Saucedo added, "We'll see many more firings like the janitors here, and more punishments for people who are just working and trying to support their families."

The Bush and Obama administrations did not need congressional approval for more enforcement. Many unions were paralyzed, finding it difficult to support increased enforcement in CIR bills in Washington, and then oppose that same enforcement when it led to the firing of their own members. The Pacific Steel and Able protests became part of a growing challenge to this paralysis.

In the Bay Area, labor councils in San Francisco, Silicon Valley, and Alameda County all passed resolutions calling for the repeal of sanctions. Twelve years ago, the Alameda council had authored the original resolution that changed the AFL-CIO position at its 1999 convention in Los Angeles. In a new resolution passed unanimously in June 2011, the council "reiterates its support for the immigration reform proposal it first proposed in 1999, which was then adopted by the AFL-CIO Convention." The three Central Labor Council resolutions, also passed by the national convention of the Labor Council for Latin American Advancement, called for support for an alternative to the CIR tradeoff called the Dignity Campaign, which called for repealing sanctions.

In November 2011, however, ICE sent Pacific Steel a letter listing the names of the individuals it insisted lacked visas. Since the workers could not provide other valid documents, ICE demanded that the company fire them. In December 2011 and January 2012, 214 Pacific Steel workers were finally fired after a year-long campaign to try to stop the terminations. They'd held meetings in union halls and churches, distributed food to families hungry because they could no longer work, and spoken to elected officials. About half the workers live in nearby Richmond and San Pablo. Richmond mayor Gayle McLaughlin condemned the firings and accused ICE of undermining the city's already devastated economy in the middle of a recession. "Their firing is a violation of their human rights," she said at a local food drive for the workers. "When they say that these raids are targeting criminals, it's not true. People who are just trying to make a living are being targeted big time."

In February 2012 hundreds of the workers, their wives, husbands, children, and supporters marched through downtown Berkeley, protesting their firing from Pacific Steel. Starting at City Hall, they walked for an hour past stores and homes, as bystanders often applauded. Teachers and students at one school along the route even came out to the sidewalk to urge them on. At a rally before the march started, fired worker Jesus Prado told the assembled crowd, "I worked for Pacific Steel for seven years. We've organized this March for Dignity because we want to stop the way they're stepping on us, and treating us like criminals. We came here to work, not to break any laws."

"Many of us are buying homes, or have lived in our homes for years," added another fired worker, Ana Castaño. "We have children in the schools. We pay taxes and contribute to our community.

What is happening to us is not just, and hurts our families. All we did was work. That shouldn't be treated like it's a crime." Berkeley City Councilmember Jesse Arreguin agreed. "We're here today to send a message to the Obama administration that the I-9 raids have to stop," he told the crowd.

The march was the culmination of months of debate in which workers weighed the consequences of making their firings public, and therefore their immigration status as well. "We know Berkeley is a sanctuary city," one worker explained. "This is about the safest place we can think of to have this march. What happened to us was unjust, and we feel we have to protest, if not for ourselves, then for others who face the same injustice." Throughout the march, chants and shouts condemned the Obama administration. Activists in the crowd pointed out that President Obama was attacking the communities of immigrants and people of color who were his strongest supporters in his 2008 presidential election campaign. At the time, candidate Obama said he'd work to reform immigration law so that immigrants could enjoy greater rights. Once in office, however, the administration vastly expanded I-9 audits and firings.

Councilman Arreguin, one of the first elected officials to support the workers last year, added, "The workers' paychecks inject hundreds of thousands of dollars into our local economy every month that support other businesses and families. All this is placed in jeopardy by the audit. It is not necessary to enforce immigration law in a way that is so destructive to workers, their families, their employer, and our entire community." Some other public officials, however, attacked the idea that local communities should defend the workers, and said the workers were "stealing jobs," despite the fact that many of those fired had worked over a decade in the foundry. Arreguin responded, "An immigration audit leading to the firing of these workers will not create a single job. Instead, it will force them into the underground economy where illegal wages and conditions are prevalent. It will not improve wages and conditions in the foundry. There is already a union contract in place that guarantees health care, pensions, and wages that can support families."

On the day of the march, the company and union released a joint statement, in which Pacific Steel declared, "These terminations were not only devastating to the workers and their families, but also to the workforce at PSC. The company is proud to have a workforce of extraordinary longevity and skill. Many PSC employees have worked here for decades, earning generous wages and benefits for their hard work and dedication to the company. . . . [We] implore the protestors to direct their attention to the Department of Homeland Security and federal policy makers." The union also criticized "the broken and unfair laws used by the government to disrupt and destroy the lives of many of our friends and colleagues."

The rallies that began and ended the march made the human cost of the firings plain. Metzli Blanco Castaño, the daughter of Ana Castaño and David Herrera, both fired Pacific Steel workers, told supporters of her concern for her own future. "I've lived in the Bay Area my entire life and now I might not be able to stay," she said. Like many others, her parents had exhausted their savings, and their home was in foreclosure. One of the justifications made by Obama administration officials for the audits is that if undocumented immigrants cannot work or find other jobs, they'll be forced to leave the country in a process euphemistically called "self-deportation." Yet among the 214 workers and their families, hardly anyone planned to return to Mexico. "We came because there was no work for us in Mexico and we couldn't survive," said David Herrera, Metzli's father. "That hasn't changed. There's nothing to return to."

Bill Ong Hing, law professor at the University of San Francisco, described the administration's justification as divorced from reality: "Employer sanctions have not reduced undocumented migration at all. They've failed because NAFTA and globalization create great migration pressure. Trying to discourage workers from coming by arresting them for working without authorization, or trying to prevent them from finding work, is doomed to fail in the face of such economic pressure. To reduce it, we need to change our trade and economic policies so that they don't produce poverty in countries like Mexico."

Reverend Deborah Lee of the Interfaith Coalition for Immigrant Rights called the firings a violation of the workers' basic human rights. "These families have done nothing wrong," she said. "They're being punished for working, which is what people in our community are supposed to do. We will not let this happen in silence, nor allow these workers to be treated as though they are invisible."

As hundreds of people filled Second Street, a block away from the foundry where they'd put in their years of labor, the fired workers were certainly not invisible any longer.

Protest Tactics Cross the Border

One of the organizations Pacific Steel workers turned to when they began organizing their march was Occupy Oakland. Although they feared conflict with the police, which might have resulted in arrests leading to deportations, they saw the Occupy protests, especially the tent encampments, as a familiar tactic. And in some cases, the young people involved in setting up those encampments not only knew about the strategies used by workers like the SME in Mexico City, but actively sought to emulate them.

When Occupy Seattle called its tent camp "Planton Seattle," camp organizers were laying a local claim to a set of tactics used for decades by social movements in Mexico, Central America, and the Philippines. And when immigrant janitors marched down to the detention center in San Diego and called their effort Occupy ICE, people from countries with that planton tradition were connecting it to the Occupy movement here.

This shared culture and history offered possibilities to the Occupy movement for survival and growth at a time when the federal law enforcement establishment, in cooperation with local police departments and municipal governments, had uprooted many tent encampments. Different Occupy groups from Wall Street to San Francisco began to explore their relationship with immigrant social movements in the United States, and to look more closely at the actions of the 1 percent beyond the borders, which produce much of the pressure for migration.

Reacting to the evictions in the fall of 2011, the Coalition for the Political Rights of Mexicans Abroad sent a support letter to Occupy

Wall Street and the other camps under attack. "We greet your movement," it declared, "because your struggle against the suppression of human rights and against social and economic injustice has been a fundamental part of our struggle, that of the Mexican people who cross borders, and the millions of Mexican migrants who live in the United States."

Many of those migrants living in the United States know the tradition of the planton and how it's used at home. And they know that the 1 percent, whose power was being challenged on Wall Street, also designed the policies that are the reason why immigrants are living in the United States to begin with. Mike Garcia, president of United Service Workers West, SEIU, the union that organized Occupy ICE, described immigrant janitors as "displaced workers of the new global economic order, an order led by the West, and the United States in particular."

Criminalizing the act of camping out in a public space is intended, at least in part, to keep a planton tradition from acquiring the same legitimacy in the United States that it has in other countries. That right to a planton was not freely conceded by the rulers of Mexico, El Salvador or the Philippines, however—no more than it has been conceded in the United States. The 99 percent of those countries had to fight for it.

Two of the biggest battles of modern Mexican political history were fought in the Tlatelolco Plaza, where hundreds of students were gunned down in 1968, and three years later in Mexico City streets, where more were beaten and shot by the government-backed paramilitary group Los Halcones. In both El Salvador and the Philippines, strikers have a tradition of living at the gates of the factory or enterprise where they work. But even today that right must be defended against the police and (at least until the recent election of the Funes and Aquino governments in those two countries) even the military.

Plantons, or encampments, don't stand alone. They are tactics used by unions, students, farmers, indigenous organizations, and other social movements. Each planton is a visible piece of a movement or organization—a much larger base. When the plantons are useful to those movements, they defend them. That connection between planton and movement, between the encampment and its social base, is as important as holding the physical space on which the tents are erected.

For the last two years that relationship was very clear in the zocalo, Mexico City's huge central plaza. During that time, fired members of Mexico's independent left-wing electrical workers union, the SME, lived in a succession of plantons. They were often elaborate, with kitchens, meeting rooms, and communications centers, in addition to the tents where people slept and ate.

At various times, the SME encampment was one of several in the huge square. In 2010 the workers were joined by indigenous Triqui and Mixtec women from Oaxaca, who protested the violence used by their state's previous governor against teachers' strikes and in Triqui towns like San Juan Copala. The social movement in Oaxaca, of which those women were a part, grew strong enough to finally knock the old ruling party, the Institutional Revolutionary Party (PRI), from the governorship it had held for almost eighty years.

In the zocalo plantons, members of different organizations mixed it up on the Day of the Indignant in September 2011, which brought together people from very diverse movements. Some saw electoral politics as a vehicle for change, while other indigenous activists and SME members didn't. Even among those who did, there were deep disagreements over how to participate in the electoral process. But the people in the zocalo had two things in common. Different plantons may not see every political question eye to eye, but each represented a social movement in the world outside the plaza. And the planton itself had value primarily because it forced public attention to focus on the crisis that led each group to set up its encampment.

The SME workers used their plantons to dramatize repression by the federal government. In 2010, several SME members conducted a hunger strike at the planton that generated front-page headlines for weeks, lasting so long that doctors warned participants they were risking death. At the height of the protest, the union battled police in front of the power stations, as it tried to exercise its legal right to strike and picket. The planton and the movement outside it were intimately connected. The hunger strikers were few but spoke for a union of tens of thousands of workers. In the end, the SME negotiated the removal of its last planton in return for government acknowledgment of its right to exist. It organized other unions to resist the government's assault on labor rights, and mobilized electricity consumers to protest rising bills and cuts in service. The planton helped to focus attention on these demands, and to pull the union's allies into action.

Clearly someone in Seattle knew this tradition of plantons in the zocalo, perhaps even as a participant. When the painter made the "Planton Seattle" banner that flew at the edge of the Occupy Seattle encampment, she or he also included, next to the word "planton," the anarchists' "A" with the circle around it. This symbol was a reminder of another aspect of cross-border fertilization. Many anarchists or anarcho-syndicalists—members of the Industrial Workers of the World—fought in the Mexican Revolution. Because of that revolutionary upheaval, even today, almost a century later, ordinary Mexicans expect certain rights, including the right to set up a tent in the Zocalo. US workers crossed the border to fight alongside Mexicans in that insurrection long ago for a government that would acknowledge that right. The planton, therefore, is a common heritage, with a history that makes it as legitimate on Wall Street as it is in Mexico City.

Not long after the Occupy Wall Street camp was set up in Zuccotti Park, the planton-Occupy movement crossed the US-Mexico border yet again. In Tijuana, home to a million people, mostly displaced migrants from Mexico's south, activists came together to set up an occupation on the grassy median of the Paseo de los Heroes. Their tents were pitched in the middle of the Zona del Rio, where the city's 1 percent meet in fancy hotels and work in government offices. Then, on October 18, police reacted even earlier than they did in most US cities, arresting two dozen activists at the urging of local businessmen. Occupy Tijuana condemned the detentions, declaring, "We are not assassins, delinquents, tramps, or crooks."

The United States has its own history of defending public space for protest, and it isn't necessary to reach back a hundred years to find it. In just the last few decades, immigrant workers have popularized the use of the planton, helping unions recover the militant tactics of their own past. In 1992 immigrants trying to join the United Electrical Workers mounted the first strike among production workers in Silicon Valley and set up a planton and conducted a hunger strike to pressure their employer. A year later, other Latino immigrants in San Francisco erected their tents on the sidewalk in front of Sprint's headquarters after their workplace was closed days before they were scheduled to vote in a union election. More recently, in 2008, when workers at the Republic Windows and Doors plant in Chicago were told that the factory would close, they occupied it until an agreement was reached with the bank holding the company's loan to keep it open.

More than a decade ago, antiglobalization activists and unions shut down the meeting of the World Trade Organization in Seattle. Young protestors chained their arms together inside metal pipes and lay down in the intersections of downtown Seattle. Tens of thousands took over the streets. Other antiglobalization protests followed, in which activists battled for their right to use public space to challenge the international policies of the 1 percent. There was extensive working-class and trade union support for the battle in Seattle, which had its roots in the impact of the North American Free Trade Agreement. Workers could see the cost of free trade in the loss of their own jobs as production moved south. Over the last two decades, many also discovered that those same agreements and policies didn't make Mexicans better off, but led to their impoverishment as well.

NAFTA and free market policies forced on developing countries produced opportunities for banks and corporations to reap profits. They drove down wages, forced farmers off their land, and destroyed the unions and livelihood of millions of people. This system was designed on Wall Street, by the same bankers Occupiers hold responsible for the current crisis of foreclosures and unemployment in the United States. The current economic crisis doesn't stop at the border. In fact in Mexico, Central America, the Philippines and elsewhere, it's been a fact of life for a long time. This is the source of forced migration—what Mike Garcia of United Service Workers West,

SEIU, condemned at Occupy ICE. The 99 percent live in all those countries where free trade agreements and structural adjustment policies are imposed. They also live in the communities of people who have migrated across borders as a result. Who, then, were more natural allies for Occupy protestors than people who'd been on the receiving end of these policies for years?

In New York, this connection wasn't lost on Occupy Wall Street. In October 2011 a group, Occupy Wall Street-Español was formed at the first Asamblea en Español. They, in turn, translated the first issue of the *Occupied Wall Street Journal*, the activists' newspaper. Participants formed a subgroup, Occupy Wall Street Latinoamericano, to spread the movement to Spanish-speaking communities, recognizing that the city is home to so many Mexicans from the state of Puebla that its nickname is Puebla York, as well as much older established communities of Puerto Ricans, Colombians, Ecuadorians, and other Spanish-speaking people. The group also sought to publish its own newspaper, with articles talking about immigration, globalization, and the specific attacks by the 1 percent on Latinos. Claudia Villegas, a women's rights activist working with the group Occupy Wall Street Latinoamericano, helped organize a demonstration of immigrant women four days after police raided the Zuccotti Park encampment. "We decided to change our original plan for a march because we were afraid they would stop it," she says. "Nevertheless, twenty-three organizations participated, including women's rights groups and, above all, those working with immigrant women."

In San Francisco, a joint march of immigrant activists and Occupy participants helped to defend that city's encampment. In the general assembly meeting preceding it, participants talked about the city's offer to move the Occupiers into an abandoned building in the Latino Mission District several miles away. Few wanted to give up the camp on the waterfront in Justin Herman Plaza, and most felt the city was just trying to move them out of sight. But many people also felt that having an Occupy camp in the barrio was a good idea.

"We're still really working in parallel," Villegas said. She drew attention to the potential power of the immigrant rights movement and what it could mean to Occupy activists. "We have to include the movement that began in 2006, when there were hundreds of thousands of people in the streets across this country. People were reacting to the injustice of the system then too." They're separate movements, though, she warned, and "our agenda has to come from immigrants themselves. We need to integrate, and at the same time the Occupy movement has to learn to accept us. But we're all on the same path."

Bringing the immigrant and Occupy movements together meant more than setting up an encampment. In San Diego, the Occupy ICE demonstration didn't set up an overnight camp, but in November 2011 it brought thousands of workers and supporters down to the ICE detention center to protest the firings of immigrant janitors. The Occupy ICE protest was intended to draw public attention to the federal government's immigration enforcement strategy of I-9 audits and firings. In Southern California, the multinational corporations that clean office buildings had threatened to terminate two thousand union members.

Garcia said ICE and the employers were in collusion. "To hide their greed, the commercial real estate industry has used the tools of government to confuse and divide the 99 percent," he charged. "They first said we were unskilled workers who should be happy to be working. They then weakened worker protections to make organizing virtually impossible. Over the last decade, the industry has used immigration as a wedge to intimidate and, if need be, replace our workers. ICE is doing what the 1 percent corporate real estate industry wants: using immigration laws to recycle well-paid janitors in the hopes of taking back gains in pay and benefits our union has won." Ironically, the week United Service Workers West, the janitors' union, organized Occupy ICE, its parent union, SEIU, endorsed the reelection of President Obama. However, four Latino members of the international union's executive board couldn't stomach the contradiction and voted against the endorsement.

For Occupy, defending workers under attack was a way to survive, grow roots and develop a strong base. Although Occupy Oakland initially ignored the firing of the Pacific Steel workers in

Berkeley, some then made contact with them and helped organize their march. Solidarity is a two-way street, based on mutual respect. In most cities, including Oakland and San Francisco, labor unions welcomed Occupy and sought to defend the encampments. In New York, Occupy activists were given resources in many union halls, and unions mobilized against police raids at Zuccotti Park. An alliance of unions, immigrants and Occupiers showed potential strength, not just in numbers but also in the exchange of ideas and tactics. Unions in particular might benefit from wider use of the planton or Occupy encampment. Occupy ICE challenged the Occupy movement to take up the firings of immigrant workers, but it was also a challenge to unions themselves, many of whom had watched in silence as long-time members were forced from their jobs.

The vision of Occupy—the 99 percent versus the 1 percent—has enormous support among immigrants and unions. In place of the tired rhetoric of politicians, shedding crocodile tears for the "middle class" while demonizing the poor, Occupy gave workers a vision of their commonality in the 99 percent. This powerful message blew away illusions that higher-paid workers have more in common with stockbrokers than with immigrants laboring at minimum wage, or unemployed young people on the streets of African American ghettos or Latino barrios.

The Coalition for the Political Rights of Mexicans Abroad shared the same vision of class-based commonality. "We are outraged," it said, "that US citizens, when they demand justice and expose the inequalities that exist in their society, are treated like criminals. With the same outrage, we condemn the criminalization of migrant Mexicans by the US government, the raids by immigration authorities [and] the militarization of the border. . . . No human being should be treated as a criminal because they struggle to find better conditions in which to live."

Marching Away from the Cold War

One sign carried in almost every May Day march of the last few years in the United States says it all: "We are Workers, not Criminals!"

Often it was held in the calloused hands of men and women who looked as though they'd just come from work in a factory, cleaning an office building, or picking grapes. The sign stated an obvious truth. Millions of people have come to the United States to work, not to break its laws. Some have come with visas, and others without them. But they are all contributors to the society they've found here. In the largest US May Day event of 2011, marchers were joined in Milwaukee by the public workers who protested in the state capitol in Madison, Wisconsin, and became symbols of the fight for labor rights in the United States. Their message was the same: we all work, we all contribute to our communities and we all have the right to a job, a union and a decent life.

May Day marches and demonstrations since 2006 have provided a vehicle in which immigrants protest their lack of human rights and unions call for greater solidarity among workers facing the same corporate system. The marches are usually organized by grassroots immigrant rights groups, increasingly cooperating with the formal structure of the labor movement and, more recently, the Occupy movement. In 2011 the attacks on public workers provided an additional push to unions to use May Day as a vehicle for protest. AFL-CIO president Richard Trumka spoke in Milwaukee, where national attention focused on the attacks on public workers and their mass resistance. Trumka's presence marked two important political changes in labor. May Day is no longer a holiday redbaited in the US labor movement, but one used to promote a defense of workers' rights, as it is in the rest of the world. And unions are slowly adopting a tradition of May Day demonstrations calling for immigrant rights, a tradition begun by immigrant communities themselves.

The immigrant-based May Day protests have responded to a wave of draconian proposals to criminalize immigration status, and work itself, for undocumented people. The defenders of these proposals have used a brutal logic: if people cannot legally work, they will leave. But undocumented people are part of the communities they live in. They seek the same goals of equality and opportunity that working people in the United States historically have fought to achieve. In addition, for most immigrants, there are no jobs to return to in the countries from which they've come. One common chant in the marches is *"Aqui estamos, y no nos vamos! Y si nos echan, nos regresamos!"*—"We're here, and we're not leaving! And if they throw us out, we'll come back!"

Instead of recognizing this reality, the US government has attempted to make holding a job a criminal act. Thousands of workers have been fired. Some have been sent to prison for inventing a Social Security number just to get a job. Yet these workers stole nothing—the money they've paid into Social Security funds now subsidizes others' pensions or disability payments. Undocumented workers deserve legal status because of that labor—their inherent contribution to society. Their marches have supported legalization for the twelve million undocumented people in the United States. In addition, immigrants, unions and community groups have called for repealing the laws making work a crime, ending guest worker programs, and guaranteeing human rights in communities along the US-Mexico border.

Undocumented workers and public workers in Wisconsin have a lot in common. With unemployment at almost 9 percent nationally and higher in many states, all working families need the federal government to set up jobs programs, like those Roosevelt pushed through Congress in the 1930s. If General Electric or Microsoft alone paid their fair share of taxes, and if the military budget were redirected toward peaceful uses, every person wanting a job would be able to find work building roads, schools, and hospitals. All communities would benefit. Immigrants and public workers need strong unions that can push wages up and guarantee pensions for seniors and health care for the sick and disabled. A street cleaner whose job is outsourced and an undocumented worker fired from a fast-food restaurant both need protection for their right to work and support their families.

Instead, some states like Arizona, Georgia, Alabama, Utah, and North Carolina have passed measures allowing police to stop any "foreign-looking" person on the street and question his or her immigration status. The states and politicians that attack immigrants are the same ones calling for firing public workers and eliminating their union rights. Now a teacher educating children has no more secure future in her job than an immigrant cleaning an office building at night. In Milwaukee, President Trumka told marchers, "It's the same fight. It's the same people that are attacking immigrants' rights, workers' rights, student rights, voting rights." He paid tribute to the role immigrants have played in resurrecting May Day as a day for worker demonstrations in the United States. "Your voices have been heard across this nation," Trumka said, "inspiring an uprising of America's working people, standing together and saying 'No' to divide-and-conquer politics. 'No!' to tearing working families down rather than building us up. 'No!' to corporate-backed politicians trying to turn us into a low-wage, no-rights workforce as payback to their CEO friends. And what is this America we want? It's a land of equal opportunity, a land of fairness in the workplace and society."

While 2011 May Day marches were smaller than the millions-strong turnout of 2006, they had a more organized participation from unions. That marks a fundamental shift in the attitude of US labor towards May Day. Although May Day was born in the fight for the eight-hour day in Chicago more than a century ago, during the Cold War US unions stopped celebrating it. In 1949, nine left-wing unions were expelled from the Congress of Industrial Organizations, and a witch hunt then purged activists, including communists, socialists, and anarchists, from leadership in most unions. The US labor movement grew more conservative, enshrining a "business unionism" model, which negotiated increases in wages and benefits while defending the corporate system. Eventually, some of the highest elements of US labor leadership collaborated with US intelligence services in supporting right-wing coups in other countries, in which labor and political organizers were murdered. At the same time, unionists in the United States who advocated celebrating May Day as a symbol of international labor solidarity were attacked and red-baited.

In the late 1970s and 1980s, however, large corporations, assisted by the government, intensified their attacks on unions and workers. President Ronald Reagan's support for that effort was made plain when he broke the air traffic controllers' strike early in his administration and sent some of its leaders to prison. The percentage of workers belonging to unions fell drastically, causing an internal crisis in the labor movement. Many Cold War–era leaders were challenged because of their support for the administration's anti-communist crusades abroad while it was attacking unions back home. Finally, at the AFL-CIO convention in New York in 1995, a contest over leadership led to the election of John Sweeney as the union's new president. Richard Trumka, who'd led a critical battle of coal miners against the Pittston Corporation, was elected secretary-treasurer.

At that time, Trumka proposed a new model for internationalism in US labor. "The Cold War has gone," he declared. "It's over. We want to be able to confront multinationals as multinationals ourselves now. If a corporation does business in fifteen countries, we'd like to be able to confront them as labor in fifteen countries. It's not that we need less international involvement, but it should be focused toward building solidarity, helping workers achieve their needs and their goals here at home." Jack Henning, past executive secretary of the California Labor Federation, one of the most vocal critics of the old Cold War policy promoted by the AFL-CIO Department of International Affairs, admitted, "We were associated with some of the very worst elements . . . all in the name of anti-communism. But I think there's an opportunity now to review our foreign activities, to stop the global competition for jobs among the trade unions of the world."

Their ideas embodied a pragmatic view of solidarity, a first step away from that Cold War past. But it was not radical enough to confront the new challenges of globalization—the huge displacement and migration of millions of people, the enormous gulf in the standard of living dividing developed from developing countries, and the wars fought to impose this system of global economic inequality.

Slowly, Cold War barriers began to come down. In Colombia, the United Steel Workers became a bastion of support for the embattled unionists of its left-wing labor federation. In Mexico, the Steel Workers supported striking copper miners in Cananea and gave refuge to their exiled union president in Canada. Under pressure from the group US Labor Against the War, the AFL-CIO publicly rejected US military intervention in Iraq. But progress was uneven. The Democratic Party's support for war in Afghanistan and for Israel's attack on Gaza was greeted with silence. In Venezuela, US labor even supported coup plotters against the radical regime of Hugo Chavez.

Among US union members domestically, the key issues were jobs and trade policy and their corollaries, displacement and migration. The implementation of NAFTA in 1994 (supported by both US political parties) and the street battles in Seattle at the World Trade Organization meeting of 1999 profoundly affected workers' thinking about their own future. Many were educated by the fight against corporate trade policy and began to understand the way neoliberal reforms displaced workers and farmers in Mexico, leading to migration across the US-Mexico border. That understanding created a base for solidarity with Mexican workers in the United States that did not exist during the Cold War era.

During the years after 1994, when NAFTA took effect, over eight million people from Mexico migrated to the United States in search of jobs. The number of people living in the United States without legal immigration status climbed to over twelve million. In 2005 and 2006, those workers faced threats of imprisonment as felons because of their immigration status in a bill passed by the US Congress, authored by Representative James Sensenbrenner (R-WI). Immigrants began using May Day marches to call for human, political, and labor rights. Many came to the United States with a tradition of using May Day celebrations to call for labor rights. May Day became their vehicle to challenge anti-immigrant hysteria.

This wave of increasingly assertive workers was hardly the first to challenge US unions, many of which were organized by earlier immigrants and their children. But US unions were organized in a working class deeply divided by race and nationality. Some unions saw (and still see) immigrants as unwelcome job competitors, and sought to exclude and even deport them. But other unions fought racism and anti-immigrant hysteria, arguing for organizing all workers together. That division and conflict is still very much alive in the modern labor movement.

Today, many undocumented immigrants wonder, "Will my union

defend me when the government tells my boss to fire me because I don't have papers?" It's not a hypothetical question—thousands of workers already have been fired. Their situation requires US unions to make critical decisions. Are unions going to defend all workers, including the undocumented? Should they support immigration enforcement designed to force millions of workers from their jobs? How can labor achieve the unity and solidarity it needs to success- fully confront transnational corporations, both internally within the United States, and externally with workers in countries like Mexico?

The firings also highlight basic questions about immigration enforcement policy. "These workers have not only done nothing wrong, they've spent years making the company rich. No one ever called company profits illegal, or says they should give them back to the workers. So why are the workers called illegal?" asks Nativo Lo- pez, director of the Hermandad Mexicana Latinoamericana, a radical grassroots organization of Mexican migrants in southern California. "Any immigration policy that says these workers have no right to work and feed their families is wrong and needs to be changed."

The justification implicit in the policy's description on the White House website—"remove incentives to enter the country illegally"— was the original justification for employer sanctions in 1986. If mi- grants can't work, they won't come. Of course, people did come, because at the same time that Congress passed the Immigration Reform and Control Act, it also began debate on NAFTA. That vir- tually guaranteed future migration. That rationale for exclusion, inequality and deportation was rejected by the AFL-CIO in its 1999 convention. At the same time, the federation also rejected NAFTA and the trade agreements that play such a strong role in creating poverty and displacement.

Before he retired and was succeeded by Richard Trumka, John Sweeney, former president of the AFL-CIO, wrote to President Obama and Canadian prime minister Harper. He reminded them that "the failure of neoliberal policies to create decent jobs in the Mexican economy under NAFTA has meant that many displaced workers and new entrants have been forced into a desperate search to find employment elsewhere." The joint immigration position of the AFL-CIO and Change to Win labor federations recognized that "an essential component of the long-term solution [to immigration reform] is a fair trade and globalization model that uplifts all workers."

Supporting work authorization and employer sanctions contradicts this understanding. Even with a legalization program, millions of people will still be living in the United States without papers, as more people come every year. For them, work without "authorization" will still be a crime. While employer sanctions will not stop their migration, they will make them vulnerable to the same firings and pressure from employers that immigrants face today.

In a speech in Cleveland in 2010, AFL-CIO president Trumka challenged "working people who should know better, some in my own family—[who say] that those immigrants are taking our jobs, ruining our country. . . . When I hear that kind of talk, I want to say, did an immigrant move your plant overseas? Did an immigrant take away your pension? Or cut your health care? Did an immigrant destroy American workers' right to organize? Or crash the financial system? Did immigrant workers write the trade laws that have done so much harm?"

Trumka accurately described the class exploitation that underlies US immigration policy. "Too many US employers actually like the current state of the immigration system—a system where immigrants are both plentiful and undocumented, afraid and available," he explained. "Too many employers like a system where our borders are closed and open at the same time—closed enough to turn immigrants into second-class citizens, open enough to ensure an endless supply of socially and legally powerless cheap labor."

He concluded by declaring that "we are for ending our two-tiered workforce and our two-tiered society. . . . We need to restore workers' fundamental human right to organize and bargain with their employers. And we need to make sure every worker in America—documented or undocumented—is protected by our labor laws." When he called for "a land of fairness in the workplace and society" in Milwaukee a year later on May Day, immigrant workers in the audience at that march, and those who read his words later, hoped this would mean a sharper challenge to the Obama enforcement policy.

Across the country, tens of thousands marched and rallied on May Day in 2011 for national immigration reform and to support workers' rights. Marchers often bore placards declaring: "Somos Uno—Respeten Nuestros Derechos," or "We Are One—Respect Our Rights." In addition to the hundred thousand in Milwaukee, ten thousand marched in Los Angeles, five thousand in San Jose (in the heart of California's Silicon Valley), and thousands more in New York, Atlanta, Houston, Buffalo, Chicago and other major cities. In Boston, marchers demanded "From Cairo to Wisconsin to Massachusetts—Defend All Workers' Rights." Smaller towns with a large immigrant population, like Fresno, in the heart of California's agricultural region, also turned out large demonstrations.

In Milwaukee, Jose Salazar, a volunteer with Equality Wisconsin, joined Trumka on the stage. "Issues relating to immigration and labor law affect us all," he told the crowd. "That is why the lesbian and gay community is joining today's May Day March for Immigrant and Worker Rights. We march to protest Governor Scott Walker's budget cuts that hurt our families and children. And we march to support the union between immigrant and worker communities."

This Law Is Very Unjust

The Story of Teresa Mina

Teresa Mina left her children behind in Veracruz and came to the United States to work and send money home. She was fired in an immigration audit.

I come from Tierra Blanca, a very poor town in Veracruz. After my children's father abandoned us, I decided to come to the US. There's just no money to survive. We couldn't continue to live that way.

We all felt horrible when I decided to leave. My three kids, my mom, and two sisters are still living at home in Veracruz. The only one supporting them now is me.

My kids' suffering isn't so much about money. I've been able to send enough to pay the bills. What they lack is love. They don't have a father; they just have me. My mother cares for them, but it's not the same. They always ask me to come back. They say maybe we'll be poor, but we'll be together.

I haven't been able to go back to see them for six years, because I don't have any papers to come back to the US afterwards. To cross now is very hard and expensive.

My first two years in San Francisco I cleaned houses. The work was hard, and I was lonely. It's different here. Because I'm Latina and I don't know English, if I go into a store, they watch me from head to foot, like I'm a robber.

After two years, I got a job as a janitor, making $17.85 per hour. Cleaning houses only paid $10. But then I was molested sexually. Another worker exposed himself to me and my friend. When we went to the company and filed a complaint, they took me off the job and kept me out of work a month. They didn't pay me all that time.

That's when my problems started, because I called the union and asked them to help me. After that, the company called me a problematic person, because I wouldn't be quiet and I fought for my rights. Sometimes they wouldn't give me any work.

When you work as a janitor you're mostly alone. You pick up trash, clean up the kitchen, and vacuum. These are simple things, and they tire you out, but basically it's a good job. Lots of times we don't take any breaks, though. To finish everything, sometimes we don't even stop for lunch.

No one ever said anything to me about immigration for four years. But then the company gave a letter to my coworkers, saying they wouldn't be able to continue working because they had no papers. About forty people got them at first. Eventually I got a letter too.

The person from human relations said immigration had demanded the papers for all the people working at the company. She said three hundred people didn't have good papers. People whose papers were bad had a month to give the company other documents. If the immigration authorities said these were no good too, we'd be fired. She said the immigration might come looking for us where we lived.

We had a meeting at the union about the letters. Some people in that meeting had papers, and came to support those of us who didn't. They said when they first came here they had to cross the border like we did, in order to find work.

They complained that so many of us were being fired that the workload increased for people who were left. The union got weaker too. We're all paying $49 a month in union dues, and that adds up to a lot. We're paying that money so that the union will defend us if we get fired like this. In that meeting, we said we wanted equal rights. No one should be fired unless the immigration arrests us. We don't want the company to enforce immigration law. The company isn't the law.

The company gave me no work in December and January. I was desperate. I had no money. I had to move in with someone else, because I couldn't pay rent. I couldn't send money home to my children.

I was so stressed I fell and broke my arm and was out on disability.

Then I went back to work, and when I went to get my check, the woman in the office wouldn't pay me until I showed them new immigration papers. She gave me three days to bring them and said if I didn't, I'd be fired. I asked her, "So you're the immigration?"

I felt really bad. I spent so many years killing myself in that job, and I needed to keep it so I could send money home. But I couldn't keep fighting. I didn't want my problems to get even bigger—I could tell things would only get worse.

I went back after three days and told the company I didn't have any good papers. I asked for my pay for the hours I'd worked and my vacation. I told them I had a flight back to Mexico and needed my check. They only paid me sixty hours, though they owed me eighty-two. They knew I was leaving and couldn't fight them over it. The union did get me something. If I come back with papers within two years, I'll get my job back.

This law is very unjust. We're doing jobs that are heavy and dirty. We work day and night to help our children have a better life, or just to eat. My work is the only support for my family. Now my children won't have what they need.

Many people are frightened now. They don't want to complain or fight about anything because they're afraid they might get fired. They think if we keep fighting, the immigration will pick us up. They have families here. What will happen to their children? Nobody knows. They worry that what's happened to me might happen to them.

I can't afford to live here for months without working. I came to this country to work for my children. But if this is what happens because I've been fighting and struggling, I'd rather leave and go home and live with my children. In the end, they need me more.

So I guess I'll go back to Tierra Blanca. I'll work in the fields or try selling food there. My family says the economic situation at home is very hard. I'm not bringing much money home. But I like to work, and I know I'll find a way.

When We Speak You Hear a Roar

The Story of Keith Ludlum and Terry Slaughter

Keith Ludlum and Terry Slaughter were leaders of the campaign to organize a union at the huge Smithfield Foods slaughterhouse in Tar Heel, North Carolina. Today they are officers of the union at the plant.

KEITH LUDLUM

When I was 22, I heard about this new hog plant, and went and applied. They put me in the livestock department, right in the belly of the beast. It was a real shock—seeing how workers were treated. I saw hogs fall on people, and then the supervisors doing everything to get the hog back on the line. They were more concerned with the hogs then with the people. A dead animal was more valuable than a live human being.

Most people working there were African American. I never thought of myself as better than anyone. My dad came from poor, rural North Carolina. He taught me, we're all the same. Treat people how you want to be treated. Work hard and you'll be rewarded for hard work. I had no idea what unions were. Like most people in the South, most of my ideas about unions came from the companies I worked for, which were very anti-union.

Then an older African American guy, a humble spirit, broke his leg. The next day when I came in he was in the break room with his leg in a cast on crutches. He said they told him that if he didn't come in to work he'd be fired. The supervisor wouldn't even let him park near the place where he worked in the plant—those places were just for management. That's when I knew I wouldn't keep working under those conditions. One of the ladies invited me to a union meeting in Lumberton, and I went.

I knew what they were doing to people was wrong. And the only fix that I could see was the union. So I took union cards into the plant. I thought the law would protect me, and if I lost my job, it wasn't the end of the world. I was naive. Now that I'm older I know corporations don't care about the law, but I was young. I thought, Americans believe in the law and everyone has to obey it.

After three weeks I had most of livestock signed up. But other workers told me the supervisors were watching me. Then they started writing me up. Finally they called me in. They had the regional guy in charge of all the farms, the livestock manager, and the assistant plant superintendent all in there to fire me. The livestock manager knew what he was doing was wrong. He couldn't even look at me. I looked up at him and said, "You can't hold it against someone for trying to make things better." They walked me out, and when we got to the lobby there were two deputies standing there to escort me to my car.

I said to myself, "You picked the wrong m———." And that started a twelve-year fight. That was 1994.

TERRY SLAUGHTER

I was born in Georgia, but we moved to New York City when I was ten. My wife's family was from North Carolina, and after we got married she decided to move down here. I didn't want to leave the city life, but finally I decided it was time to grow up.

When I came down here, it was the first time I had a regular job, where I was paid by the hour. Before, I was never paid on the books. At first I worked at a Black and Decker factory on the line. In 2002, after three years, I came to Smithfield. It was a whole new world.

I started in the livestock department, taking animals off the truck. I was scared of the hogs the first week. I called them pigs. They told me, they're not pigs. That's a city name. The plant was killing thirty-two thousand hogs a day. In eight years there was never a day they didn't have hogs.

If a hog gets crippled or falls, someone has to pick it up. They weigh four hundred pounds. You have to push it into a barrel, and if you're a man, they say, you do it by yourself. With all the walking and carrying hogs, I lost seventy-five pounds the first year I was there.

At first I liked it. Then in 2005, reality set in. I started seeing the way management was treating the employees. Hogs would run over a worker and managers would move the person to the side so they could keep the animals moving. The hogs were more important than the people. But what could I do? One person alone couldn't do anything.

In July 2006 I heard people start talking about forming a union. That was what I was waiting for. I knew about unions in New York. Some were skeptics and some were scared. But I thought, if we don't stand for something, we won't count for anything.

One morning, it was almost 100 degrees outside. Keith and a couple of others went to get water from the cooler, but it was hot and had ants in it. We said, "We're not going to work if we don't have clean and cold water." So twenty-five of us got some chairs and we sat in the middle of the barn. We crossed our arms and said, "We're not going to do anything until we get what we deserve." For eight hours we did nothing.

The supervisors started to go crazy. When livestock stops, the rest of the plant does, too, since it doesn't have any more hogs on the line. The hog trucks were lined up at the gate, and the animals were dying from heat in the trucks. When they started losing money and realized we weren't going back to work, supervisors tried to run the hogs themselves. But they couldn't do it. They'd never done that work before.

I thought for sure we were going to get fired. But they realized they weren't going to be able to produce if we weren't working. The very next day we got clean and cold water. That's when I knew we had a chance. From there it snowballed.

KEITH LUDLUM

I won at the labor board, and all the appeals later in court. Finally they reinstated me in 2006. By then the whole community knew what was happening. By the time I came back there were only a few people in livestock who remembered me. I wore a Justice at Smith-field shirt when I went back in, and even had my company ID photo taken with the shirt on.

The first day I started asking people to sign cards. Some people thought I had the plague, but other people were really excited. I always let the company throw the first punch, but I always hit them harder, and workers saw that. You can't show any kind of weakness or make any mistakes. So we slowly built a core group in livestock. That department controls the whole plant. Terry and some of the others joined. They started believing, and we started doing actions in the plant.

By then there were a lot of immigrants in the plant. After Smithfield ran through the workforce around here, you started seeing a lot more immigrants working in the plant. The company thought the undocumented would work cheap, work hard, and they wouldn't complain. It happened very quickly, and there wasn't an established community here before. Someone made a personal effort to get the workforce here. The company had to make that happen.

I went back in July of 2006, and the walkout over the firings happened in November 2006. At first, African Americans and others viewed the firings as just a Latino problem, but during the walkout I tried to explain that it was a worker problem. People are just trying to earn a living and raise a family. The company took advantage of them, and then made them pay the price.

They'd fired fifty or seventy people, and they said more were coming. People were panicked. They knew they were going to be next. Were they going to wait, or do something about it? That's when they said, "Let's shut them down." It was really empowering to see all those workers stand up together. We just took over the parking lot. We had total control. When you've got enough people, nothing can stop you.

We were trying to buy some time for people, and the company agreed to extend the time by two months [that is, the time before which workers had to provide new documents, or be fired]. It was the best we could do, but it did show people we can change the way the company makes a decision.

The next February ICE hit this area again, and Eduardo and I followed them around with cameras. With cameras on them, ICE would handle going into people's houses differently. You could tell they were mad at us, and kept trying to push us back. They surrounded one trailer, and turned off the power to try to smoke the people out. It was a hundred and some degrees, and the air conditioning was cut off. There were children in there.

But you could see that staying just wasn't worth it to people, and they were going to move on. They didn't know if they were going to be arrested, or how their family might be split up.

TERRY SLAUGHTER

If you're a good worker, they should let you work. Granted, you're supposed to be documented. We know that. But this was a tactic by Smithfield at the time when we were trying to get the union in.

They wanted people to believe that the union had called ICE on the people, so we'd lose the Latino vote. I would say a vast majority of the Latino workers were a yes vote for the union. But people were scared if they were undocumented. If I was undocumented, I wouldn't want to be out in front either.

There were more Native Americans and African Americans coming into the workforce at that time. I don't think the change in the workforce made a big difference by the time of the election. The union won because it was time.

KEITH LUDLUM

I think there had to have been cooperation [between ICE and the company]. The company wants someone they can exploit—the dream employee. You were supposed to come to work, take whatever they paid you and however they treated you, and if you didn't keep your mouth shut you should go back home. It was a perfect employee for a corporation, other than a slave.

But I'm sure the company saw these people were getting organized. That's not what the company wanted.

For a while relationships between Latinos and African Americans were strained. Some African Americans thought Latinos were taking jobs they could do, and keeping the wages down. But there was also a sense of envy after Latino workers walked out over the firings, and showed their power. Many started saying, we need to do something, and started demanding the MLK holiday. The following year Smithfield named MLK an official holiday for the whole company. People started building bridges, standing together.

Everyone saw the power of that unity in the walkout. But it was something people did out of necessity. Afterwards, they had to start getting ready to leave. It would have been different if we'd been able to stop the terminations permanently. That would have made a difference. Once people started leaving, it broke up those core groups that made things happen. The damage had been done to the immigrant population, and the undocumented started leaving, getting away from the hotspot. You can't blame them. Who wants to get arrested, with your kids waiting to be picked up? Immigrants have that extra fear. We all have to worry about being fired. They have to worry also about being arrested, separated from their families and deported.

The company terminated me again in 2007. They wanted me out of there. So I worked for the union on the campaign here. After we won the election in 2008 we always wanted the union here to be run by workers from the plant. It's got to be people who live here, not just someone for whom it's a job. I've been a member of the local since it was chartered in 2009, so I ran for president after the first contract had been negotiated.

The union has been able to improve the wages, even though we've been in the worst recession since the depression. Thirty people who were fired unjustly are back on the job with back pay. To me that's enough—firing is like a death. People in this country are two paychecks away from being homeless. The company can't fire people for getting hurt the way they did before, and we can time the lines and slow them down.

When the union made the agreement with the company for the election, they had to agree that I couldn't go anywhere near the plant. I couldn't even be on the grass on the roadway outside. Now I'm the local president.

TERRY SLAUGHTER
Relations between Latinos and African Americans today are great. When you look at the culture in the plant today, everyone's together.

Supervisors can't yell at you—no more. They can't downgrade you—no more. It used to be that if you said anything you got fired—no more.

Between all the shop stewards and elected officers, there's over a hundred of us. When we speak, plus the five thousand people who work there, you hear a roar. When it's a few of us together, we're a force. But when it's all of us together, we're a union.

SIX

HUMAN BEINGS OR JUST WORKERS?

How Do You Say Justice in Mixteco?

Erasto Vasquez was surprised to see a forklift appear one morning outside his trailer near the corner of East and Springfield, two small rural roads deep in the grapevines 10 miles southwest of Fresno, California. He and his neighbors pleaded with the driver, but to no avail. The machine uprooted the fence Vasquez had built around his home, and left it smashed in the dirt. Then the forklift's metal tines lifted the side of his trailer high into the air. It groaned and tipped over, with the family's possessions still inside. "We were scared," Vasquez remembers. "I felt it shouldn't be happening, that it showed a complete lack of respect. But who was there to speak for us?"

Eight farmworker families lived in this tiny *colonia*, or settlement, on the ranch of Marjorie Bowen. Their rented trailers weren't in great shape. Cracks around the windows let in rain and constant dust, which carried with it the pesticides used to kill insects on the nearby vines, or sometimes evil-smelling fertilizer. Some trailers had holes in the floors. None had heat in the winter or air conditioning in the summer.

Still, they were home. Vasquez had lived in his trailer for seventeen years. His youngest daughter, Edith, was born while the family lived there. By the time the forklift appeared she had started middle school, while her brother Jaime was in high school and her sister Soila had graduated. "Señora Bowen was a nice lady, and even though we had to make whatever repairs the trailers needed ourselves, sometimes she'd wait three or four months for the rent, if we hadn't been working," Vasquez says. The families had labored in her vines for years.

But Marjorie Bowen died in 2005. Her daughter, Patricia Mechling, inherited the ranch and wanted the trailers removed before selling it. That September, she sent the families letters, giving them sixty days to clear out. It was the picking season, however, when there are many more workers in the San Joaquin Valley than places for them to live. Vasquez's family couldn't immediately find another home, nor could the others. They asked for an extension. Mechling refused.

At the last moment, the farmworkers actually did find someone to speak for them—Irma Luna, a community outreach worker at California Rural Legal Assistance (CRLA). They had their first meeting at CRLA's Fresno office that November, before the forklift arrived. Luna and attorney Alegria De La Cruz informed their clients and Mechling's attorney, James Vallis, of the legal requirements that must be followed before carrying out evictions. Vallis denied that Luna had notified him she had met with Vasquez. On November 14, 2005, the forklift cut short the legal process. "Destroying the trailers in front of the families that lived in them wasn't a reasonable or legal way to evict them," Luna said. "The families didn't really understand their rights in the legal process. Many speak only Mixteco."

Luna, a soft-spoken Mixtec woman in her thirties, migrated from Oaxaca with a brother when she was eleven. Growing up in a mostly white community in Oregon, she remembers, "They looked at me as if I were a Martian." She learned English at school, and because she arrived speaking only Mixteco, she learned Spanish at home. "I even began to wonder why I should speak my native language if nobody was going to understand me," she remembered. "Sometimes when I was alone or in the shower, I would talk to myself in Mixteco, to reassure myself that I wasn't forgetting."

She was stubborn, however. By the time she finished school she was fluent in all three languages. Then, after moving to California, she was caught up in the political ferment in the Oaxacan communities of the San Joaquin Valley, eventually joining the FIOB. Not long after, she was also hired as one of the first indigenous community outreach workers for CRLA. At first foremen would underestimate this quiet Mixteca when she came out to the fields to see if they were providing bathrooms and drinking water. She looked just like the women in the rows, in dusty jeans and tennis shoes. After a few years, though, her reputation spread. Foremen who'd yell at workers when no one was there to hear, would speak deferentially to her. Contractors learned to fear her. Women from their crews would walk into the CRLA Fresno office after work, covered in dust from the vines, some still with bandannas across their noses and mouths. Luna would listen, she and the attorneys would file cases, and eventually the contractors would have to cough up the back wages or unpaid overtime they owed.

Vasquez and his neighbors from Marjorie Bowen's ranch had heard about Luna. Some came from the same Mixtec hometown she did. So, like the others, they climbed the three flights of stairs to the CRLA office and filed their case. De La Cruz and the Fresno law firm Wagner & Jones, who provided pro bono co-counseling, sued Mechling in August of 2006. They accused her of committing prohibited acts to get the families to move out and making threats. De La Cruz also alleged that the eviction was in retaliation for complaints the families had made over substandard living conditions in the trailers. Attorney Vallis called the suit "a shakedown." But eventually CRLA won the immigrants compensation for destroyed belongings, rent abatement, withheld security deposits, and emotional suffering. The suit was settled the day before trial for $55,500, and Mechling later sold the property.

Seven of the eight families in the little *colonia* came from San Miguel Cuevas, a tiny town in the Mixtec region of Oaxaca, an area they poetically call the "land of the clouds." And while speaking only Mixteco created great difficulty for many in understanding the legal proceedings, their strong cultural traditions also gave them a sense of responsibility toward each other. During the period before the case was settled, Vasquez was elected in absentia as San Miguel's "sindico." That is a position responsible for ensuring that members of the community take an equal part in the collective work of building roads, schools, organizing fiestas, or other tasks called "tequios." Election meant he had to return to Mexico for a year to fulfill this duty.

When Vasquez was required to give a deposition in Fresno, however, Luna appealed to that same sense of collective responsibility.
Vasquez paid $600, at a time when he wasn't working, to travel from
Oaxaca back to California. "I wanted the landlord and lawyer to pay
for what they'd done, so that they'd feel what we felt," he explained.
"I was also the one who convinced the other families that we had
to do something. When it was my turn to give a deposition, I felt
responsible to them, and to the case."

Today there are many farmworkers in California with indigenous
roots who feel that same sense of collective responsibility. While
farmworkers twenty and thirty years ago came from parts of Mexico with a larger Spanish presence, migrants today come increasingly from indigenous communities like San Miguel Cuevas. Rufino
Dominguez estimates that 75 percent of the indigenous migrants
from Oaxaca and other states in southern Mexico arrive in California with no immigration visas, an increase from 50 percent a decade
ago. "A few of us benefited from the immigration amnesty in 1986,
but not many," he explains. "The reality is there are no visas available in Mexico to come here, so even though it's harder, more expensive and more dangerous than ever to cross the border, many people
still come because their need is so great. Neither the United States
nor the Mexican government are willing to look at the root cause
of migration."

Vasquez's case highlighted the need for legal services for these families—some of the state's poorest. It also demonstrated dramatically
the challenges facing legal aid providers. This demographic change
convinced CRLA to create an innovative program to bring legal services to indigenous rural communities. But providing those services
is complicated by the fact that a large number of people lack legal immigration status. Restrictions on the money CRLA receives from the
Legal Services Corporation, the part of the federal government that
funds legal aid agencies for the poor, bar them from providing any
services to undocumented migrants. Jose Padilla, CRLA's executive
director, explains that until the Clinton-era immigration and welfare reforms of 1996, CRLA could still use funds it raised from other

sources to defend those workers. "In 1996, however, Congress said that so long as we receive even $1 in federal funding, we can't represent undocumented people," he says. "The same legislation also prohibited us from collecting attorney fees and filing class actions."

CRLA was particularly affected by that legislation because it had started reaching out to indigenous communities just a few years before. In the late 1980s, the agency opened an office in Oceanside, just north of San Diego. "We found people living in the bushes, in open country, ravines and canyons," Padilla recalls. "We began to understand that the people living in these extreme conditions came from a different part of Mexico. Although we've always had bilingual outreach workers who speak English and Spanish, here we found people with an indigenous language and culture we weren't prepared to serve."

At the same time, indigenous migrants were becoming critical of CRLA for not responding to their needs. A network of Mixtec and Zapotec organizations, which eventually came together to form FIOB in 1992, met with Claudia Smith, who headed the Oceanside office, and eventually with Padilla. As a result, CRLA decided to hire its first indigenous staff member, Rufino Dominguez. "We began to work on the basic problems of our communities," Dominguez recalls. "When we went out to the fields we often found no bathrooms or drinking water. Some were working with the short-handled hoe [prohibited by state law], or weren't getting paid and had no rest breaks. Many people were living outside, or in unclean housing in bad condition. So we held workshops in homes and fields, and got on the radio."

At first Dominguez, and a second Mixtec-speaking outreach worker, Arturo Gonzalez, traveled all over the state educating people about their rights in Mixteco, the language spoken by the largest number of indigenous farmworkers. As word spread, complaints began to surface. At the Griffith Ives Ranch in Ventura County, two Mixtecos tunneled under fences that held laborers in virtual peonage, going first to the Mexican consulate, and then to CRLA. With the assistance of Munger, Tolles & Olson in Los Angeles, CRLA lawyers filed suit in federal court alleging enslavement as well as violations of the Agricultural Worker Protection Act and the RICO (Racketeer Influenced and Corrupt Organizations) Act. Eventually Edwin Ives pleaded guilty to RICO charges in a related criminal prosecution, in the first federal organized crime conviction in a civil rights case. Some three hundred workers shared $1.5 million in back wages.

Outside of Fresno, a group of thirty-two Mixtec families were found living in a trailer park located on an old toxic waste disposal site. Dominguez began the investigation of their situation, which was completed by Irma Luna when she was also hired as an indigenous outreach worker. Following negotiations between CRLA, Chevron and the Environmental Protection Agency, the area was declared a superfund site, and Chevron paid to relocate the families in new homes in a community called Casa San Miguel, named after their hometown in Oaxaca.

In October 2003 another indigenous outreach worker, Fausto Sanchez, investigated the case of families exposed to chloropicrin, a toxic pesticide, when an onion field was sprayed near Weedpatch in the San Joaquin Valley. The subsequent case and settlement required Sanchez to give 167 separate clients an ongoing understanding of a complex legal case in Mixteco for three years.

"Relations between CRLA and FIOB were difficult at first, and some people said they didn't need us, or complained about our work," Dominguez says. "But we have a very close relationship now, and each of us recognizes the importance of the other." Dominguez left CRLA to become FIOB's binational coordinator in 2001. By 2010 CRLA had six Mixtec-speaking outreach workers based in offices around the state and had hired Mariano Alvarez, its first Triqui-speaking staff member. Some are active in FIOB, and others aren't. Antonio Flores helped start a separate organization in Oxnard, the Mixteco/Indigena Community Organizing Project.

"We respect our differences," Dominguez emphasized, "because it's good for us. When we work together we have a greater impact." Jeff Ponting, CRLA attorney in Oxnard, is the coordinator of CRLA's Indigenous Farmworker Project. "We've become an example to other legal aid organizations," he says. "We employ more indigenous people than the state and federal governments combined, which indicates their lack of commitment to providing services to a growing and important community."

Predictably, cases generated by this work get CRLA into trouble with growers. "There are always employers who will not respect the basic labor rights of their workforce to minimum wage, overtime or rest periods," Padilla says. "We do more employment work—about 16 to 20 percent of our cases—than 99 percent of legal service organizations, where the average is 2 percent."

Because of the restrictions imposed in 1996, CRLA now cooperates much more extensively with private lawyers—far beyond the legal requirement to use 12.5 percent of its resources to do so. Because private attorneys may collect fees, cooperation means that opponents face serious financial penalties, while the poorest workers don't have to pay for legal representation with a percentage of recovered wages. And private lawyers, unlike CRLA, are not barred from representing undocumented clients. "Not only can they represent individuals where we are barred," says Padilla, "but they also can ensure that farmworkers and the poor continue to have access to quality litigation. So long as CRLA doesn't directly represent any ineligible immigrants, it can participate in litigation that might benefit both eligible and ineligible case members."

By keeping strictly to the letter of the regulations, CRLA held its critics at bay for more than a decade. Early in 2000, however, CRLA began filing complaints against powerful dairy interests in the Central Valley, settling one on behalf of dairy workers for $475,000. According to Padilla, in late 2000 the first of several federal investigations of CRLA began, requested by congressmen from rural California. In 2006, the Legal Services Corporation issued a report, requested by Congressman Devin Nunes (from a conservative Republican ranching family in Visalia), that found "substantial evidence that CRLA has violated federal law" by engaging in conduct prohibited by funding restrictions. A year later Kirt West, outgoing LSC inspector general, issued a subpoena demanding thirty-three months of data on thirty-nine thousand clients to determine if CRLA "disproportionately focuses its resources on farmworker and Latino work." CRLA refused to comply with the subpoena, Padilla said, "because California law protects clients and their confidentiality."

"The Office of Inspector General can make no conceivable use of the thirty-nine thousand client names and their spouse names it is seeking," said Marty Glick, a San Francisco attorney who represents CRLA. "One has to wonder what the purpose is. Why is the effort to give people redress for the failure to pay legal wages or overtime so controversial?" Added Padilla: "The message we get is that CRLA should change the way it advocates for low-wage and Latino workers. We're being punished for protecting our clients."

To indigenous communities, the prohibition on representing undocumented people is a critical problem. "That prohibition doesn't change the conditions that uproot our communities and turn us into migrants," Dominguez explained. "But ranchers know there's no one to defend us. People decide not to file complaints because they're afraid, and bosses sometimes use undocumented status to threaten people if they try. In some places, just walking on the streets is dangerous if you have no papers."

Some members of Congress argue that more enforcement of employer sanctions would stop the abuse. Workers without documents would be forced to leave the country, the logic goes, and growers would be forced to hire other, less vulnerable workers. "That won't stop migration either," Dominguez says, "since it doesn't deal with why people come. Whatever workforce is in the fields should have basic rights." CRLA and most labor unions say it would be better to devote more resources to enforcing labor standards for all workers. "Otherwise, wages will be depressed in a race to the bottom, since if one grower has an advantage, others will seek the same thing.

"The governments of both Mexico and the US are dependent on the cheap labor of Mexicans. They don't say so openly, but they are," Dominguez concluded. "What would improve our situation is legal status for the people already here, and greater availability of visas based on family reunification. Legalization and more visas would resolve a lot of problems—not all, but it would be a big step. Walls won't stop migration, but decent wages and investing money in creating jobs in our countries of origin would decrease the pressure forcing us to leave home."

Meanwhile, Erasto Vasquez said, "it's important to have someone like Irma."

Something Less Than Citizens

Undocumented workers are not the only population of vulnerable immigrant laborers in California fields. Increasingly, growers are turning to federal programs that allow them to bring workers into the country on temporary visas—so-called guest workers. The current H-2A visa program, set up by the federal Immigration Reform and Control Act of 1986, expanded an earlier H-2 labor scheme, which in turn was a remnant of the notorious bracero program. Like its predecessors, the H-2A system allows an agricultural employer to employ workers recruited outside the United States. First, however, the employer must obtain Department of Labor certification that it can't find local labor to meet its needs, and that hiring foreign workers won't drive down the wages and working conditions of domestic laborers. The recruited foreign workers are then given H-2A visas, but can only work for the company recruiting them, and only for less than a year. At the end of the contract they must return to their country of origin. Federal regulations govern wages, housing and other conditions. An H-2A visa does not lead to permanent residence, or a "green card."

Despite the minimum wage and housing requirements, a 2007 report by the Southern Poverty Law Center documented extensive abuses of workers under this visa program. No one gets overtime, the report said, regardless of the law. Companies charge for tools, food, and housing. Guest workers are routinely cheated. They go into deep debt to raise the money to migrate, making the cost of losing a job in the United States the loss of their home, or hunger among family members dependent on the money they send back from working in the United States. When the recruiters who profit from that system are challenged, their response can be murderous.

In 2006 Santiago Rafael Cruz, an organizer for the Farm Labor Organizing Committee, was tortured and killed when the union set up an office in Mexico to monitor hiring by Manpower and the North Carolina Growers Association, in an effort to end the corruption among the contractors who recruit guest workers.

California's seven hundred thousand farm laborers comprise a third of the nation's agricultural workforce. About 1 percent of those laborers are here on H-2A visas—a lower proportion than on the East Coast. However, numbers don't tell the full story. For more than a decade, pressure for expanding guest worker programs in California agriculture has been coming from growers and the politicians close to them. More than half of the state's farmworkers are undocumented, and though their labor is cheap, growers can't always rely on having it when they need it. And if the prohibition on hiring undocumented workers is seriously enforced in agriculture—as it has been increasingly in other industries—most farms and packing sheds would not be able to function. Under grower pressure, therefore, every major immigration reform bill proposed over the past decade has called for the expansion of guest worker programs. In 2012 alone, three separate grower-supported bills to expand the H-2A system were debated in Congress.

In the fall of 2006, Irma Luna got a phone call with an anonymous tip. The call precipitated a legal case that opened a window into the conditions endured by workers in the guest worker system. Hundreds of farm laborers, the caller said, were living in the Siskiyou County Fairgrounds. Many were being fired and sent back to Mexico. To investigate, Luna and CRLA attorneys Alegria De La Cruz and Mike Meuter drove five hundred miles north to the tiny town of Tule Lake. They found a hundred angry migrants waiting at the local library. Over six hundred people, workers said, had been contracted in Mexico by Sierra Cascade, a large nursery, to spend six weeks trimming the roots of strawberry plants. The company owns over a thousand acres of nursery ranches in far northern California and southern Oregon, where it grows rootstock for berry plants, selling to clients around the world.

The attorneys took declarations and prepared a suit, beginning one of the largest and longest guest worker cases in the program's history. These farmworker advocates sought to enforce the limited legal protections available to migrants on H-2A visas. But their suit was also a means to highlight the fundamental structural imbalances built into this temporary visa system. Five years after the case was filed, many workers were still just getting their checks to settle their claims. For people living from one paycheck to the next, waiting that long wasn't just a delay—it was proof that the legal process could not overcome the vast inequality in power between Mexican contract workers and their US employers.

One of the H-2A workers who met Luna and the lawyers in the library, Ricardo Valle Daniel, later described in a declaration the way he and many others were hired by Sierra Cascade's human relations director, Larry Memmot. While still in his hometown of Nogales, Mexico, Valle said, Memmot offered him an H-2A visa and a contract guaranteeing six to eight weeks of work at $9 an hour. The company would supply housing and transportation. On the night of September 20, 2006, Valle recounted, "Sierra Cascade transported me and other workers by bus from Nogales to Susanville" in Lassen County. Nine buses of workers made the trip in about twenty-four hours. Though the company had promised to provide them with food for the journey, the workers were given only water, Valle said.

In Susanville, more than a thousand miles from the Mexican border, "we were given documents to fill out and sign. . . . In addition, I was given a new copy of the employment contract. There were significant differences between the information we received in Mexico when we were recruited and the employment contract we were forced to sign at that time." The big difference was that the contract specified they'd have to meet production standards requiring them to process over a thousand plants per hour, or one every four seconds. "I was told by Mr. Memmot," Valle said, "that the new provisions were [due to] clerical errors . . . and that I had to sign the documents—otherwise I would be sent back to Mexico."

After the stop in Susanville, the workers were taken to Tule Lake and bunked in a warehouse at the fairgrounds, sleeping in a large room on cots densely packed together. Valle and his wife, Ana Luisa

Salinas de Valle, were among more than a hundred workers who slept in bunk beds in a mixed-gender dormitory. Around six the next morning, they boarded company buses to the nurseries. From the beginning, however, they had problems with the quota. As former factory workers, they had no experience cutting the roots of strawberry plants. "This is not a common job," he explained, "and it has taken me some time to learn to do it without damaging the plant. In fact, if I don't do it correctly the cuttings that are used to credit my piece rate are thrown away by my forelady and I don't get any credit for them." When Valle and his coworkers couldn't make the quota, the supervisor threatened to fire them and send them home.

At the fairgrounds, life was grim. "During the first two weeks, on many occasions we would have a cup of coffee for breakfast, a small portion of greasy tough meat with rice for lunch, and cereal, coffee and bread with jelly for dinner," Valle remembered. After the workers met with the CRLA lawyers, the food got better. But in the warehouse couples like Rosa Ignacia Guzman Castro and her husband were housed in a barracks-type room where many men and women were mixed together, despite what she said were promises of family quarters.

Guzman's first paycheck for two weeks' work totaled $1078.12. The company deducted $130.20 for the food, leaving her with $947.93. Like the other H-2A workers, she didn't take breaks and worked through her lunch period, trying to make the quota. She put in more than 125 hours—over eleven hours a day (eight on Saturday)—making her hourly rate just over $7.50. She wasn't paid time-and-a-half for overtime. Finally, at the end of her third week, she and fifty others, including Ana Luisa Salinas de Valle, were fired for not meeting quota and told to get on a bus to Mexico. "I came with my husband, and he has not been fired. I do not want to be separated from him, or to have to travel without him back to Mexico," Guzman said she told the bosses. She was already sick from the cold. "I am afraid to travel alone in this condition," she worried.

By then she'd already met with Luna and De La Cruz, so she knew the company was supposed to pay her final check immediately if they fired her. When the foreman wouldn't do so, she and others refused to get on the bus, and he called the sheriff. "I think if the sheriff hadn't agreed to talk with our attorneys we would have been put in jail or sent back without our pay," Guzman said.

What followed was a tortuous legal process as workers and their lawyers were bounced between state and federal courts. Even with committed advocates they had a very difficult time using the legal system to remedy the abuses inherent in guest worker programs. CRLA lawyers filed suit in Superior Court for Siskiyou County in Susanville, asking for a temporary restraining order. The suit, filed less than a month after the contract workers had arrived, was brought under California's Unfair Competition Law and accused Sierra Cascade of breach of contract and violations of California labor laws—failure to pay minimum wage, provide break and meal periods, or pay wages due on discharge, as well as unlawful wage deductions, misrepresentation, housing violations, enforcement of penalties and unlawful competition.

CRLA attorneys believed the company was also guilty of violating federal regulations governing the H-2A program. Sierra Cascade had failed to pay the required wage, called the adverse wage rate, which at $9 an hour is set just higher than the minimum wage. It hadn't paid overtime after 10 hours a day or 60 a week, violating federal wage and hour laws. Compensation also has to comply with prevailing practices, which CRLA litigation director Cynthia Rice believed meant the quota and piece rate system wasn't legal either. Failure to disclose the production requirement violated the H-2A regulations, which hold that a written contract must set forth all the terms and conditions at the time people are hired.

Further, if workers complete half of their contract, the company has to reimburse transportation to and from the US worksite, and provide subsistence payments to allow people to eat on the way. While the fired workers hadn't completed half their contract, a Florida judge had decided in the Arriaga case that the first weeks' wages, minus the unreimbursed transportation expense, must total a wage above the legal minimum. CRLA attorneys believed Sierra Cascade hadn't met that standard either.

Yet although the company had violated the rules of the federal program, CRLA filed suit in Superior (state) Court, alleging violations of state statutes rather than in federal court. By doing so, the lawyers sought to avoid a basic problem in enforcing labor standards for H-2A workers. "There's no private cause of action that can enforce the federal regulations governing their employment," Rice explained. "The law doesn't recognize the right of H-2A workers to go to federal court." Workers can file a complaint with the US Department of Labor, but the process is very slow. And since the Bush administration was still in office, the outcome seemed uncertain.

CRLA attorneys wanted to change conditions, especially to stop the firings, while workers were still in the United States. They argued that California's Unfair Competition Law gave them standing to request a restraining order in Superior Court. Sierra Cascade had failed to pay the H-2A program's required "adverse effect wage rate," and by maintaining illegal conditions, CRLA argued, the company was able to lower costs and thus unfairly compete with other employers who obeyed the law.

Instead of litigating these issues in Siskiyou County, however, lawyers for Sierra Cascade removed the case to federal court anyway. The company's answer to the complaint, filed by Merrill F. Storms Jr. of Piper US LLP, admitted some basic facts, but denied all allegations of illegal conditions, and even challenged the constitutionality of the California Unfair Business Practices Act.

In federal court CRLA argued that the company had violated the regulations on recruiting H-2A workers because the quota requirement hadn't been disclosed when they were hired, and was only included in a contract they were required to sign once they were a thousand miles north of the border. "At that point they had to sign because they were already in the country and had to work," Rice charged.

The company fiercely defended its production standards and its right to fire workers and return them to Mexico if they couldn't meet them. Sierra Cascade CEO Steve Fortin argued in a declaration, "If there are no production standards, Sierra Cascade is concerned that a substantial number of workers, particularly the H-2A workers who have indicated a dislike for the trimming work, will simply produce little or nothing and draw their $9 per hour pay plus free housing." In another declaration, Larry Memmot, Sierra Cascade's HR director, added that "since the start of the [company's] H-2A program, approximately 170 H-2A workers have voluntarily resigned. In addition, approximately 100 workers have been terminated for failure to meet a production quota." Fired workers were provided with bus transportation back to Nogales, he said.

Seven days before the employment contract for the remaining workers was due to end, federal judge Garland Burrell granted a partial restraining order. He told the company to comply with basic standards on bed spacing, heat in the bathrooms and meals. He accepted CRLA's arguments that food should meet the standard of the Child Nutrition Act. But he refused to declare the production standards illegal, or prohibit the company from firing workers if they failed to meet them.

The root-cutting work ended soon after the federal order was granted, and the workers returned to Mexico. Finally, on January 24, 2007, Judge Burrell accepted CRLA's argument that although some conditions were governed by federal regulations, the allegations in the complaint involved state rather than federal law, particularly violations of California worker protection statutes. He therefore remanded the case back to Siskiyou County. Once the case was back in state court, CRLA and the company began settlement negotiations. A year and a half later, in October 2008, they reached agreement.

The final settlement paid workers for three violations. One H-2A regulation guarantees that workers will be paid at least three-quarters of the hours promised under their contract. The California Labor Code section 226.7 says workers must be paid an hour's wages for each missed break period. And Labor Code section 203 requires an employer to pay workers thirty days' pay if it terminates their employment without paying their wages immediately. The total settlement included $59,000 for unpaid wages and rest periods, $57,000 for the guaranteed number of hours under the contract, and $210,000 in penalties and damages. The company was required in the future to pay travel time from housing to the workplace, to disclose all contract provisions in Spanish in Mexico, to reimburse transportation expenses from Mexico to the US worksite, and to provide legal housing, heat, toilet and laundry facilities, meals, and meal and rest periods.

Nevertheless, while the settlement ended the suit, it took a two-and-a-half-year effort to track the workers down and ensure they received their share. That was much longer than even the litigation itself. Long before agreement was reached with the company, the workers were back in Mexico. To ensure that plaintiffs knew what was happening with their case and were able to agree on the terms of the settlement, Luna set up a communications network. While fifty-two were named in the suit, the company gave the lawyers a list of 242 people entitled make claims under the terms of the agreement, either because they were owed reimbursement for travel or because they hadn't been paid for three-quarters of the hours promised in their contract. "We generally knew where the plaintiffs were, but for most workers, the company listed an address in Susanville. Since we knew they were actually living in Mexico, we had to look for them," Luna remembered. "So I compared the names, and found people in the same family. I went over the list with the plaintiffs by phone, and they knew where others were."

Workers came from all over Mexico—some from Sonora and Chihuahua near the US border, but others from more remote states, including Zacatecas and Guanajuato. Luna realized that there was already a network used by the recruiters in small towns. When she called someone saying she was looking for "the guys who went to California," word spread through that network. "In Casas Grandes, Chihuahua, for instance, we found one person who helped us find the others. In each place workers had been recruited, we found a contact. People would go to that person's house, and sign the papers we needed."

The hunt began in October 2008, and workers had until October 2010 to make a claim. "We never did find everyone," Luna said. "There were still about forty we couldn't locate when the time expired." CRLA staff went to Nogales, Arizona, where they held a press conference on the border, hoping that news of the settlement in the Mexican press would encourage more workers to claim their share. Slowly, she began to collect signatures on forms authorizing payment, turning them over to the company. Beginning in May of 2009, Sierra Cascade began issuing checks, deposited first in CRLA's trust account. But getting money to claimants also turned out to be complicated. Workers in Mexico couldn't cash CRLA checks. The wire-transfer companies used by workers to send wages home charge high fees, and couldn't handle the many individuals involved.

Finally, CRLA asked the Center for Migrant Rights (Centro para los Derechos de los Migrantes, or CDM) in Zacatecas to distribute the money to each person. CLRA's Rice is a member of its board. CDM located its office in Zacatecas because of that state's role in encouraging its residents to enroll in guest worker programs. With over 50 percent of Zacatecans working abroad, remittances are the state's largest source of income. Even with CDM's help, however, it was hard to determine sometimes whether the person claiming the money was who they said they were. Finally, CRLA and CDM developed a unique code for each person. At the bank where CDM deposited money, claimants had to have the code and show their voting credential, an identification document most workers already had before they came to the United States to work. "It was very complicated and difficult," Luna concluded.

Despite Sierra Cascade's six-figure payout in the case, the company continued to use the H-2A program. On the California-Oregon border, there's not much in the way of a permanent farm labor force. In 2009 Sierra Cascade obtained 742 H-2A visas. The following year it was certified for 310 guest workers. Department of Homeland Security records indicate that in 2011 Sierra Cascade had applied for at least forty-five H-2A visa workers to be housed in a dormitory and barracks at Susanville, and another fifty-five at Tule Lake. According to its application, the nursery company still held workers to a production quota.

After the legal ordeal, Luna hoped word of the Sierra Cascade settlement would spread among H-2A workers in Mexico and encourage more of them to sue their employers over similar abuses. That might, she felt, put California growers on notice that workers' rights must be respected, even for guest workers. Sierra Cascade was one of a number of cases that raised the same issues. Over the past decade, CRLA attorneys have used legal action or the threat of it to win settlements for H-2A workers employed by other growers. It sued Ralph de Leon, a labor contractor in Ventura, in 2002, and Harry Singh, a San Diego grower, in 2004. Both were early users of the H-2A program in California. In 2008, it filed suit in Sacramento for workers brought from Colima, Mexico, by Salvador Gonzalez, Farm Labor Contractor, with promises of work for $100 a day. CRLA is far from alone in challenging conditions for H-2A workers. In May the Southern Poverty Law Center won a $2 million summary judgment for fifteen hundred workers harvesting tomatoes for Candy Brand, a grower in Bradley County, Arkansas. Legal aid agencies in North Carolina, Florida, and other states also have a long history of filing cases over guest worker abuses.

Enforcing Labor Rights for Border Crossers

Suits by legal aid organizations in the United States, especially those serving farmworkers, have been coupled with work by CDM and another similar organization, Global Workers Justice Alliance (GWJ), in a cooperative strategy. Its object is to win settlements for guest workers whose rights are violated and to ensure that workers receive their share of those settlements, even after they've returned to their home countries. That strategy, called "portable justice," uses the legal system both in the United States and in the countries where workers are recruited.

The GWJ statement of purpose defines portable justice: "Global Workers Justice Alliance (Global Workers) combats worker exploitation by promoting portable justice for transnational migrants through a cross-border network of advocates and resources. Global Workers believes that portable justice, the right and ability of transnational migrants to access justice in the country of employment even after they have departed, is a key, under-addressed element to achieving justice for today's global migrants."

The CDM and GWJ efforts both respond to a growth in guest worker programs in the United States over the past decade. Legal action by CRLA and others has not slowed their recruitment. The number of visas issued for guest workers in one category alone, agriculture, increased rapidly just before the recession hit in 2008. The Department of Homeland Security certified 87,316 H-2A visas in 2007 and almost twice that number in 2008, for a peak of 173,103. Then the number dwindled with the economy, falling to 149,763 in 2009. In 2011, 74,000 farm labor jobs were filled by H-2A workers, according to the Department of Labor. California H-2A employment followed a similar, if less pronounced, course. According to the Department of Homeland Security, 7,422 workers were admitted to California under the H-2A program in 2007 and 8,889 the next year, but the total dropped to 5,018 in 2009.

California has a century-old tradition of immigrant labor in its fields, where employers hire huge numbers of undocumented workers. But the employment of undocumented workers is very high everywhere in US agriculture. "It's likely that over 70 percent of farmworkers in America lack proper work authorization and immigration status," says Craig J. Regelbrugge of the American Nursery and Landscape Association. Because H-2A workers' wages are set slightly higher than the federal minimum wage, hiring through that program has been less attractive to growers, who generally pay undocumented workers the minimum wage—and sometimes less. Growers also complain that having to advertise for local workers before they can hire guest workers is a cumbersome burden.

But that calculation has started to change. From 2007 to 2009, California ranked among the top five states in applications for H-2A visas, twice ranking second only to Arizona. CRLA's efforts responded to that growing popularity. "We've seen in other states that H-2A programs have been accompanied by serious labor and housing violations and the displacement of local US workers," says Rice. "We believe that litigation to vigorously enforce labor standards can help keep that from happening in California."

As immigration enforcement efforts increase, so does the appeal of foreign contract labor programs. The current administration has placed much more emphasis on workplace immigration enforcement, including the E-Verify electronic database and audits of the I-9 immigration status forms each worker fills out at the time of hiring. A proposed Legal Workforce Act would phase in the E-Verify system for all employers, including growers, over four years.

Democrats in Congress, including California senator Dianne Feinstein and Los Angeles representative Howard L. Berman, have long championed the Agricultural Job Opportunities, Benefits, and Security Act, or AgJOBS, a plan to legalize limited numbers of undocumented workers in agriculture in exchange for relaxing requirements on the H-2A program. The bill would lower the adverse wage rate to its 2008 level, permit a housing allowance for workers in lieu of actual housing, and give workers a private right of action in federal court to enforce contract provisions. The measure failed to become law, however, despite many years' efforts.

Meanwhile, political campaigns to enact criminal sanctions against undocumented workers have slowed the supply of agricultural labor, especially in states in the South and Southwest. In June 2011, a federal court granted a temporary injunction in a constitutional challenge to the Georgia law—but not before the state agriculture commissioner reported that farmers would need more than eleven thousand additional workers to harvest that year's crops. These pressures have increased growers' interest in the H-2A program.

In 2012, grower interests proposed four separate bills in the US Congress. At the same time, Senator Feinstein, the main sponsor of the AgJOBS bill in the past, did not reintroduce it—the first time she'd failed to do so in a decade. The bills that were introduced had none of the negotiated character of AgJOBS, which was the result of a deal struck between growers and farm labor unions.

The American Specialty Agriculture Act would set up a new H-2C category, which would allow growers to recruit half a million workers per year, who would only be able to stay for ten months, and would then have to spend the next two months in their countries of origin before returning. Instead of having to certify that they'd tried to hire workers locally, growers could simply say they'd done so. The housing guarantee would be replaced by a voucher, which, given the lack of housing in most rural areas, would simply drive up rents without providing workers with a place to live. The adverse wage effect rule would be eliminated, and workers would only get their transportation costs reimbursed if they worked more than half their contract.

The Legal Agricultural Workforce Act would have no numerical limit on the number of available visas, and would be administered by the grower-friendly Department of Agriculture. To show they'd tried to hire local workers, growers would post jobs on the Electronic Job Registry maintained by the Department of Labor. Most farmworkers have very limited Internet access and almost no farm labor hiring is done electronically, so the requirement is basically meaningless. Guest workers would have to pay for their own transportation and housing. They'd also have Social Security and unemployment insurance deducted from their wages, but these funds would then be used to administer the program instead of providing benefits. Western growers favor this proposal.

The Better Agriculture Resources Now Act would cut the waiting time for growers who apply for H-2A workers to thirty days and allow dairies and other employers with year-round work to hire them for periods of up to two years. Here growers would also provide housing vouchers instead of actual housing, in a USDA-administered scheme. It would cut the adverse effect wage in most areas. Growers could reject local job applicants who don't have what they consider adequate experience doing farm labor.

The Agriculture Labor Market Reform Act would allow up to a million undocumented workers to apply for a "blue card"—a visa that would give them a probationary legal status that could lead to eventual residence status. Growers would then have to use the E-Verify database to screen all job applicants and would be penalized under employer sanctions for hiring undocumented workers.

If agricultural guest worker programs expand as growers would like, the number of workers needing "portable justice" will undoubtedly increase dramatically. Yet even some of the attorneys who file lawsuits on workers' behalf in the United States have doubts that legal efforts can counteract the structural abuse inherent in guest worker programs. Cynthia Rice points to the isolation of the workers, corruption in the recruitment system, and the temporary nature of their presence in the United States as root causes of vulnerability. "Our agricultural industry is sustained by cross-border labor—we have to acknowledge that," she says. "But these workers have only a quasi-legal status, controlled by growers."

In 2007 the Southern Poverty Law Center's report, *Close to Slavery*, said the program was structurally flawed because workers "are bound to the employers who 'import' them. If guest workers complain about abuses, they face deportation, blacklisting or other retaliation." Regulations to protect workers "exist mainly on paper. Government enforcement . . . is almost nonexistent." A GWJ report, *Visas, Inc.*, explains: "Foreign workers are wholly dependent on their employer for their fragile status in the US. As a general matter, if they are fired, they must leave the country quickly, or face deportation. Combined with other tools of control, this creates a culture of fear that effectively prevents workers from reporting any abuse or exploitation."

H-2A wages have been especially controversial. The adverse effect rule says wages must be set high enough that they don't depress wages of farmworkers in the surrounding community. At the end of the Bush administration, the methodology for calculating this wage was changed, resulting in a $1 to $2 wage cut for H-2A workers. The Bush administration also challenged the Arriaga (Florida) decision that CRLA had used as a precedent in its Sierra Cascade case, arguing that it was "wrongly decided." In March 2010, Obama administration labor secretary Hilda Solis reinstated the old wage methodology and withdrew the challenge to Arriaga. Her new rule also requires employers to document efforts to recruit local workers, and to provide workers with contracts before they leave for the United States.

The *Visas, Inc.* report documents the mushrooming use of temporary migrant labor far beyond the H-2A program. GWJ estimates, using US government statistics, that between seven hundred thousand and nine hundred thousand migrants are working in the United States on many kinds of temporary work visas at any given time. In 2010, for instance, the State Department issued a total of 220,733 H1-B, H-2A and H-2B visas—the traditional visas used for guest worker employment. However, another 120,579 workers received visas for domestic labor, media work, or as workers transferred to the United States by a multinational corporation. Students on work visas did an additional 385,210 jobs, some on campuses but others in retail stores or even information technology. And that's not counting the 320,805 people who came to teach in a school or university, or youth who sought to experience US culture under the wings of the State Department. The abuse of that visa program alone was highlighted in 2011 by a strike by four hundred young people who signed up to work in a cultural exposure program, and found themselves instead doing hard labor in the Hershey chocolate plant in Pennsylvania. Others in that program work on dairy farms, ski resorts, seafood processing plants, or as staff in hospitals or au pairs in private homes.

In the wake of the Hershey strike, Secretary Solis vowed to tighten up the restrictions limiting the kinds of work that would qualify for visas under the cultural exposure program. But even with a labor secretary committed to workers' rights, the nature of guest worker programs reinforces low wages and precarious employment. No employer brings guest workers into the country to pay more than absolutely necessary, so the programs provide a flood of workers at minimum wage or very slightly above. The *Visas, Inc.* report argues that "US employers have substantial economic incentives, built into the visa framework, to hire foreign workers in place of a potential or existing US workforce."

The programs also accelerate the transition from permanent to contingent employment across the US economy, the report says. "The abuse and misuse associated with temporary foreign labor are closely linked to the larger crisis of decent work in the US. The shift away from full-time, living wage jobs as the standard for American workers, to ever more precarious employment, is only accelerating. The use of temporary foreign labor is not responsible for the crisis, but it is both a contributing factor and an alibi." The report adds, "US workers are pushed out of entire industries and regions by the systematic erosion of wages and underlying work conditions. This is followed by the recruitment of foreign workers." These are the judgments, not of anti-immigrant nativists, but of advocates for the rights of guest workers themselves.

"Some improvement is possible with changes in the regs," argues Mary Bauer, legal director for the Southern Poverty Law Center. She suggests raising wages and policing recruitment. "But the structure of the program is the real problem," she says. "Workers need a visa that's not dependent on employment. They should come with a visa that lets them shop their labor around, like any other worker." Both Rice and Bauer argue against immigration reform proposals based on guest worker programs. "How we bring human beings into the economy is a fundamental question of policy and morality," Bauer concludes. "Will they be prospective citizens, or something less? Programs for disposable people are convenient for some, but they're not my vision of what our world should look like."

Canada's "Model" Guest Worker Program

Guest workers in Canada, who work under a program like H-2A, report similar conditions. Facing abuses like those in the United States, many guest workers in Canada have been interested in joining unions, and Canadian unions, especially the United Food and Commercial Workers (UFCW), have a decade-long history of trying to organize them. Today the UFCW Canada and the Agriculture Workers Alliance (AWA) run ten agriculture-worker support centers in Canada. The experience of these unionization drives, however, has dramatized not just the problems of retaliation for union activity, but of even more serious imbalances in power between guest workers and the alliance between growers and the Canadian and Mexican governments.

In March 2009, Mexican and Jamaican farm laborers at Sidhu and Sons Nursery in British Colombia voted for a union, UFCW Local 1518. In November 2010, the company signed a contract. The union bargained for the guest workers under provincial law, negotiating an agreement that said workers who completed a season with the grower had seniority rights and could return to work the following year. It also included wage increases and a grievance procedure. Sidhu and Sons was the latest of several efforts by the union to organize guest workers brought to work in Canadian nurseries, mushroom sheds and farms. But the union says that the nature of the program not only places workers who organize in danger of deportation, but that the Mexican government cooperates in threatening them.

In 2011, petitions were circulated in another nursery where UFCW had signed a contract representing guest workers, Floralia Plant Growers Limited, to have the union decertified. The labor organization accused the Mexican consulate of "choreographing" the signature collecting. According to UFCW, consulate officials told Honorio Corona Martinez, a worker brought to Canada under the Seasonal Agricultural Workers Program, to get the union thrown out. The complaint said guest workers at two greenhouses were threatened with losing their jobs unless they signed a decertification petition. As in the US H-2A program, getting fired in Canada means a guest worker must leave the country.

Presumably, the Mexican consulate was worried that if guest workers started earning higher wages and joining unions, it would make them costly, militant and uncompetitive. Canadian growers might then prefer to import workers from other countries, depriving Mexico of remittances.

Canadian labor involvement in organizing foreign workers on farms dates back to 1994, when the labor-supported New Democratic Party government of Ontario adopted the Agricultural Labour Relations Act. Under that law, workers were given the right to organize and bargain collectively, but strikes and lockouts were prohibited. In 1995 the UFCW then organized two hundred workers at a Leamington farm belonging to Highline Produce Limited. That became a national test case for the right of farmworkers in Canada, including guest workers, to join unions. When the Conservative Party came back into power in Ontario, it repealed the law. The union appealed the repeal. In 2001 the Canadian Supreme Court seemed to uphold union rights, ruling that the Ontario government either had to pass another law allowing farmworkers to organize, or drop its appeal of the Agricultural Labour Relations Act.

Meanwhile, efforts by workers to protest and organize continued. On April 29, 2001, Mexicans laboring in Mastron Enterprises' tomato greenhouses in Leamington, Ontario, stopped work over complaints of abuse by a foreman. The day following the protest, twenty-four were deported. More than one hundred other workers signed a petition in protest and told representatives of the United Farm Workers that they had been working twelve-hour days, six and a half days a week, without overtime pay, for $7 an hour. They said they had no protection when spraying pesticides on the tomatoes in the enclosed greenhouses. In the labor barracks they were packed together, the sewer and plumbing backed up, and if they complained they were told to go back home. "What I've realized here in Canada is that employers don't hire us as human beings," one worker told the UFW. "They think we're animals. The first threat that they always make is that if you don't like it, you can go back to Mexico." When reporters called the company to ask about the workers, the company referred them to the Mexican consulate in Toronto.

Having regained power, Ontario's Conservative Party in 2003 passed the Agricultural Employees Protection Act, which said workers had the right to form associations but that they couldn't bargain collectively. Michael Fraser, the UFCW national director, said that without collective bargaining, an association had no power.

The union appealed the new law again to the Supreme Court, in a case involving three hundred workers in a mushroom shed belonging to Rol-Land Farms near Windsor, who voted for UFCW in 2003. Workers complained that the foremen would only call them by numbers, instead of their names, and said they could only speak English at work. Work in sheds involves climbing up stacks of trays on which the mushrooms grow on sanitized manure, in the steaming dark, a job for which they were getting the Canadian minimum wage. Furthermore, they were threatened that if they didn't work fast, they'd be sent home to Mexico, Cambodia, or the Sudan. "Every year," Fraser charged, "thousands of unemployed men and women come from developing countries to work on Canadian farms. But provincial health and safety standards don't apply to the vast majority of these workers. For many, the right to work under safe and healthy conditions, their right to fair treatment and to justice if they fall victim to the abuse or negligence of an employer, is not protected by law."

Finally, in April 2011, the Supreme Court went back on its earlier decision and upheld the Conservative Party's law. It said an association would lead to "meaningful" negotiations, but that it wouldn't mandate actual collective bargaining. "What is protected is associational activity, not a particular process or result," it held. Two of the justices even denounced the court's earlier ruling, saying the Canadian Constitution "does not protect a right to collective bargaining nor does it impose duties on others, such as the duty to bargain in good faith on employers." The earlier ruling "was not correctly decided. It should be overturned thus disposing of the constitutional challenge in this case."

The International Labor Organization called the court decision a violation of human rights, and Wayne Hanley, the national president of UFCW Canada, declared "These are farmworkers, not farm animals, and people have human rights including the right to collective bargaining." The court decision was also criticized by Justicia for Migrant Workers, a Canadian migrant rights organization, for its particular impact on guest workers. "The Supreme Court," it said, "failed to address issues raised by Justicia for Migrant Workers relating to agricultural worker self-determination, to ongoing racism in Canadian society and to the inherently exclusionary impact of Canada's immigration laws. The Court's ruling . . . reinforces the hyper-exploitative and apartheid-like conditions faced by hundreds of thousands of migrant workers across Canada."

"Migrant workers are treated like second-class workers in Canada," says Chris Ramsaroop of Justicia for Migrant Workers. He charges that the Canadian government discriminates against guest workers, who pay into employment insurance funds but are disqualified from collecting benefits, receive lower wages than other workers doing the same job, and are not covered by health and safety legislation. Workers who demand better conditions are sent home. "To change their situation migrants must be guaranteed the right to form unions, the right to social and economic mobility in Canada, and most important, the right to regularization. Workers must have the right to apply for citizenship in Canada," Ramsaroop declares.

The UFCW and the Canadian Labour Congress published a report in 2002, *The Status of Migrant Farm Workers in Canada.* "The Government of Canada refers to its Seasonal Agricultural Worker program as 'managed migration,'" the report said. "We would attest to that. The program is managed quite well by the federal government, applicable consulates, and representatives of farm employers to meet all their respective needs and requirements. To date, however, the needs of the workers have not been part of the equation. We view the Special Agricultural Workers program more clearly as exploitation. It is Canada's shameful little secret."

While restricting the ability of guest workers to organize and join unions, the Canadian government continues to bring more into Canada. From 2006 to 2010, the number of temporary workers on guest worker visas shot up from 139,000 to 182,276, according to the Institute for Research on Public Policy. On June 26, 2011, Citizenship and Immigration Canada announced changes in the country's immigration policy that places further barriers on keeping those migrants from establishing a normal, permanent residence. According to immigration analyst Usman Mushtaq, "Jason Kenney, the Citizenship and Immigration Minister, has charted a course for Canadian immigration policy that treats migrants as disposable labor. Under the new policy changes, temporary foreign workers and students are no longer eligible to apply for residency even if they have the necessary points for immigration. Instead, they are rewarded for their contribution to the Canadian economy with a 'thank you' and 'good-bye' from the government."

Canada's changes are reminiscent of proposals made in some of the comprehensive immigration reform bills debated in the US Congress. Canadian temporary workers can stay for four years, for instance, but then have to go home, and are barred from reentering Canada for the next six years. "This made it harder for temporary workers to gain residency or skilled employment through experience, creating a disposable workforce," Mushtaq explains. At the same time, the number of occupations that qualify applicants for residence has been reduced from thirty-eight to twenty-nine. Those are generally skilled jobs, very different from those in which almost all guest workers are employed, such as farm labor or clerical work.

And because they come into Canada on guest worker visas, they still have to go home for six years before they can apply for residence.

Jenna Hennebry, associate director of the International Migration Research Centre at Wilfrid Laurier University, points out in an Institute for Research on Public Policy report, *Permanently Temporary*, that the conditions faced by farmworkers are at the bottom even of the temporary worker category. Every year, thirty thousand laborers are put to work in Canada fields, recruited under three programs administered by the national government—the Temporary Foreign Worker Program, the Seasonal Agricultural Worker Program (SAWP), and the Low Skill Pilot Project (LSPP). Most of them work in Ontario. The oldest of those, SAWP, has been in effect since 1966, which began two years after the US bracero program was abolished. SAWP first brought workers from Jamaica, then Trinidad and Tobago, then Barbados, and finally from Mexico in 1974. The program is a negotiated, bilateral system, much as the bracero program was.

Although these workers can only work less than a year, many come back every year, a status Hennebry calls "permanently temporary." Like US H-2A workers, they can only work for the employer who recruits them. "Despite Canada's long experience in agricultural labor migration, our programs do not measure up," she charges. "Temporary migrants face significant impediments to the labor market and social integration, including work permits that are tied to employers, weak enforcement of contracts, language barriers and social isolation, especially for the large share of these workers who live in employer-provided housing."

Most farmworkers come to Canada under the SAWP and LSPP schemes, but Hennebry says growers play the programs against each other, looking for the least expensive way to import agricultural labor. The *Visas, Inc.* report points to a similar pattern in the United States, where employers barred from using workers in one visa category then import them using another. The impact, she says is "potentially driving wages and conditions down while pitting one group of workers against another based on gender, race or country of origin."

Overall, the number of workers coming to Canada under the

SAWP has grown dramatically, to 23,898 in 2010. Those from Mexico, 203 in 1974, mushroomed to 15,809 in 2010. Most return every year, asked for by name by the growers who employ them. In addition, new streams of workers are coming to Canada to work in the fields from the Philippines, Thailand, and Guatemala. The recruitment of these workers is sponsored by the International Organization for Migration and the Fondation des Entreprises en Recrutement de Main-d'œuvre agricole Etrangère, both of which have opened recruitment offices in the countries of origin. Those workers are often placed into competition by nationality. One told Hennebry: "Supervisors threaten to replace us with Cambodians if we don't work hard enough. Employees are repatriated for reporting abusive supervisors."

In September 2010, the UFCW organized a demonstration in front of the Canadian Embassy in Guatemala City, accusing Canadian growers of deporting back to Guatemala farmworkers hurt at work in Canada. The union also accused the International Organization for Migration of promoting the Canadian program without concern for the consequences for workers, since IOM recruits over four thousand Guatemalans to work on Canadian farms.

In the SAWP, employers must pay a prevailing wage, provide transportation to and from workers' countries of origin, and provide medical coverage. They also have to provide housing, although they can deduct 7 percent of workers' pay for it. The LSPP has fewer mandates, although it allows workers to change employers. The SAWP allows workers to return every year indefinitely, but the LSPP, while it allows workers to work under two consecutive two-year contracts, then forces them to return home for four years before they can go back to Canada.

Mexico considers the Mexico-Canada program a model. According to Carlos Obrador, Mexican vice consul in Toronto, the SAWP should be an example for those in other countries, including the United States. He calls it "a real model for how migration can work in an ordered and legal way." According to the Mexican government, 80 percent of Mexican workers return each year, and very few try to leave and live as undocumented migrants. Temporary status is not the choice of the workers involved, however. When Hennebry asked, half the workers from Mexico and almost two-thirds from Jamaica said they would rather have permanent resident status.

Coming to Canada involves a considerable investment, including at least two trips to Mexico City at workers' expense for medical exams and documentation. Men must be between twenty-two and forty-five, married or living with a woman, and must have children. Women must be twenty-three to forty, heads of households, and mothers of children older than two. Neither men nor women can take their children with them when they migrate for work, however. Presumably, having children is used only to indicate family stability, without concern for the effect of a long parental absence on those children. Both must have gone through third grade, but no further than elementary school. Once they get to Canada, they then find conditions like "lack of access to clean drinking water, lack of safe food storage (e.g., refrigeration), insufficient food preparation and cleaning amenities, proximity to pesticides and fertilizers, inadequate bathroom facilities, and improper management of food [and] household and human waste," according to Hennebry. A third of workers brought from Jamaica reported long-term illness or injury suffered from work in Canada.

Hennebry defines the migration of farmworkers to Canada as circular migration, rather than temporary migration, because many workers return year after year. But circularity doesn't necessarily produce a satisfactory life. One migrant told her, "We think that when we are separated, in this way, during eight months, from our family, well . . . in reality we are living our lives in halves. This is how I see it, because we can't live completely when we don't have either place." Hennebry says that her years of research shows that "many migrant workers have spent the better part of their lives in Canada, working on Canadian farms, shopping in local stores, going to local church services and so on." Yet despite that, "research has shown that these workers' lives are characterized by inequality and lack of freedoms when compared with those of their Canadian counterparts." A Jamaican worker told her, "We have no rights— not allowed visits, even prisoners get visitors. We are always afraid of repatriation. The employers try to keep us intimidated, afraid of being sent home."

Hennebry calls for regulating Canada's guest worker programs more strictly, and improving protections for workers. "Given the growing presence of temporary migrant workers in communities across Canada and the reality that there is nothing temporary about these migrants, who play an essential role in Canada's economy, it is certainly time to make improvements," she says.

Adriana Paz, cofounder of Justicia for Migrant Workers, however, calls for ending the programs. "Since 2000, farm operators in BC have been complaining of a shortage of labor to harvest their crops," she argues. "Little science is needed to find the cause. When wages are low, often less than the legal minimum, and working conditions are substandard, workers are unwilling to work in agriculture if they have a choice." By restricting permanent residence and family-based migration, she says, "the federal government is closing the door to permanent immigration of farmworkers while steadily moving toward a US-style policy based on temporary migration."

Echoing the debates in Oaxaca, Paz concludes, "The creation of this oppressed migrant workforce must be answered by a migrant labour movement with its feet and heart in the countries of both origin and destination, one that seeks real and lasting solutions to the migrant workers' problems. This movement must be based on grassroots organizing initiatives that empower workers to lead their own struggle. Real changes happen only when those most affected, those who suffer the most, are at the forefront of the struggle. If this is not the case, changes if any will be superficial and short-lived."

The Pitfalls of Regulating Guest Worker Programs

The case against the guest worker system made in the *Visas, Inc.* report, like that in the Oxfam report on tobacco workers, is a powerful one. Yet those reports' recommendations call, not for ending the programs, but for modifications to make them less abusive. The main recommendation of the *Visas, Inc.* report, for instance, is the consolidation of the many work visa categories: "[a] long-term vision must be of a unitary visa system with uniform oversight, rather than a multiplicity of visas, regulated differently." It is a call, basically, for a better-managed or better-regulated system. It accepts, in effect, the system's basic structure—displacement and expulsion in communities of origin, and work-based visas that treat displaced people as a labor supply. The abuses are built into this system because it is premised on employers' desire to pay as little as possible. This places guest workers in those programs into low-wage competition with local residents.

Without addressing the sources of the displacement that pushes people into the guest worker stream, recommendations for better management assume an inherent desire on the part of workers to come to the United States, to which US government policies and corporate actions have no relation. This is the basic assumption challenged by the call for the right to not migrate. It is a call for the right to an alternative course of economic development that makes migration truly a voluntary choice, rather than one brought about by the need to survive.

Representatives of the Mexican government have little interest in the implementation of that right. Instead, they also call for a better-managed system. They often accuse the United States of dictating, by unilaterally establishing visa categories, the terms governing the flow of Mexican migrants to the United States, rather than negotiating them with Mexico. Conservative Mexican administrations, whether of the PAN or the PRI, have been increasingly dependent on remittances from Mexicans working in the United States and seek to manage that flow of labor and money. The change from a PAN to a PRI administration in Mexico City will not change this.

About 11 percent of Mexico's population lives in the United States, according to the Pew Hispanic Center. Their remittances, which were less than $4 billion in 1994 when NAFTA took effect, reached $25 billion in 2006. Even after the recession started, Mexicans sent home $21.13 billion in 2010. At the same time, the public funds that used to pay for schools and public works leave Mexico in debt payments to foreign banks. Remittances, as large as they are, cannot make up for this outflow. According to a report to the Mexican

Chamber of Deputies, remittances accounted for an average of 1.19 percent of the gross domestic product between 1996 and 2000, and 2.14 percent between 2001 and 2006. Debt payments accounted for 3 percent annually, according to Frank Holmes, investment analyst and CEO of US Global Investors. By partially meeting unmet and unfunded social needs, remittances are indirectly subsidizing banks.

In the United States, every administration since President Ronald Reagan's has supported the idea of using the flow of displaced people to meet the labor needs of US employers. It is unlikely, therefore, that the governments of the two countries would negotiate anything other than another labor supply scheme. The likely outcome would be an even more entrenched system dominated by the same economic interests who hold power in the current system—employers, recruiters and the governments that protect them.

Faced with the impact of guest worker programs on US jobs and wages, liberal reformers in Washington, DC, including former labor secretary Ray Marshall, propose a commission that would make an "independent" assessment of labor shortages, and then regulate immigration in order to fill them. Marshall seeks objective verification of the constant claims by growers and other employer groups, who predict dire labor shortages without expanded guest worker programs. But this proposal also assumes that the purpose of controlling migration to the United States is to ensure a rational supply of labor to US employers, regulating it in their interest. The *Visas, Inc.* report agrees that the biggest obstacle to immigration reform is "this refusal to regulate the temporary foreign labor system in an integrated way."

Another liberal advocacy group, Bread for the World Institute, published an article by its immigration policy analyst, Andrew Weiner, which concluded, "The H-2A program—or some version of it—is the future of agricultural labor in the United States. Under almost any scenario, including under the AgJOBS proposal, use of the H-2A program will increase. A regularization of unauthorized [undocumented] farm workers should be accompanied by a guest worker program that farmers use and whose protections are enforced." Members of this organization's board include Iowa Democratic senator Tom Harkin and former Kansas Republican senator Bob Dole.

Bread for the World called for integrating migrant-sending communities into the program as well, through the efforts of the Independent Agricultural Workers Center. The center's founder, Chuck Barrett, proposes to help growers recruit workers and to make loans to prospective migrants to help them cover the cost of visas. It is supported by Catholic Relief Services, in addition to fees paid by growers.

These recommendations for regulating guest worker programs highlight a basic question debated in migrant communities and among their advocates and supporters. How should people respond to a system of displaced communities in poor countries, and low wage labor supply schemes for migrants in rich ones? Should such a system be regulated and managed, or changed more fundamentally? This is a historical question in the United States and Mexico, as well as a current one. Recruitment programs in US agriculture, especially, go back over a century. The bracero program, established in 1942 during World War II, and ending in 1964, was the largest.

The bracero program was halted when the US Congress, under pressure from Chicano civil rights leaders Ernesto Galarza, Cesar Chavez, Bert Corona, and others, repealed Public Law 78. The Chicano labor and civil rights activists of that day contended that farmworkers would be unable to organize unions so long as strikers could be easily replaced by braceros. And in fact, the grape strike that led to the organization of the United Farm Workers Union began in 1965, the year after the bracero program ended. To replace the abolished contract labor system, they pressured Congress to establish family preference criteria for issuing residence visas ("green cards"). In effect, a system for basing migration on the family and community relationships of migrants replaced one that prioritized the labor needs of employers.

In 1986, however, the Immigration Reform and Control Act moved US immigration policy back in the other direction, expanding the H-2 visa program into the H-2A system for supplying workers to growers (along with a similar, H-2B system for unskilled, nonagricultural labor). Other labor-based categories were added in the following years, leading to the current recruitment total of slightly less than a million a year, according to the *Visas, Inc.* report.

Guest worker proposals, advanced now even at the negotiations of the World Trade Organization, have two characteristics. They allow employers to recruit labor in one country and put it to use in another, and they tie the ability of workers to stay in their new country to their employment. These inevitably lead to an inferior social, political, and economic status, in which workers don't have the same rights as people living around them, and can't receive the same social benefits.

Guest worker programs are the heart of the corporate program for immigration reform, and are combined with proposals for increased enforcement and a pro-employer program for legalization of the undocumented. The meatpacking industry started lobbying for guest workers in the late 1990s, when companies organized the Essential Worker Immigration Coalition—made up of the likes of Walmart, Marriott, Tyson Foods, and the Associated Builders and Contractors. Though Republicans are strong guest worker supporters, the proposals in Congress have been bipartisan, supported also by Democrats.

Some bills in the US Congress in recent years would have allowed some of the largest corporations to recruit and bring into the country, through labor contractors, as many as eight hundred thousand people a year. In the middle of the final debate in 2006, just before his proposal failed, President George Bush tried to eliminate all family-based immigration and allow people to come to the United States only when recruited by employers, under a so-called "merit" or point system in which migrants would accrue points based on their employability.

Because of the record of abuse of guest worker programs, and because working outside those programs offers an attractive alternative, a necessary element of corporate reform is an increase in enforcement against undocumented labor in the workplace, and unauthorized border crossing. These proposals seek to end spontaneous migration, in which people decide for themselves when to come and where to go, by making it impossible to work without a work visa and contract. In its place they substitute a regimented system in which people can only migrate as contracted labor. Employer lobbies in Washington, DC, therefore oppose E-Verify and I-9 audits as stand-alone policies, but support them when they're combined with work visas and labor supply programs.

The corporate program also includes legalization of the undocumented but in programs tailored more to protect employers from legal charges for hiring undocumented workers than inclusive programs helping families adjust their status. Even the more "liberal" of Congress' comprehensive immigration reform bills would have imposed waiting periods from eleven to eighteen years on immigrants applying for legalization, usually with high fees and fines and barriers excluding many applicants. Employers, however, would have been protected from penalties for violating employer sanctions, while they recruited new workers through guest worker programs.

This is the same general three-part structure of the Obama administration's immigration reform program. Its goals were outlined in a report from the Independent Task Force on US Immigration Policy, sponsored by the Council on Foreign Relations. Edward Alden, senior fellow at the Council on Foreign Relations, stated, "We should reform the legal immigration system so that it operates more efficiently, responds more accurately to labor market needs, and enhances US competitiveness." This essentially calls for continuing the use of migration to supply labor at competitive, or low, wages. "We should restore the integrity of immigration laws," Alden went on to say, "through an enforcement regime that strongly discourages employers and employees from operating outside that legal system." This couples an enforcement regime, with its raids and firings, to the labor supply scheme.

US and Canadian guest worker programs are one part of a much larger, global system, which produces labor and then puts it to use. In Mexico and Central America, economic reforms promoted by the United States and Canadian governments through trade agreements and international financial institutions displace workers, from miners to coffee pickers. They then join a huge flood of labor moving north. When they arrive in the United States and Canada, they become an indispensable part of the workforce, whether they are undocumented or laboring under work visas. Displacement creates a mobile workforce, an army of available workers that has become an indispensable part of the US and Canadian economies and of wealthy countries like them. The same system that produces migration needs and uses that labor.

The creation of a vulnerable workforce through the displacement of communities is not new. Africa became "a warren for the hunting of black skins" during the bloody displacement of communities by the slave traders. Uprooted African farmers were transported to the Americas in chains, where they became an enslaved plantation workforce, from Colombia and Brazil to the US South. Their labor created the wealth that made economic growth possible in the United States and much of Latin America and the Caribbean.

Displacement and enslavement produced more than wealth. As slave owners sought to differentiate slaves from free people, they created the first racial categories. Society was divided into those with greater and fewer rights, according to skin color and origin. When anti-immigrant ideologues call modern migrants "illegals," they use a category inherited and developed from slavery. Calling another human being an "illegal" doesn't refer to an illegal act. Illegality is a social category, defined by a lack of basic human rights and by social inequality. In this context, both undocumented workers and guest workers have a similar "illegal" status. In fact, Rigoberto Garcia, a former bracero who also at times crossed the border as an undocumented worker, uses the terms bracero and "illegal" interchangeably. "I came as an *alambrista* [undocumented], and then back came as a bracero," he explained. "Eventually I got my papers and lived like any other person. But I always remembered how I got here. Illegal, a bracero."

In this system of displacement and migration, US immigration policy determines the status of migrant labor. It doesn't stop people from coming into the country, nor is it intended to. Its main function is to determine the status of people once they're in the United States. When President George W. Bush said the purpose of US immigration policy should be to "connect willing employers and willing employees," he was simply restating what has been true throughout US history. Providing labor is the reason Chinese migrants were brought from the Pearl River Delta to build the transcontinental railroad in the 1850s. Providing labor was the motivation for the slave trade. In the 1920s and '30s, Filipinos were kept moving from labor camp to labor camp, while antimiscegenation laws kept them from settling down and forming families. They, too, provided labor, as did the Mexican farmers brought to the United States during the bracero program. US industrial agriculture has always depended on a migrant workforce, formed from waves of Chinese, Japanese, Filipinos, Mexicans, and, more recently, Central Americans. Today a growing percentage of farmworkers are indigenous people speaking languages other than Spanish, an indication that economic dislocation has reached far into the most remote parts of Mexico's countryside.

Whether undocumented or bracero, illegality creates a low-wage worker as a foundation of a system that's inexpensive and profitable for employers. So-called illegal workers produce wealth, but receive a smaller share in return than workers who labor for the average wage in the United States or other industrial economies. That wage difference is a subsidy, a source of profit for those who employ them. And those employers depend not just on the workers in the fields and factories but also on the communities from which they come. If those communities stop sending workers, the labor supply dries up. But no US employer pays for a single school or clinic in Mexico, nor any taxes in workers' communities of origin. Workers pay the social costs of producing more workers through the remittances they send home. This is the part of the system challenged most directly when people in those communities assert that they have a right to a different future, other than remittances and more migration.

Today displacement and inequality are as deeply ingrained in the free market economy as they were during the slave trade. Mexican president Felipe Calderon said during a 2008 visit to California, "You have two economies. One economy is intensive in capital, which is the American economy. One economy is intensive in labor, which is the Mexican economy. We are two complementary economies, and that phenomenon is impossible to stop." When Calderon says intensive in labor, he means that millions of Mexican citizens are being displaced, and that the country's economy can't produce employment for them. To Calderon and employers on both sides of the US-Mexico border, migration is therefore a labor supply system.

US and Canadian immigration policy determines the rules under which that labor is put to use in each country. Employers see migrants as a source of labor and seek to organize the flow of migration, to direct it where it's needed. "The economic interests of the overwhelming majority of employers favor borders as porous for labor as possible," according to economist Jeff Faux. But employers want labor in a vulnerable, second-class status, at a price they want to pay.

Companies dependent on this migrant stream gain greater flexibility in adjusting for the highs and lows of market demand. The global production system has grown very flexible. Its employment system is based on the use of contractors, which is replacing the system in which workers were directly employed by the businesses needing their labor. This has been the employment model in the garment and janitorial industries and in agriculture for decades. Displaced migrant workers are the backbone of this system. Its guiding principle is that immigration policy and enforcement should supply migrants to industries when their labor is needed, and remove them when it's not.

Guest worker and employment-based visa programs were created to accommodate these labor needs. When demand is high, employers recruit workers. When demand falls, those workers not only have to leave their jobs, but the country entirely. The price of that flexibility is paid in migrants' communities of origin, which have to absorb both the demand and the unemployment. No wonder that the call for the right to not migrate is growing.

The Future Doesn't Exist for Us Here

The Story of Miguel Huerta

Miguel Huerta came to North Carolina from Veracruz to work in the tobacco fields. Today he looks for alternatives to forced labor migration.

There are various reasons why we came to this country. Each of us has a goal. Many of us are escaping poverty and marginalization and are looking for what our country couldn't give us. Most of us arriving from Veracruz come from poor families and we come to work, not to visit. We contribute toward the development of this country.

We all had different goals coming here. Some of us came to better ourselves economically, or to own a home. In our case we wanted to provide our child with an education. He came to us when he was seventeen years old and asked if we were able to send him to college. I didn't know what to answer him. He was going to work in the fields instead.

Our parents didn't know how to read or write, but they gave us the opportunity to go to school up to high school. We didn't want our child to be illiterate. We wanted him to have more. This is why we chose to only have one child and not seven. But we didn't have the money in Veracruz to send him to college. So I came to the US.

I arrived by myself with an H-2A visa to work in the tobacco fields. When the contract ended, I looked for work elsewhere. In those years, there weren't many immigrants. In fact, we all knew each other. There was a lot of work and you could find something in a week. Now it takes you two to three months to find something.

After a few years, I brought my wife, and later my son graduated from a university in Puebla with a mechanical and electronics degree, which wasn't available in Veracruz. A German company in Mexico, Volkswagen, was looking for engineers and he was hired. They sent him to Germany to learn the language, where he lived for three years. Then, after he got additional training, he returned to their assembly plant in Puebla. Our son designs and makes car parts, and recently designed the Ford Fiesta clutch. We are very proud that what we came to do, we did. We are very thankful to this country for giving us so much. As the Americans say, "God bless you."

Now we're thinking of returning to Mexico, because the future doesn't exist for us here. Our son was able to expand his horizons. We were able to experience this country and see how it works. But now we're focused on finding a way for Mexicans to stay and work in their native country, because life here is very difficult now. It's very hard to find work because of the economy, and there is a lot of discrimination. Many have decided to go back to Mexico, because if they're going to be poor, they would rather be poor in Mexico, where they can be close to family.

Our next goal is to prevent more Veracruzanos from immigrating to this country. We can accomplish this if folks from this country buy our products from Veracruz. At the same time, we need the small growers in Veracruz to get together.

The large growers always know the selling price at export, but the small growers never know what the products they raise are sold for. We never get the profit; just whatever it costs us to grow them. With the Free Trade Agreement, small growers were left out. We only sell our products to the middleman, who will export them. And with the Free Trade Agreement, what we sell to the US is a lot less than what the US sells to Mexico. The benefits of the agreement went to a few and not the majority of the growers.

Small farmers in Mexico are at the mercy of the US market, and the companies that control access to it. That's what happened with the orange crop. Overproduction made prices go down. The orange-juice companies in the US purchased oranges for very little money—just enough for citrus farmers to feed and clothe their families, but not to pay for an education for their children. Growers need to be able to sell to the US directly, avoiding the middleman. This change would allow families to stay in Veracruz and not migrate elsewhere.

Veracruz is a state where we could live well. We wouldn't have the need to look for the dollar in the US. But only if the dollar can get to our agricultural lands.

Our coast has many climate regions and our production is varied, which is a great advantage. If the US bought our products directly in the winter months, we wouldn't need to come to this country. Veracruz also has a port and can transport what we produce anywhere in the world. The Carolinas also have a port and could easily bring in our products, which come from much closer markets than Asia, for instance. And if politicians actually listened to their constituents, maybe this could become a reality.

There are millions of Hispanics living in the US. We can easily tap into that market, as well as the American market. It's a simple way to get the dollar to Veracruz without us having to come to this country. We grow our cucumbers, tomatoes, and chilies in November, December, January, and February. Everything people consume here in the winter, we can produce in our country. It isn't necessary for us to be here.

Instead, it's scary to see a few large companies dominate the world's production. Small farmers in Mexico are already struggling. We're going to see them displaced completely by these large companies and chains. They will disappear. Look at Walmart and Lowe's. These stores are making the small businesses disappear and this can happen in Mexico too. In this country we've seen these large businesses settle into a town and the merchant area disappear. You have politicians who support these large businesses and even approve new roadway construction around the new businesses instead of supporting their constituents.

These large companies have tremendous power, and in the long run will also take a hold of Mexico. This will not only happen with the Smithfield hog farms. We have seen the way large meat producers operate and how fast they fatten up the animals they raise. But we really don't know what is in the meat that we eat in our hamburger. We don't know how it was produced and what effects it will have on our health.

SEVEN

THE RIGHT TO NOT MIGRATE AND RADICAL REFORM

Following the 2012 US national election, in which President Barack Obama was returned to office, immigration reform once again became a national issue. Seventy percent of Latino voters cast ballots for Democrats, and Latino politicians demanded the party move on legalization in recognition of that fact, and as a way to create a larger pool of new citizens able to vote in future elections. Even the Republican Party was divided between its anti-immigrant right wing and those who saw some recognition of changing demographics as a key to maintaining political viability.

The following spring the administration and bipartisan groups in both the US House and Senate unveiled principles for new comprehensive immigration reform bills. For some immigrant rights organizations, however, these principles sounded very familiar. "The idea of the three-part tradeoff, that is, that we get some legalization in trade for guest worker programs and increased immigration enforcement, has been around for a long time," said Lillian Galedo, executive director of Filipino Advocates for Justice in the San Francisco Bay Area. "We need a new alternative, based on much more progressive ideas. I don't think the Dignity Campaign is the only alternative, but it's an effort to get us to talk about what we actually want, not just what politicians in Washington, DC, tell us is politically possible or necessary."

In Tucson, the Coalición de Derechos Humanos called comprehensive immigration reform "primarily a vague promise used to attract immigrant and Latino voters, [while] border communities have suffered the costs of irresponsible and brutal enforcement-only policies, resulting in death and violence." A study by the Migration Policy Institute found the federal government was spending more on border and immigration enforcement than on all other federal law enforcement agencies combined.

Galedo and Isabel Garcia first saw the tradeoff in 1986, in the Immigration Reform and Control Act, and campaigned against it because it contained employer sanctions and set up today's H2-A visa scheme. "We've lived with the consequences ever since," Galedo says. "That's why, when we look at Obama's principles, or the CIR bills of the last decade, we think not just about our need for legalization but that we'll have another twenty-five years of enforcement and more guest workers. Because we've lived with those costs, we believe the best starting point for immigration reform is a discussion of what immigrant communities actually need and want, and what we know will actually solve the social problems around migration."

Challenging the Washington, DC, Consensus

One of the most direct challenges to labor-based migration came from the FIOB assembly in Oaxaca in 2011. In the year leading up to it, then Coordinator Gaspar Rivera Salgado organized a series of workshops for the organization's chapters in California. In the first one in Los Angeles, a meeting of thirty active members divided themselves into groups to analyze the impact of NAFTA, the 1986 Immigration Reform and Control Act and the 1996 Clinton-era immigration reform bill. They then regrouped to put forward proposals for changing both trade and immigration law in the United States. Rivera Salgado told them that in the United States, "migrants need the right to work, but with labor rights and benefits." In Mexico, he said, "We need development that makes migration a choice rather than a necessity—the right to not migrate. Both rights are part of the same solution."

The Los Angeles meeting outlined a broad set of principles for fundamental change—an FIOB program for immigration reform. That document was taken to FIOB chapters in other areas of California for discussion, and the California delegates then brought it to the binational assembly in Oaxaca in the fall of 2011 for adoption. Irma Luna chaired the assembly subgroup that discussed immigration reform. She was later elected FIOB's statewide coordinator for California.

The organization's process for determining its own program was unique because it brought together discussions among migrant community activists on both sides of the Mexico-US border. This produced a creative tension at the Oaxaca assembly between members living in Oaxaca, those from Oaxacan migrant communities elsewhere in Mexico and FIOB members living in California. California delegates brought with them the product of their dialogues, which concentrated on changing US immigration and trade law. Delegates from Oaxaca were insistent on producing a position that called on the Mexican and Oaxacan governments to implement economic development that would make migration a voluntary option rather than a necessity for survival. They also called for the defense of the rights of Central American migrants traveling through Mexico to the United States. And delegates from Mexico City and Baja California talked about the need to protect the political rights of Oaxacan migrants living in other Mexican states, as well as economic rights like housing, education and higher wages.

A common thread through their different perspectives was a rejection of the idea that Oaxacans should simply be a source of cheap labor for guest worker programs. "We have seen what happens to us in these programs," one delegate said during the discussion. "The things that are important to us as people—our families, our culture and language—have no place or importance in them. We're just valued for our ability to work. Once that work is done, we have no place in that world our labor creates."

The FIOB proposal is similar to that advanced by the Dignity Campaign, the loose coalition of organizations around the country that has proposed an alternative to the comprehensive immigration reform bills. Most of the campaign's constituent organizations participated in earlier coalitions opposing employer sanctions and guest worker programs. The Dignity Campaign brings together immigrant rights and fair trade organizations, encouraging each to see the global connections between trade policy, displacement and migration. It connects unions and immigrant rights organizations, seeking to spur opposition to immigration enforcement against workers and highlighting the need to oppose the criminalization of work.

The Dignity Campaign proposal draws on previous proposals, particularly one put forward by the American Friends Service Committee called "A New Path"—a set of moral principles for changing US immigration policy. Several other efforts were also made earlier by the National Network for Immigrant and Refugee Rights to define an alternative program and bring together groups around the country to support it.

The critique shared by all these organizations contends that the comprehensive immigration reform (CIR) framework ignores trade agreements like NAFTA and CAFTA. Without changing US trade policy and ending structural adjustment programs and neoliberal economic reforms, millions of displaced people will be forced to migrate, no matter how many walls are built on the border. The CIR proposals were built on the three-part structure of guest worker programs, increased enforcement, and legalization of the undocumented. Most conditioned legalization on "securing the border," a Washington, DC, euphemism for a heavy military presence augmenting twenty thousand Border Patrol agents that creates a climate of wholesale denial of civil and human rights in border communities. Changing corporate trade policy, however, was not part of any of the CIR proposals, because corporations were not only a central part of the alliance supporting them, but in some cases even wrote them.

The Dignity Campaign proposal, in contrast, begins by requiring Congress to end the use of the free trade system as a mechanism for producing displaced workers. It calls for delinking immigration status and employment, which would involve giving migrants green cards, or residence status, instead of work-based visas, as well as ending workplace enforcement. To raise the low price of immigrant labor, it calls for reinforcing the ability of immigrant workers to organize. Permanent legal status makes it easier for workers to organize, while guest worker programs, employer sanctions, and raids make organizing more difficult.

Some of the basic points of the Dignity Campaign proposal include

- giving permanent residence visas (green cards) to undocumented people already in the United States, and expanding the number of green cards available for new migrants
- eliminating the years'-long backlog in processing family reunification visas, strengthening families and communities
- allowing people to apply for green cards in the future, after they've been living in the United States for a few years
- ending the enforcement wave that has led to thousands of deportations and firings
- repealing employer sanctions and enforcing labor rights and worker protection laws
- ending guest worker programs
- dismantling the border wall and demilitarizing the border, restoring civil and human rights in border communities
- responding to recession and foreclosures with jobs programs to guarantee income and remove the fear of job competition
- renegotiating existing trade agreements to eliminate causes of displacement and prohibiting new trade agreements that displace people or lower living standards
- prohibiting local law enforcement agencies from enforcing immigration law, ending roadblocks, immigration raids and sweeps, and closing detention centers

The FIOB proposal and the Dignity Campaign agree that the root problem with migration in the existing global economy is that it's forced migration. Both agree that people should have the right to not migrate. At the same time, they both call for basic human and labor rights for those who do migrate. They both oppose denying people rights or benefits because of immigration status and envision a popular coalition that can push back against raids and anti-immigrant hysteria, toward more equal status.

Proposing programs for reform implies building a political coalition capable of fighting for it. The Dignity Campaign strategy is based on seeking mutual interest among workers, calling for jobs and rights for everyone in order to unite diverse communities. Bringing together African American and immigrant constituencies is a basic part of that strategy. Black unemployment, high even in boom times, reached catastrophic levels in the current recession. Very little of this unemployment, however, is a result of displacement by immigrants; instead, it is caused mostly by a decline in manufacturing and cuts in public employment. In the 2001 recession alone, three hundred thousand out of two million black factory workers lost their jobs.

Nevertheless, unemployed workers and immigrants are often pitted against each other in low-wage job competition in some industries. In the growing service and high-tech industries, African American and Chicano workers are often anathema to employers because they demand high wages. Many of the organizations who later joined the Dignity Campaign therefore supported a 2006 immigration proposal by Texas congresswoman Sheila Jackson Lee, which included job training and creation programs for unemployed workers combined with legalization and labor rights for undocumented immigrants.

Jackson Lee proposed to attack job competition by requiring Congress to move toward a full-employment policy. In her view, progressive reform, whether on jobs or immigration, needs an alliance between working people—immigrants and native-born, Latinos, African Americans, Asian Americans, and whites. In contrast, the strategy that supported the CIR bills was an alliance with employers based on new guest worker programs. Those would increase job competition, push wages down and make affirmative action hiring much more difficult.

The Dignity Campaign and FIOB proposals, therefore, represent not just an alternative program but also an alternative strategy of alliances among communities and constituencies based on their mutual interest in rights, jobs, and higher wages. The CIR alliance with employers made it impossible to include in its proposed immigration bills any proposal for renegotiating NAFTA or opposing displacement caused by trade agreements—one of the principle causes of migration. By contrast, the Mississippi Immigrants Rights Alliance, one of the most active Dignity Campaign members, has a political strategy that calls for bringing together African Americans, immigrants, and union members. All have an interest in opposing free trade agreements because they eliminate jobs in the United States, while displacing communities in Mexico.

Over the last decade, a loose network of groups has grown that generally opposed most CIR bills, and that also organized much of the grassroots opposition to increased enforcement and raids in immigrant communities. Outside the Washington beltway, community coalitions, labor and immigrant rights groups have advocated a number of alternatives. Some of them are large-scale counters to the entire CIR framework. Others seek to win legal status for a part of the undocumented population as a step toward larger change.

One of those proposals is the DREAM (Development, Relief, and Education for Alien Minors) Act. First introduced in 2003, the bill would allow undocumented students graduating from a US high school to apply for permanent residence if they complete two years of college or serve two years in the US military. Estimates are that it would enable over eight hundred thousand young people to gain legal status and eventual citizenship. For seven years, thousands of young *sin papeles*, or people without papers, have marched, sat-in, written letters, and mastered every civil rights tactic to get their bill onto the Washington, DC, agenda. Their movement has been so vocal that in June 2012, the Obama administration told the Department of Homeland Security to stop deporting young people brought to the United States by their parents as children if they're in school, have graduated or are veterans. They would also receive permission to work. But they wouldn't receive visas, leaving their long-term status and future in the air.

Supporting the DREAM Act and other partial protections for the undocumented are many worker centers around the country. This movement is based on organizing contingent workers, mostly undocumented. Some of the centers have anchored the protests against repression in Arizona, or fought to pass laws in California, New York, and elsewhere prohibiting police from turning over people to immigration agents. They've developed grassroots models for organizing migrants who get jobs on street corners, and these projects have come together in the National Day Labor Organizing Network. The National Domestic Worker Alliance was organized in 2010, in part using the experience of day labor organizing, to win rights for domestic workers, almost all women. It won a bill of rights in New York and passed the same bill of rights in California in 2012, although it was vetoed by Governor Jerry Brown in 2012.

On the Canadian border, in the far northwest corner of Washington State, Community2Community (C2C), a women-led grassroots organization, developed a process for discussing migration similar to that of FIOB called dignity dialogues. C2C is based in Whatcom County, where eight thousand mostly undocumented farmworkers are the workforce in the largest raspberry-growing area in the United States. C2C's director, Rosalinda Guillen, is a former union organizer of farmworkers, who then started setting up co-ops among northwest field laborers.

Immigration raids have become much more frequent in Mexican communities near the Canadian border. In Forks, a tiny town on the Olympic Peninsula, migrant families say they've been driven out by a wave of roadblocks and detentions. In an effort to escape one, a local worker fled into the forest and died. Guillen and C2C combined grassroots efforts to defend migrants in this border region with the dialogues. "We have to deal with this fear, and at the same time, try to organize so that we can improve our lives as farmworkers," Guillen explains. In meetings in rural communities north of Seattle, people talked about that work and fear, and at the same time debated immigration reform proposals. In over thirty meetings, their movement spread to other parts of Washington and Oregon as well.

Guillen explains, "We wanted to just ask ourselves, 'What kind of changes could we imagine that would really meet our needs?' We went section by section, idea by idea. We not only saw the sense in the Dignity Campaign proposals, but we added some of our own. These dialogues became a catalyst for developing leaders in our own communities. They eventually met with Senator Patty Murray [D-WA] and Congress members, to tell them we wanted an alternative to the bills they'd been debating in Washington, DC. It helped us decide what we stand for."

Two of the issues that got the most attention in the dignity dialogues were guest worker programs and the right to not migrate.
Guillen says, "Many of us are children or grandchildren of braceros.
Like Latinos across the country, we have roots in that experience.
Our families tell stories of the abuse we went through. When we
hear how people are treated now, the stories sound the same. The
guest program proposals coming from DC are just looking for a cap-
tive workforce at low wages. What we want is respect and recognition in the communities where we live, as well as the ability to come
and go with rights."

As in the discussions at the FIOB meetings in California and Oaxaca, dignity dialogue participants saw opposition to guest worker
programs connected to the right to not migrate. "A lot of the families in Whatcom County would rather be home, working their own
land," Guillen says. "But they can't because the free trade agreements have made farming so difficult. Coming as a guest worker, or
coming without papers, is a means to survive. Now we see these bills
in DC that won't do anything about what's displacing people, but
they will facilitate the recruitment of a cheap workforce. That won't
help farmworkers here, and it won't solve their problems as farmers
in Mexico either. It's just a corporate free-for-all. Our most important
conclusion from the dialogues was that proposals for reform should
come from the people they affect. They should deal with the issues
that affect us the most, including the militarization of the border
and the huge number of undocumented people in detention." C2C
members travel to Tacoma once a month to hold a vigil outside the
big Immigration and Customs Enforcement detention center.

In Mexico and Central America, other organizations and forums
have also called for the right to not migrate, and for protecting the
rights of migrants at the same time. In 2010, the Forum on Migration
and Development met in Cuernavaca, Mexico, and agreed on a two-
part program. Saying "No to forced migration," it called for public
policy "based on human rights, to confront the causes of migration
forced by lack of good jobs, environmental degradation, unequal opportunities, political and social exclusion, and human insecurity." It
then said "Yes to development based on transnational citizenship."

Included in this point were financial support for communities of origin, defense of food sovereignty and sustainable agriculture and forestry, and vesting decision-making power with migrant organizations, indigenous people, and organizations in peoples' communities of origin.

The forum proposed an alliance between migrants, civil society organizations, groups fighting for sexual equality and indigenous and migrant rights, and human rights groups generally. Participants included FIOB, the National Alliance of Latin American and Caribbean Communities (NALACC) and other US immigrant organizations, and groups in Mexico, Guatemala, and Honduras.

Oscar Azmitia, representing the Latin American Association of Development Organizations, and rector of La Salle University in Costa Rica, summarized the agreements reached at the forum in five points: stop treating migration as a national security issue and instead as a social one; recognize the right to not migrate through building a just society, including policies to eradicate poverty; demand that countries respect international treaties and their own laws; create local credit alternatives, like microbanks, in communities of origin; change public perception of migration and migrants, giving them a chance to put forward their own programs; and develop research and studies of labor, legal, and economic rights.

Rodolfo Garcia Zamora summarizes the declaration from the Latin American Migrant Communities Summit, held in Morelia, Michoacan, in 2007. It declared, he says, "that in essence migrants should stop being the object of study, and become instead transnational social actors, promoting new forms of civic participation, and designing public policies both in their countries of origin and their destinations." Proposals made by Garcia Zamora and Oscar Chacon, representing NALACC, suggested that every country should have a long-term policy for development and migration, that the organizations of migrants and their communities of origin should be strengthened and given more resources, and that they should develop alliances with other parts of civil society.

A third declaration, by a meeting in Tapachula, Chiapas, in 2008, made a similar call to link the rights of migrants with the right to not migrate. Included among its ten demands were respect for the dignity and human rights of migrant workers, punishment for those committing violence or acts or racism against them, and a call that the United States sign and ratify international agreements on the rights of migrants. The signers included the independent Mexican labor union, the Authentic Labor Front, Global Workers Justice, FIOB and several religious human rights organizations.

Chacon believes that the right to not migrate is emerging from indigenous culture in Latin America as part of the growing asser-tiveness of indigenous communities. "These communities don't be-lieve in borders, and have a different concept of sovereignty," he says. "How you belong to a community doesn't depend on the place you live, but on your relations with other people." Chacon sees similar ideas emerging from the growth of indigenous political movements in countries like Ecuador, and believes they're connected to the rise of left-leaning governments and political movements throughout Latin America. "Going back twenty years, those governments gave up any notion of national development policy," he explains. "Now the economies of countries like Mexico and El Salvador are depen-dent on remittances and drugs. When you talk about the right to not migrate, you're talking about a drastic change in direction and a completely different alternative."

The Right to Not Migrate Is a Social Movement

The right to not migrate, then, is not an idea or demand that exists separately from the debates over the direction of economic policy—who it should benefit, and who has the right to decide on it. For in-digenous communities in Oaxaca, or for the farmers in the Perote Valley, gaining the kind of support that will allow people to stay on their land requires political change. Economic development based on human needs requires changing the priorities that govern how the resources of Oaxaca or Veracruz, or of Mexico as a country, are used. So long as those resources go to debt payments and subsidies to corporate investors, they won't be available for community develop-ment on any significant scale.

Today, countries like Mexico that send migrants to the United States, Canada, and the developed world depend on remittances to finance social services and keep the lid on social discontent over poverty and joblessness. Meanwhile, government resources are used to make huge debt payments. This creates a common interest between conservative governments in migrant-sending countries and the corporations using displaced labor. Both have an interest in regulating the system that supplies that labor. Increasingly, the mechanisms for regulating the flow of people are contract labor programs—whether called "guest worker" or "temporary worker" programs in the United States, or "managed migration" in Canada or the EU.

As communities assert their right to not migrate, they are challenging the basic way this international system functions. The reason FIOB and C2C challenge guest worker programs is not just because they abuse migrants or undermine the wages and jobs of host country residents. It's because they are challenging the way the economic system is geared to produce displaced people and make migration a matter of survival.

This is the reason the right to *not* migrate is integrally connected to the right *to* migrate and the rights of migrants themselves. Migration should be a voluntary process in which people can decide for themselves if and when to move, and under what circumstances. It is a profoundly democratic demand, one that asserts that the ability to make individual decisions over where to live is meaningless unless people also have the ability to decide how the resources of their communities and countries are used. As Rivera Salgado says, "The right to not migrate is not meaningful if it is not also the right to go to school, the right to make a living from farming, or the right to health care and decent housing." People in communities of origin, therefore, not banks and corporations, should control the economic development choices that either make it possible for people to stay, or that force them to leave in order to live.

The same organizations asserting the right to not migrate also apply these democratic principles to migration itself, and to the rights of migrants. C2C, for instance, calls for balancing the needs of migrants with those of farmworkers in the communities in which both work together. Both residents and newcomers have an interest in ensuring that everyone enjoys rights and security. To ensure they aren't pitted against each other, both need jobs. Both need the right to organize and raise wages. That makes the immigration status of migrants a critical issue. Guest worker status denies people rights, makes it harder for them to organize, and keeps them in isolation from the other working people in the communities in which they live. Permanent residence visas give people choices. A green card allows a migrant to decide for herself whether or not to work or where to live. And getting fired, as painful as that is, doesn't mean being deported.

If the family preference system is supplied with enough visas to eliminate the decades-long backlog in applications, many migrants can use it. For those who have no relatives or community connections in the United States, a system for applying for green cards with a realistic hope of getting one would be a far preferable alternative to recruitment as an H-2A guest worker. The purpose of migration is not to supply to labor needs of employers, but to fulfill the human needs of people. While work is a human need, so is the need for family and community. Vulnerability is only increased by the social exclusion and second-class status imposed by guest worker programs. Delinking immigration status and employment is a necessary step to achieving equal rights for migrant workers. Healthy immigrant communities need employed workers, but they also need students, old and young people, caregivers, artists, the disabled, and those who don't have traditional jobs.

Employers who want workers can offer higher wages and better conditions to make their jobs more attractive. They can negotiate with unions, giving workers some job security and expectation of fair treatment. The Coalition of Immokalee Workers, with its demand that fast-food chains pay more for tomatoes so that tomato pickers' wages rise, and the UFW's demand for a "5¢ for fairness" increase in the price of a basket of strawberries to give those pickers a raise too, both make an important point. The workers who provide field labor get only a tiny percentage of the supermarket or restaurant price for the fruits and vegetables they pick. Their wages could double, and the impact on the final consumer price would be negligible. The same logic applies to the women who sew clothes, the framers who put up the walls in homes, or the janitors who clean office buildings. Employers do not need indentured low-wage labor programs to survive. Their cost is brutal—to migrant workers themselves, to the communities around them, and to the communities from which they come.

The right to not migrate is therefore not just a demand but also a social movement. People have to be able to organize to win the political power to implement it. When the miners in Cananea have an enforceable right to a union, they can ensure their jobs are secure and their wages are capable of sustaining their families. When they lose that right, they lose their very ability to remain in Mexico. In Oaxaca, the alliance between FIOB, the teachers union, and other indigenous social movements made it possible to achieve partial political power—enough to begin reordering the state's priorities to make the right to not migrate real. But it is not yet a complete change.

The right to not migrate is a movement that crosses borders. The solidarity of communities and organizations in the United States has a big impact on the ability of people to achieve it in Mexico. Solidarity from the United Steel Workers has helped to keep the miners' union alive in Cananea. The FIOB chapters in California helped convince voters in Oaxaca to seek an alternative to the expulsion and remittance policies of the former PRI governors. The integration of the economies of the United States, Canada, and Mexico, and the enormous migration of Mexicans to the United States and Canada, have created new possibilities for building social movements that span borders. They make possible new tactics and strategies that are built on the growing closeness of the United States, Canadian, and Mexican people.

Migrants are human beings first, and their desire for community is as strong as the need to labor. As the old shop floor saying goes, "We work to live; we don't live to work." The use of neoliberal reforms and economic treaties to displace communities, to produce a global army of available and vulnerable workers, has a brutal impact on people. Rather than reduce migrants to a factor of production, or a commodity to be exported and imported, migration policy must acknowledge migrants as human beings and address their dignity and human rights.

Migration policy, which includes the right to not migrate as well as political and social rights for migrants, is an integral part of a broad agenda for change both in sending and receiving countries. The needs of people in each are really not so different. They include jobs, better wages and housing, a national health-care system, and the right to organize without fear of retaliation and repression. To end job competition in the United States, workers need the four million jobs promised by the Obama administration, paid for by an economy reordered away from military spending. In Mexico, people need a national development policy instead of a policy of expulsion and remittances.

The global economy has turned insecurity into a virtue, praised as necessary to increase flexibility and competitiveness. But working communities need a system that produces security, not insecurity. In evaluating proposals for migration reform, the watchwords should be security, equality, organization, and community. Immigration policy should make movement possible, instead of seeing the threat of terrorism everywhere. Freedom of movement is a human right. But selling workers to employers should not be the price for gaining it. Nor should migration be the only possibility for survival and a decent future.

ACKNOWLEDGMENTS

I owe a great deal of thanks to many people who have helped me. They include Juan Manuel Sandoval, Bill Ong Hing, Gaspar Rivera Salgado, Rufino Dominguez and all the people whose personal narratives are included, Carolina Ramirez, Baldemar Velasquez, Tim Wise, Jonathan Fox, Robin Alexander, Dan La Botz, Laura Carlson, Isabel Garcia, John Womack, Jeff Faux, Enrique Davalos, Mary Bauer, Cynthia Rice, Irma Luna, Alegria De La Cruz, Cathleen Caron, Rosalinda Guillen, Bill Chandler, Jim Evans, Patricia Ice, Jose Padilla, Bill Fletcher, Nativo Lopez, John Grant, Mike Garcia, Javier Murillo, Rafael Morataya, the Pacific Steel workers, and my wife, Lillian Galedo.

I want to thank also some of the magazines and media that have paid me to write about the movements and events described here. Without their support this book wouldn't exist, and I wouldn't be able to continue as a writer and photographer. They include the *Nation* and the Nation Investigative Fund, the *Progressive*, *TruthOut*, *California Lawyer*, *Dollars and Sense*, and New America Media. I thank especially the editors at these publications, many of whom have supported this work for many years. I also want to thank the Institute for Transnational Social Change at the University of California, Los Angeles, Labor Center and the Rosa Luxemburg Foundation for their support.

SOURCES

To provide more information for interested readers, the following is a selected list of sources used in this book.

Alvarado Juarez, Ana Margarita. "Migration and Poverty in Oaxaca." Institute for Sociological Investigation, Universidad Autonoma Benito Juarez de Oaxaca.

American Friends Service Committee. "A New Path." January 31, 2009. http://afsc.org.

Bacon, David. "Displaced, Unequal and Criminalized." Rosa Luxemburg Foundation. November 2011. http://www.rosalux.de.

Carlson, Laura. CIP Americas Program website. http://www.cipamericas.org.

Delgado-Wise, Raul, and Humberto Marquez Covarrubias. "The Reshaping of Mexican Labor Exports under NAFTA: Paradoxes and Challenges." *International Migration Review* 41, no. 3 (September 2007): 656–79.

Diaz, Miguel Angel, and Felipe Casanova. *Pueblos Unidos.* Film. Universidad Veracruzana, Xalapa, Veracruz.

Fernandez-Vega, Carlos. Mexico SA (Mexico, Inc.) column, *La Jornada* (Mexico City).

Fox, Jonathan, and Libby Haight. "Subsidios para la desigualdad: Las políticas públicas de maíz en México a partir del libre comercio." Woodrow Wilson Center. 2010. www.wilsoncenter.org.

Griswold, Daniel T. *Willing Workers: Fixing the Problem of Illegal Mexican Migration to the United States.* Cato Institute. October 15, 2002. http://www.cato.org.

Guthrie, Woody. "Ballad of Pretty Boy Floyd" and "Deportee." YouTube. http://www.youtube.com.

Hennebry, Jenna. *Permanently Temporary? Agricultural Migrant Workers and Their Integration in Canada.* Institute for Research on Public Policy. February 28, 2012. http://www.irpp.org.

Hernandez Diaz, Jorge, and Leon Javier Parra Mora. "Violencia y Cambio Social en la Region Triqui." Universidad Autonoma Benito Juarez de Oaxaca, Oaxaca.

Hing, Bill Ong. *Ethical Borders: NAFTA, Globalization, and Mexican Migration.* Philadelphia: Temple University Press, 2010.

Imagen de Veracruz. Daily newspaper.

Lopez Barcenas, Francisco. "San Juan Copala: dominacion politica y resistencia popular." Universidad Autonoma Metropolitana, Xochimilco, Mexico City.

Lopez Barcenas, Francisco, and Mayra Montserrat Eslava Galicia. "El Mineral o

La Vida." Centro de Orientacion y Asesoria a Pueblos Indigenas Autonomous Metropolitan University (UAM) Xochimilco.

Meissner, Doris, Donald M. Kerwin, Muzaffar Chishti, and Claire Bergeron. *Immigration Enforcement in the United States: The Rise of a Formidable Machinery.* Migration Policy Institute. January 2013. www.migrationpolicy.org.

Mexican Labor News and Analysis. United Electrical Workers. http://ueinternational.org.

Mines, Rick, Sandra Nichols, and David Runsten. *California's Indigenous Farmworkers.* Indigenous Farmworker Study. January 2010. www.indigenousfarmworkers.org.

Morales Vasquez, Jorge. "Los estragos de Granjas Carroll en Perote." Milenio, Xalapa.

Oxfam America. *A State of Fear: Human Rights Abuses in North Carolina's Tobacco Industry.* http://www.oxfamamerica.org.

Paley, Dawn. "Another Mexican Mining Activist Assassinated: Bernardo Vásquez Killed in Oaxaca." Pacific Free Press. March 15, 2012.

Paz, Adriana. "Harvest of Injustice: The Oppression of Migrant Workers on Canadian Farms." *Socialist Voice.* June 22, 2008. http://www.socialistvoice.ca.

Pew Hispanic Center. "Mexican Immigrants in the United States, 2008." Fact sheet. April 15, 2009. http://pewhispanic.org.

Rural Migration News. University of California, Davis. http://migration.ucdavis.edu.

Southern Poverty Law Center. *Close to Slavery: Guestworker Programs in the United States.* March 2007. http://www.splcenter.org.

Sukthankar, Ashwini, et al. *Visas, Inc.: Corporate Control and Policy Incoherence in the U.S. Temporary Foreign Labor System.* Brooklyn, NY: Global Workers Justice Alliance. May 31, 2012. http://www.globalworkers.org.

La Tijereta. http://latijeretabcs.blogspot.com.

Trumka, Richard. Speeches on immigration reform. AFL-CIO website. http://www.aflcio.org.

United Food and Commercial Workers Canada. *Report on the Status of Migrant Workers in Canada.* January 2011. http://www.ufcw.ca.

US Department of Homeland Security. "Fact Sheet: H-2A Temporary Agricultural Workers Program." http://www.dhs.gov.

US Department of Labor. "Fact Sheet #26: Section H-2A of the Immigration and Nationality Act." http://www.dol.gov.

US Immigration and Customs Enforcement. News releases. http://www.ice.gov.

Vargas, Zaragosa. *Labor Rights Are Civil Rights: Mexican American Workers in Twentieth-Century America.* Princeton, NJ: Princeton University Press, 2004.

Wise, Timothy. "The Impacts of US Agricultural Policies on Mexican Producers." In *Subsidizing Inequality: Mexican Corn Policy Since NAFTA.* Jonathan Fox and Libby Haight, eds. Washington, DC: Woodrow Wilson Center, 2010. www.wilsoncenter.org.

Wise, Timothy, and Betsy Rakocy. "Hogging the Gains from Trade: The Real

Winners from U.S. Trade and Agricultural Policies." Policy brief no. 10-01. Global Development and Environment Institute, Tufts University. January 2010. http://www.ase.tufts.edu.

Organizations and Resources

Asamblea Nacional de Afectados Ambientales, Mexico City
http://www.afectadosambientales.org

Center for International Policy Americas Program, Colonia Tortuga, Mexico
http://www.cipamericas.org

Centro de Investigacion Laboral y Asesoria Sindical, Mexico City
http://cilas.org

Coalición de Derechos Humanos, Tucson, Arizona
www.derechoshumanosaz.net

Community2Community, Bellingham, Washington
http://foodjustice.org

Dignity Campaign, Oakland, California
http://www.dignitycampaign.org

Farm Labor Organizing Committee, Toledo, Ohio
http://www.supportfloc.org

Frente Indigena de Organizaciones Binacionales, Fresno, California, and Oaxaca, Mexico
http://fiob.org

Global Forum on Migration and Development
http://www.gfmd.org

Instituto Oaxaqueno de Atencion al Migrante, Oaxaca, Mexico
http://www.migrantes.oaxaca.gob.mx

Meatingplace, Chicago
http://www.meatingplace.com

Mississippi Immigrants Rights Alliance, Jackson, Mississippi
http://www.yourmira.org

Occupy Wall Street en Espanol, New York
http://owsenespanol.nycga.net

Servicios Para Una Educacion Alternative AC, El Topil, Oaxaca, Mexico
http://educaoaxaca.org

Sindicato Mexicano de Electricistas, Mexico City
http://www.sme1914.org

Sindicato Minero Seccion 65, Cananea, Mexico
http://www.sindicatomineroseccion65.com.mx

INDEX